T0367023

THE

PUBLICATIONS

OF THE

SURTEES SOCIETY

VOL. CCI

At a COUNCIL MEETING of the SURTEES SOCIETY, held on 14 June 1993, it was ORDERED—
"That the edition of Darlington wills and inventories prepared by a group led by Dr H. J. Smith should be printed as a volume of the Society's publications."

A. J. Piper, *Secretary*
5 The College
Durham

THE

PUBLICATIONS

OF THE

SURTEES SOCIETY

ESTABLISHED IN THE YEAR
M.DCCC.XXXIV

VOL. CCI

IN MEMORIAM

CHRISTOPHE ROY HUDLESTON

13.x.1905 – 8.ii.1992

Editor of the Society

1966 – 79

DARLINGTON WILLS AND INVENTORIES

1600 – 1625

EDITED BY

J. A. ATKINSON, B. FLYNN,
V. PORTASS, K. SINGLEHURST

AND

H. J. SMITH

PRINTED FOR THE SOCIETY BY
ATHENAEUM PRESS LIMITED, NEWCASTLE UPON TYNE
1993

CONTENTS

Preface

This collection of wills and inventories and the introduction and glossary which accompany it are the work of a group of adult students, who met under the auspices of Durham University and the W.E.A. at Bennet House in Darlington. Having worked together at Darlington for two years studying palaeography, they went on to spend several more, transcribing and editing the documents in this collection. The Teddy Allen Fund of the W.E.A. Northern District generously made a grant towards the costs of obtaining copies of the documents.

The members of the group, Mrs Joy Atkinson, Mrs Brenda Flynn, Mrs Valerie Portass and Mrs Kate Singlehurst, and their tutor Mr John Smith, are grateful for help in the initial stages from Mrs Edna Hugill, Mr John Maddison and the late Mrs Betty Ellis.

Miss Margaret McCollum of Durham University Library, Archives and Special Collections, as the original tutor of the group, gave much assistance and encouragement. The first draft of the glossary was prepared by Mrs Catherine Ferguson and help was subsequently given by Miss M. Hartley and Miss J. Ingilby of Hawes, by Mrs Kate Mason of Ilkley and by Mr Bill Cowley of Northallerton. Mr John Creasey of Dr Williams Library, London, was very helpful in identifying books in Isaac Lowden's inventory; Dr Ian Doyle, formerly Keeper of Rare Books and now Honorary Reader in Bibliography at Durham University, generously identified the most difficult and elusive titles in that inventory. Great assistance was rendered by the staff of Durham University Library, Archives and Special Collections, and of the reference libraries at Darlington and Newcastle-upon-Tyne. The editor of the Surtees Society, Mr Alan Piper, both kindly and sternly oversaw the final stages of this work. Thanks are due to all other colleagues, friends and spouses who helped with advice and expertise or by their forbearance.

Editorial method

The wills and the inventories have been numbered 1 to 58 but they are arranged in chronological order of probate. They are normally called for by name and date at the Durham University Library, Archives and Special Collections, where nos 1 to 57 are preserved. One, no. 58, is preserved at the Borthwick Institute in York and is called for by volume number of register.

The punctuation of the wills has been wholly modernised and the use of capitals regularised. All abbreviations and contractions in the wills and in the inventories have been silently expanded except where there is doubt, when the letters supplied are in italics. The Latin endorsements, mostly of the stages of probate, have been omitted.

All values in the inventories have been rendered in uniform columns of pounds, shillings and pence, and arabic numerals have been substituted for what was the most frequent practice of using roman forms. Where the roman forms occurred in the wills, they have been left.

Introduction

This collection of wills and inventories comes wholly from the parish of Darlington which had a population of just under 2,000 in the year 1600. Almost forty years before, in 1563, with a total of 366 householders, it had formed the third largest parish in the county of Durham.[1] Although less than half the size of Durham City, it was only just behind Bishop Auckland and much larger than Sunderland, Gateshead, Stockton and Hartlepool. It was clearly a market town of some importance and was a palatine borough by 1183. The burgesses were freeholders with a borough court and their principal trades were organised into guilds. The chief officer, the bailiff, was an appointee of the bishop but appears to have been active in the performance of his duties and of the self-conscious ceremony which always accompanied the opening of the market. After 1560, the office acquired more prestige with its occupancy by a member of the peerage family of Eure until 1586 and thereafter by a nephew of Bishop Barnes to 1605. A curious feature was that both had been married to Barbara Palmer, daughter of the town's principal merchant before 1600, and their successor in the office, John Lisle, married her too.

The town's trading horizons extended throughout the North: into Cumbria, Northumberland and Berwick-upon-Tweed and into the West and North Ridings of Yorkshire. Its shopkeepers and market supplied the local nobility, such as the earl and countess of Westmorland (before 1569) and the bishops of Durham and principal gentry families such as Bowes, Conyers and Hilton. Until the Reformation, eight religious houses, including Rievaulx and Jervaulx, possessed property in Darlington and the parish church had enjoyed status as one of the county's six collegiate establishments. Location on the Great North Road gave an added significance to the town and its market. During Henry VIII's last wars with Scotland, Darlington was from time to time a convenient seat for the Council of the North. It was also an official post town on the important diplomatic and strategic route between London and Edinburgh.

Yet Darlington was actually in decline, a decline apparently not reversed before the eighteenth century. By the 1510s, the once prosperous woollen trade was in retreat and the dyehouse and fulling mill were out of use. Although the production of linen had come largely to replace woollens by 1600, various records suggest that the number of weavers had decreased. It was the leather trade which now predominated. Moreover, Darlington suffered two disastrous experiences in the reign of Elizabeth. Firstly, in 1569 the town was deeply involved in the Northern Rising: perhaps half of its able-bodied males joined the earls of Westmorland and Northumberland in their desperate enterprise. In June 1569, before the rebellion, the official muster had enumerated 232 men. By early 1570, after the rebellion, a document states that 115 had joined the earls at Darlington and it seems most probable that the reference is to men of serviceable age. Twenty-three persons were executed.[2] Thirty-eight purchased pardons. No other town was so much involved, revealing either the extent of its political conservatism and traditional dependency or simply the pressure the earls could exert on a town through which they marched on their way south. The low rate of pardons and the high number of executions imply a degree of willing involvement. Secondly, the spectacular fire of 1585 destroyed a great part of the town and inflicted a total loss on some of the leading merchants at a time of wholly uninsured risk. Over the period 1563-1666, Darlington fell well behind the rest of the county, in which the population increased by about 45%. Along the Tyne and the Wear, the rate of increase in the ports and the mining settlements ranged from 200% to 320%. Darlington's increase was a mere 15%.[3] In absolute numbers of households, the town fell from third to tenth place. It remained active as a town of around 2,000 persons but, after the 1680s, it was to be outranked in its own neighbourhood and among its own local customers in South Durham and North Yorkshire by the rising seaport of Stockton-on-Tees.[4]

The Documents

The Probate Act Books[5] show that the estates of 143 persons of Darlington were the subject of testamentary proceedings between 1600 and 1625. Only about half the wills and inventories actually made in that period have survived. This collection consists of the 46 wills and 57 inventories of 58 persons of Darlington for which administration was granted. All were proved at Durham except for the will of Peter Glover (58) which was proved at York.

If Peter Glover is excluded, documents survive for 57 or 40% of the 143 Darlingtonians in the Act Books. The survival rate is much better for wills : of 66 proved at Durham, 45 survive or 68%. Of the 110 inventories produced at Durham, 57 have survived, or 52%. The wills made by Isabel Ward (5) and John Sober (33) survive but not their inventories; Robert Dent's (19) inventory is to be found but not his will. These are exceptions because usually the losses are of both documents relating to an individual estate. Durham archives were beset with dangers until the middle of the 19th century. Testamentary records were especially favoured for lighting pipes[6]. Although an inventory and sequestration exist for Robert Garnett (52), his name does not appear in the Act Books. As a Roman Catholic, it may be supposed that he was excluded from the benefits of testamentary law. The nuncupative or oral will of Elizabeth Wood also appears not to have been proved, although it was the subject of proceedings in the Consistory Court.[7]

What proportion of persons buried left estates to be proved? In the year 1600, eleven persons capable of making wills or leaving estates were buried. They were five adult males, one manservant, two widows and three single women. The Act Book shows that wills were proved for three adult males and administration was granted in the estate of a fourth, and a will was also proved for a manservant, William Wilson or "Crooked Will". But of these five persons, two do not occur among the burials at Darlington. Hence we have a ratio of five actual to at least thirteen potential testators. In fact, the will and inventory of only one of them, Christopher Collyn (1), a bachelor and a tanner, survives to be reproduced in this text.

In the period 1600 to 1625, 67 wills were made (including the one proved at York) and administrations were granted in another 77 cases, a total of 144. The parish registers show 522 potential testators buried in that period. This is to exclude wives, wanderers and non-residents, and all males and females referred to as somebody's child, despite the likelihood that some were young adults. This suggests that testamentary jurisdiction was exercised in over 27% of all potential cases. The percentage must actually be lower than this, because eight Darlington persons leaving wills to be proved and 25 who died intestate do not occur in the Darlington burial register. This is not only because of defects in the register. Ralph Thursby (54) was buried at Heighington in 1622 and Ann Surtees (39) at St Oswald's in Durham City in 1616. Perhaps the normal percentage was between 20 and 25%. The figures for adult males are highest : 121 of 304 burials or 40%; ten of 136 widows or 7%; ten of 56 single women or 18%. One will and one administration occurred among 13 male servants buried and one will among 26 female servants, none of which is now extant.

The making of the wills

The making of wills appears to have been almost without exception a deathbed event. A rare local example of longer foresight seems to be that shown by Leonard Chambers of Darlington, who declared his will in 1589 before he set out for the South, saying it was his intention to join the Portugal expedition. He did uncommonly well to survive that costly military fiasco and to return to die in the plague year, 1597, when his nuncupative will of 1589 was finally proved. In the period 1600-25, there is apparently no such example. The date of the will and of the burial are known in 41 cases. There were 11 persons who died within two days of making their wills, 30 who died within two weeks and 34 who died within three weeks. No one survived making a will by as much as six months. Thomas Catherick (22) held out for 155 days.

In 36 wills, the testators describe themselves in the usual phrases as "being sick but of sound mind". William Bower (51) and Peter Glover (58) refer to themselves as "decrepit". Edmund Fawell (37) made no reference at all to his state of health but perhaps anticipated dying of whatever caused the death of his mother, Jane Surtees (38). They made their wills within three days of each other and were both dead within three weeks. Ralph Hugill's (10) will was made in sad circumstances, on the day of his daughter's burial. The funerals of his wife and son had taken place during the previous two weeks and Ralph himself was buried on the following day, November 3rd, 1605. More awful was the case of John Hall (12), who had buried three sons and two daughters and a servant in the month before he dated his will. He was buried five days later on September 17th, 1606. It seems that the widow of Richard Fawcett was moved to make a will with the utmost speed. Her husband was buried on September 29th, 1605. She was buried the next day. The Act Books show a will in her name which has not survived. This she could only have written during the few days of her life as a widow, since she could not have made a will in her husband's lifetime.

Only four testators made statements which imply the existence of earlier wills. Another four wills were nuncupative. They were not written down at the time of making but subsequently from the memory of witnesses. Isabel Catherick's (24) statement was not dated and took into account the possibility of a further lease of life. She declared that she was giving her keys to Jenet Russell and Alison Hodgson for delivery to her brother, who would then find her money and her valuables. If she rallied, her two friends were not to reveal what they knew. Her witnesses, being all women, were most probably illiterate and unable to write down her wishes. The nuncupative will of William Dockera (25) in the same year, 1610, has none of the usual pious preliminaries and simply records his legacies. Another example of an oral will was that of Jane[t] Surtees (38) who lay sick in bed at her Cockerton house, "accompanied with manie wives of that towne". She summoned Ralph Blackwell who joined with Thomas Bowbank to hear her last wishes after the local wives had left the room.[8] Although the document is dated January 2nd, 1614/15, five days before her death, the two witnesses were to testify that it was not put into writing until her goods were appraised. The inventory actually bears the date May 21st, 1615.

The formality and certainty of the terms of the wills conceal the declining physical and mental condition of the testators upon their death-beds. Nevertheless, William Thompson (4) of Cockerton was well enough when making his will eleven days before his burial in 1603, to answer the challenge of Thomas Mason who was writing down his bequests. William had singled out his son Matthew to receive £100, "...not suffering to come nere that proporcion to the rest of his children". Thomas asked him if it was really his intention to be so generous to that one son. William insisted, saying that in his age it was Matthew who had been his chief support and who had taken care of him. This will was later disputed.[9] On the other hand Ann Surtees (39), a 30-year old spinster of Cockerton, was barely conscious at her will making. Apparently summoned to Durham to assist in resolving the legal and financial tangle which had arisen from the deaths within days of each other of her half-brother Edmund Fawell (37) and her mother Jane Surtees (38), she lay dying in John Walker's house in Elvet. Thomas Atkinson told her he would make her will, to which her reply was an apparently philosophical "Well, well". As he later testified, Atkinson then wrote the preamble and took down the first bequest at her dictation. Then, as he asked what other bequests she would make, she replied, "Noe Moe". Another witness testified that she was "growing sicker and sicker" and "past her memorie" and did not answer Atkinson, when three or four times he asked what other bequests she would make. He finally asked if she would make John Walker her executor, to which she answered "Yes". This will too was later disputed. The evidence in the case of her mother Jane Surtees showed that Ann was regarded as a simple woman who could not "govern her own goods".[10]

The suddenness with which death struck may account for over

half of the administrations in the Act Books, 77 of 143, being of intestate estates. Some were of considerable value: the lost inventories of Henry Browne, £281, Christopher Nicholson, £165, and Cuthbert Robinson, £257; or the inventory of Anthony Dennis (28), occurring in this collection, with an estate worth about £500. Nor were there wills for the two ministers who died during these years, Isaac Lowden (31) and Brian Grant. They above all knew the necessity and the form. Isaac Lowden was moreover not surprised by death because he was sick for the five weeks before. There was payment to two women who nursed him during this time. The failure to make a will suggests an illness which paralysed his senses.

The importance of making final arrangements, albeit in the agony of the deathbed, is exemplified by the plight of Janet Townend, a widow of Darlington. Her son William, a petty chapman, was the executor of her husband's will and had £20 in his hands for her widow-right. She was heard to ask him often for the money, in his shop and elsewhere. He would respond with talk of his liquidity problems and with vague promises,

> "Mother I ame not furnished with so much money at this present as will satisfie yow but I will Come over to Blackwell and paie the same Twenty Poundes unto yow or part thereof at the Least."[11]

This was never done nor did she receive the interest of 40 shillings a year which he promised to pay her. He died in February 1611/12, intestate. Janet was now obliged to sue her son's executors in the County Court and in Chancery and to make complaint in the Consistory Court where at one point the executors were excommunicated for non-appearance.[12]

Family, kin, and executors

Of the 46 wills, 39 were made by men and seven by women. The men were made up of three singlemen, of whom two may have been childless widowers (7) and (49); 24 married men, three of whom were remarried widowers (12), (15) and (22); and 12 widowers. The seven women were two spinsters and five widows.

Excluding the two spinsters, the three bachelors and Mary Throckmorton who clearly named only one of her children, there were 40 married or formerly married persons making wills. Five left no children. Fourteen left no more than two children. Almost two-thirds, 22 persons, left four or fewer children. These figures tell only crudely a story of survival but it is a fact that the five who left seven children or more were among the very wealthiest. Cuthbert Cornforth (41) left seven children and William Barnes (8) left the highest total of ten. Thomas Robinson (30), Peter Glover (58) and the more modest William Sober (47) left seven children each. Arguably, this proves that the longest purses had the best chances of ensuring the survival of the greatest number of children. It may also point, indrectly, to the fertility of the better-nourished.

Thirty wills referred to family relationships beyond wife, husband and children. In 15 wills, sisters were mentioned; in 12, brothers; in ten, nephews; in eight, brothers-in-law and cousins in eight too; in seven, nephews, and in six, grandchildren were mentioned. Christopher Collyn (1) was a singleman whose father and mother were dead so of necessity he called on or made benefactions to his grandfather, his uncles and their children, and made a cousin executor. If the cousin refused, then his son, Collyn's second cousin, was asked to act. Cuthbert Cornforth (41) was a man of wealth in trade and in remembering three brothers-in-law, five nephews and a neice, as well as his own wife and three daughters and four sons, he may either have been mindful of a moral obligation to less fortunate kin or acknowledging a range of business contacts cemented by marriages. Thus, it is interesting that his three brothers-in-law were named but only one of his sisters, their wives.

The age as well as the wealth of the testator meant an increase in the numbers to be remembered. Thus Lawrence Catherick (56) mentioned sons, daughters, daughters-in-law and thirteen grandchildren. William Bower (51) made bequests to servants, his brother, a nephew, a kinsman and late servant, his son-in-law and ten grandchildren. John Atkinson (49), another gentleman but apparently unmarried and childless, mentioned a grandnephew as well as a nephew and servants.

In the 46 wills and 57 inventories, about 1,600 names occur or about 15 per document. William Bower's (51) will yields 32 and Anthony Dennis's (28) inventory 102 names. At the other extreme, Mary Throckmorton's (48) will mentioned by name only one child. The existence of her other children is merely implied.

Six testators, of whom three were women, did not name executors. Of the 39 wills made by men, nine made the wife sole executrix. George Marshall (50) declared it was his wife Helen "to whom I wholly refer my trust and confidence for theducation of my children during their minority and to be sole executrix". The second and third husbands of Barbara Eure (born Palmer), William Barnes (8) and John Lisle (55), made her the sole executor of two long and complicated wills, but Barnes prayed her to be guided by his cousin John in respect of their ten children's education and the government of their portions.

In eight cases the wife was joined with others as executors but in another six, a living wife was not made the executor. Cuthbert Cornforth(41) made three sons, all apparently minors, his executors. He appointed a brother-in-law, two nephews and a fourth person to be supervisors, with the injunction that they were to assist his wife and children and "not to suffer them to take any wrong wherein they may right them".

There appears to be no consistency in the naming of executors. Sometimes it appears that the executor is the key nominee for the performance of the will. William Robinson's (35) children were all under age and so it would appear that for this reason he made his brother-in-law executor. Christopher Fawell made his wife and daughter executors jointly but not his son who was still under 21. Yet in other cases the nomination of executors appears to be a formality. In such cases, a supervisor or supervisors were sometimes nominated, being apparently the effective performers. Ralph Hugill (10) made his son Richard, a minor, his executor with his brother Henry the tutor. Robert Dale (11) made his wife, a son, and a child still in the womb co-executors but his father-in-law, his brother and two other persons supervisors. Stephen Ward (44) made the executors his five children, including one newly born but not yet baptised. Thomas Pape (3) appointed his two daughters his executors although their mother and grandmother were still living. He appealed to his mother, ".., for God's sake, to be kind and good unto my poore wif and succourlesse children", which suggests that his executors were minors. Edmund Fawell's (38) wife was joined with two daughters in their minority as executors. Seniority or responsibility was not the invariable qualification for the task. Perhaps it was a way of signalling or protecting their priority as beneficiaries, or to protect children against a mother's remarriage.

Twenty three testators left widows but formal reference to their legal entitlement of widowright or thirds occurs only in four wills. Shares among children were unequal in a number of wills. William

Thompson's (4) reward to the son who had looked after him has been noticed. Isabel Ward's (5) instructions were that her daughter Margery would have nothing if she married a certain Marmaduke Carnell, alias Carnaby.

Six testators remembered godchildren. Isabel Ward (5) left twelve pence to a godchild and Margery Lassells (42) left twelve pence to every child she christened. Richard Hudless (14) was perhaps the most generous. After his wife's death, his house was to go to Thomas, the son of his godson John Lumley. Apparently without children, he made his godson's child his heir. Ralph Wren (27) was godfather of his brother's son and left him five shillings. Cuthbert Cornforth (41) left the same sum to his godson. Stephen Ward (44) left 26s 8d to his godson when he reached the age of 21.

The religious preamble

The Reformation had wrought great changes in the wording of the religious preambles of wills and testaments. When Thomas Hodgson of Cockerton made his will in 1559, he bequeathed his soul to

"Allmyghtye God maker of hevn & Earth & to our blyssed Laedy scent Marye & to all the hollye Coumpani of Heven".

When his namesake, Thomas Hodgson (53) of Morton, formerly of Cockerton, died in 1622, he contented himself with bequeathing his soul to "almighty god which was my maker and my rede[e]mer". Protestant doctrine taught that redemption was only possible through faith and through the merits and suffering of Jesus Christ. The intercession of the Holy Virgin and the saints was totally rejected for the saving of a man's soul. By 1600, England had experienced over forty consecutive years of Protestant rule. Most of the population had conformed. Any who clung to the "old" religion were liable to be fined for non-attendance at church, imprisoned for attending mass and even executed for harbouring or aiding a Catholic priest. Any hopes that the accession of James I in 1603 would lead to an improvement in the lot of his Catholic subjects were temporarily dashed by the fiasco of the Gunpowder Plot of 1605 which resulted in further anti-recusant legislation. Non-payment of fines could lead to sequestration of lands and goods, while probate of a Catholic's estate presented great problems. Of the 58 people whose wills and inventories form the basis for this study, only Robert Garnett (52), a gentleman, can be definitely identified as a Catholic.

His inventory is described as one "of all the goods and Household stuffe that could be found" and at £8 12s 8d was a low valuation for one of his status. The sequestration of his goods states that there was much old timber belonging to him lying about and "so subject to stealth and in danger to spoil and rott". His widow was therefore given licence to sell it immediately.

Indications of strong Puritan views occur in the wills of two of the Darlington gentry. When John Atkinson (49), referring to Christ as "my onely savio[u]r and Redeemer", bequeathed his soul to God the Creator in the hope that He would receive it into glory and place it in "the company of the heavenly angels and blessed S[ain]ts", he was likely to be meaning the company of the elect. In the long preamble to his will, William Barnes (8) not only emphasised his commitment to "... those articles of doctrine and faith now publicklye p[ro]fessed through his divine mercye by this Church of England ..." but also signalled his acceptance of the Calvinistic doctrine of predestination in his hope of a "joyfull resurrection and future glorie with the elect of God". Perhaps only Ann Surtees (39) displayed a conservatism in asking to be prayed for by the poor of Cockerton.

Leaving aside the four nuncupative wills, the religious preambles to the remaining 41 wills and testaments fall mainly into four groups. The first group of 15 wills consists of those who gave, bequeathed, committed, or commended their souls to Almighty God, Creator, Maker or Redeemer, with the wills of Ralph Wren (27) and Ann Surtees (39) further expressing their assurance of being saved. The wills of Michael Jeffreyson (32), Thomas Robinson (30) and Christopher Foster (45) substituted "Saviour" for "Creator", thereby putting all their hope of salvation in Christ. Thomas Robinson also pleaded for the forgiveness of his sins and offences.

The second group laid special emphasis on the merits, death and passion of Christ: Matthew Lambert (2) "... hoping assuredly by his Merets and holie passion to be saved..." and William Sober (47) "... trusting and fully assuring myselfe to possesse the heavenly Joyes of his kingdome through the merits of his Sonne Jesus Christ my Saviour and Redeemer ...". The writing of a significant number of the wills in this group of fourteen can be attributed to Richard Pickering, the parish clerk.

A further small group of four – William Thompson (4), Toby Colling (7), John Marshall (20) and Christopher Fawell (26) – placed their faith in the merits of Christ and further showed their commitment to Protestant doctrine by the addition of the telling phrase "and by none other means". These four wills have other details in common, those of Thompson, Marshall and Fawell, all Cockerton men, being in the same hand and all having witnesses in common. Thomas Mason wrote and witnessed all four.

Redemption through Christ's sacrifice upon the Cross was stressed by William Bower (51) and by Robert Loryman (14) whose will further spoke of Christ "... who hath geaven himself for me to be an offeringe and a sacryfice of a sweete smelling savoure to God his father ...". Another four – John Hall (12), Richard Hudlesse (14), John Glover (40) and John Lisle (55) – put their faith in the redeeming qualities of the shedding of Christ's precious blood.

It should, of course, be borne in mind that the preambles to most wills owe more to the style of the scribe than to that of the testator. Yet, it may be that the long, individually phrased, introductions to the wills of the gentry, William Barnes (8), William Bower (51), John Atkinson (49) and John Lisle (55), were written at their dictation. Nevertheless, since almost all wills were dictated at the deathbed, the testators mostly left the exact wording to the scribe, who could well have had a number of stock phrases in his repertoire to offer to his clients. The historian Duffy is very sceptical of conclusions, drawn from preambles, about personal beliefs. Writing of the period of the Reformation, the 1540s and 1550s, it is his view that they reflect external pressures much more than internal convictions.[13]

In a largely illiterate society, it is surprising that the clergy of Darlington did not serve often as witnesses to their parishioners' final wishes. There were only seven instances in the period under study: Robert Thomlinson witnessed the will of Thomas Pape (3); on the evidence of handwriting, his presence as a witness and one bequest of 3s 4d, Isaac Lowden can be tentatively identified as the writer of the wills of Richard Hudlesse (14) and Robert Loryman (13) and the inventories of Gawen Ratcliffe (18) and Robert Dent (19); and Brian Grant witnessed the wills of Ann Dent (36) and Margery Lassells (42).

Darlington's possession of a small grammar school would have provided the town with a nucleus of literate citizens willing to put their skills at the disposal of friends and neighbours. Indeed Richard Pickering, the parish clerk, chiefly acted as a professional scribe. To him can be attributed the writing of eighteen wills or inventories in the period 1604-1623. In the list of expenses for George Marshall's

(50) funeral appears the entry "to Rich[ard] Pickering for writing the will and inventories 3s 4d". He also features as a beneficiary in the wills of Ralph Wren (27), Ann Dent (36) and as one of John Atkinson's (49) creditors.

Charitable bequests

Over one third of the testators, 21 out of 57, left gifts to the poor in their wills. Although most were for local people, Margery Lassells (42) also wished to give to the poor of her native parish of Auckland as well as to those in Darlington. It is necessary to distinguish between the bequests which took the form of money to be invested and those which were indiscriminate hand-outs. John Lisle (55) and Cuthbert Cornforth (41), who were important men of wealth, left their gifts to the poor in the hands of the churchwardens. Thereafter the interest would have been distributed among the local townships to help the deserving and to put others to work. Other legacies were distributed at the discretion of executors or friends and relatives and were probably distributed among friends as a remembrance or without distinction among paupers present at the funeral. As late as 1625, Peter Glover (58) willed that his gift be given out "at the church door". Ann Surtees (39) left five shillings to the poor of Cockerton in the hope that they would pray for her.

Charitable bequests varied from Ralph Wren's (27) 2s 0d to that left by Toby Colling (7), £3 6s 8d each year for a term of three years. This large legacy was the most generous by far, not only in monetary terms but as a percentage of resources, representing 26% of his total assets. More representative was Lawrence Catherick (56) whose gift of £3 was equal to 1% of the value of his estate. The average amount from all donors was £1 16s. Cuthbert Cornforth (41) and Thomas Pape (3) also honoured the wishes made in their fathers' wills concerning bequests to the poor. Cornforth gave a further £2 "which my father did wyll" and in accordance with the will of John Pape of 1599, his son Thomas left a legacy of the income from his burgage on High Row, which was to provide four horse-loads of coal at Christmas and 3s 4d in bread at Easter for the poor of Darlington. Donations for the maintenance of public works were another form of charitable bequest. Matthew Lambert (2) left 5s and Michael Jeffreyson (32) 3s 4d for the repair of the causeway leading to the Hermitage, a location in the vicinity of what is now Bank Top station.

Bequests to clergymen were infrequent: "to Isaac Lowden 3s 4d"

(14), "to Mr Brian Grant Viccar for his paines in visiting me 3s 4d" (36), "unto Mr Robert hope now Curate at darlington one halfe peece or in liew thereof 11s in monie" (49). It is, rather, as debtors and creditors that the clergy appear in the inventories and as buyers and sellers. Isaac Lowden (31) owed 9s 4d to Anthony Dennis (28), the draper, a debt apparently still unpaid at the time of his own death, his list of debts including "to Mrs Dennise 9s 6d". Others of Dennis's debtors were Robert Hutton, rector of Haughton-le-Skerne (1590-1625) and his son-in-law, John Vaux, curate and wizard of Auckland St Helen. Many entries were for professional services rendered: "to Mr Hope for his fees 5s 4d" (49); and several inventories listed the mortuary, the payment due to the priest on the death of a parishioner. Among these occur two references to the payment of a mortuary to "Mr Gifford" (30) and (35). It would seem likely that this was Robert Gifford, the assistant curate at the beginning of the century. In 1601, his Puritan views had led to his presentment for "christening children without the sign of the Cross, and for the marriage of divers persons without the ring".[14] However, he and his family had obviously found favour with Elizabeth Jennison of Walworth who bequeathed him in 1604 "a booke, being a conference betwixt Doctor Whitguifte and Mr Cartwright,[15] and 40s and to his wief six silver spoones with apostles' heads and to his brother Symon Gifford 40s". The same lady also bequeathed 10s to Mr Throckmorton and his wife.[15] The latter must surely be Mary Throckmorton (48) "lait wiefe and Relict of Robert Throckmorton Clarke deceassed" who made her will in September 1620 and whose social status was such that her goods were appraised by the bailiff John Lisle (55), Timothy and Thomas Barnes and Simon Gifford. Her mother-in-law, Thomazine Heath, had left most of her property to Robert after her death in 1596 in a will which referred to gold rings, including one with a diamond. This generous legacy helps to explain why the widow of the vicar of Aycliffe in her turn disposed of more earthly goods than the vicar of Darlington, Isaac Lowden.

The making of the inventory

It was usual to make inventories of all estates of £5 value and above. Houses and land were not valued in inventories but the value of leases was quite often stated and sometimes houses or burgage property were distributed by wills.

There is much variation in the interval between burial and the making of the inventory. The most valuable estate, that of Cuthbert Cornforth (41) worth £816, was appraised within ten days of his burial. Gawen Ratcliffe's (18) modest belongings valued at £5 8s were inventoried within a day of burial. Thomas Robinson's (30) inventory is dated October 17th, 1612, the day before his burial which suggests it was made immediately after he died. However, it includes the costs of probate which was not granted until December 5th, showing that the document was actually made in stages and that doubt must exist about the dating of such documents. The quick appraisal of such an important estate, valued at £238, was perhaps necessary before the mourners in their grief inadvertently bore off any of the belongings of the deceased. On the other hand, John Hall's (12) inventory was not made until fifty days after his burial. His death was preceded by the burials of five of his children and servant and his goods had quite possibly to be left in quarantine for that period. The minister Isaac Lowden's (31) inventory was not made until 193 days after his death. Although modest in value, it records the titles of many books. Conceivably, it was left to await the arrival of his successor as one who would be knowledgeable about books. His successor was indeed one of the appraisers. The fallibility of the appraisers is implied in the entry for Margery Lassells's (42) stable, "divers other thinges in divers places now remembred 5s."

The valuations

Because the Act Books include inventories which have been lost, it is possible to state a range of values for 110 Darlington inventories in the period 1600-25. They range from 11s 8d to £816 17s 5d. Over half the inventories were for £30 and under, two thirds were for £50 and under and three quarters were for £86 and under. The median figure is £29 2s 4d.

The range of values for the 57 inventories in this collection extends from £2 17s 10d to £816 17s 5d. Half are for £50 and under, two thirds are for £86 and under, and three quarters are for £150 and under. The median is £46 8s 4d. Thus what survives narrows the range to favour the more prosperous.

The inventories prompt many obvious questions. How much deliberate undervaluing was there? How near to current market prices were the valuations? How actively were the appraisers concerned to keep the court in the dark about the value of the estate? The wink and the nod at inventory-making are suggested by the comment made to the widow of William Townend, whose inventory of 1611/12 has not survived. According to the widow, one of the executors "called me aside" to urge acceptance of the administration, saying,

> "Yow may well enough take it for the goodes being valued to Thre score and seaven poundes are well worth a hundred poundes..."

She was, however, to complain of this undervaluation, the executors having sold for only £24 the lease of her husband's farm at Great Burdon which still had four years to run and which she said was worth £9 a year.[16]

A statement exists of the money actually raised from the sale of goods appraised. Edmund Fawell's (37) inventory may provide a test of valuation and market prices because it is accompanied by "a true inventory of all [th]e goods... as they were all sold". However, the prices in the two documents correspond so closely that it is doubtful whether the goods were "freely" sold. Perhaps there was a system of charitable "insider-bidding" at such sales.

All of the inventories and some of the wills have been compared to get an idea of standards of living. Defying 17th-century tradition, all seven women have been classed as equal to their menfolk for the purposes of this exercise in pounds, shillings and pence. Three people had to be excluded from some of the calculations for lack of sufficient detail. Richard Dack's (21) inventory was only a list of debts. John Sober (33) and Peter Glover (58) had wills but no inventories. Although the wills give an indication of their finances – Peter Glover promised £436 in legacies – the absence of detailed figures make it impossible to include them in some of the statistical analyses.

The precise value of personal estates is difficult to determine. The value of household goods, together with any farm, shop, or trade stock, would seem a fair guide to a person's financial situation, but such a valuation fails to take into account any debts or credits unsettled at the time of death. For example, Cuthbert Cornforth's (41) goods were appraised at £340 but addition of his credits would more than double the value of his estate to £818. Even with the deduction of his debts, the value would still be £761. At the other end of the scale John Lomley's (29) goods, worth only £2 17s 8d, were insufficient to cover his debts of £9 1s 4d.

In an attempt to assess the figure which most accurately reflects the true value of estates, reference was made to the Probate Act Books. The values given there were compared with all the possible combinations of appraised, gross and net totals for each individual. In 19 cases, the Act Book figures are missing or illegible. In 14 cases, they were totally dissimilar to any figure, gross or net. Only in the case of Christopher Fawell (26) did the Act Book figure give both gross and net valuations.

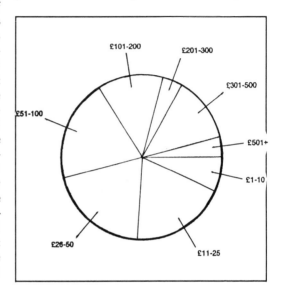

The values found to be the most consistent with those in the Act Books were those which combined the appraised value of goods with the debts due to the deceased. Values are therefore calculated in this way for comparison and for the pie-chart above.

The pie-chart demonstrates the distribution of wealth through the sample of 54 used. They divide neatly into two parts: two-thirds had assets of under £100, while the remaining third had £100 or more. Cuthbert Cornforth (41), a farmer of Blackwell, headed the list with £818. Of the ten next most wealthy, six were yeoman farmers, with the other four the two borough bailiffs, Barnes (8) and Lisle (55), the wealthy merchant Anthony Dennis (28) and Mary Throckmorton (48), widow of the vicar of Aycliffe.

Further down the scale, with assets of £100-200, yeoman farmers still dominate the scene, in company with John Atkinson (49), a gentleman and Miles Guy (15), a cordwainer who was the only craftsman with assets of over £100. The rest were the smaller farmers, the shopkeepers, most of the craftsmen and Isaac Lowden (31), the vicar of St Cuthbert's.

With the great scarcity of coin and the absence of banks, cash flow was much more of a problem in 17th-century Darlington than it is today. Gold coins occur sometimes as legacies. Their rarity was such that they were normally regarded as heirlooms rather than as currency. Thus reference was made to "gold" as well as to "money" in Miles Guy's (15) purse. Thomas Catherick (22) left his newly-born grandson an "Angel of gold", a coin worth 6s 8d depicting St Michael defeating Satan. William Bower (51), who had £40 in cash, bequeathed to each of two "very loving and kind friends" a "Jacobus", a hammered gold coin, first struck in 1604 and worth 20s.

Only six persons appear to have been completely clear of both debts and credits. Debts totalling £2,317 5s 4d were outstanding in 608 individual amounts, averaging out at 15 debts for every person to whom money was owed. It seems that the whole town owed Richard Dack (21) for his pieces of cloth, as he had 88 names in his debtors' list. For the most part, these were relatively small sums and in total amounted only to £28 19s 7d. Anthony Dennis (28) also had a large number of credit customers but was owed over £250; Sir George Conyers and his wife owed between them £29 1s 3d. A substantial number of his customers had also run up accounts that were considered "desperate" by his appraisers. By contrast, William Dockera (25) was owed only 7s 1d and that by five different individuals.

Cuthbert Cornforth (41), a farmer of Blackwell, was owed by far the largest amount of money, £478 15s 1d, mostly by neighbours and local people. Although one item in his list of debtors specifies the nature of the debt, namely that Ralph Bayles owed £6 for a horse, it would seem likely that many other sums would have been for stock or goods rather than money. Stephen Ward (44), another Blackwell farmer, was also owed a substantial sum, with some debtors outside Darlington, at Middridge, Girsby and Redworth. Thomas Nawton (17) appears to have conducted much of his wool business some distance away, with debts due to him from Berwick-upon-Tweed, Ripon, Horncastle in Lincolnshire, and Shibden, near Halifax.

The deceased themselves figured again in the cycle of credit, owing to others a total of £946 18s 1d. In the majority of instances, the reasons for the debts were not given but there were references to goods, services and rents: William Robinson (35), a weaver, "for yarne and coales"; Isabel Catherick (24), "for tow kie wintringe"; William Sober (47), "for Rent of the beck feilde". Debts also included such items as funeral expenses and costs of probate, gifts to the poor and fees to craft guilds.

Appraisers, those "four honest men" who valued the goods of the deceased, were generally enlisted from friends and neighbours, and should normally have included relatives and creditors. A creditor can be clearly identified as an appraiser in twelve of the inventories in this collection, including three where two creditors acted. Some men were, particularly favoured to perform appraisals, perhaps for reasons of local standing. Lawrence Catherick (56) was present at ten of the appraisals, Robert Ward at nine, with a further fourteen men attending to this duty on five or more occasions. It is apparent that cordwainers generally acted as appraisers of their fellow-craftsmen's goods. Normally, also, a relative or relatives occur among the appraisers but few cases can be securely identified. Thomas Pape's uncle Chambers and Cuthbert Cornforth's cousin Ward are examples.

Apparel and Arms

In a society where the majority lived in the grimmest poverty, absolutely every type of article had a value because of its potential for re-use. Thus clothing, however unmodish, worn or foul, was worthy of pricing. In just over half of all cases, apparel was put together with the purse which almost asserts equal convertibility. It is not possible to separate the two, although it may be supposed that the value of clothing in the figure of £10 for the purse and apparel of gentleman and town bailiff, John Lisle (55), and for the gentlewoman Mary Throckmorton (48) was high. However, to guess at the ratio of purse and apparel for the prosperous farmer, Stephen Ward (44), which was stated to be £10 4s 6d, or for the affluent merchant, Anthony Dennis (28), which was £4, is even more difficult. The weaver, John Corker (46), had £8 14s in money but his clothes were worth only 11s. His was one of some twenty cases where separate values were given for money and for clothing. The clothing of the town bailiff, William Barnes (8), amounted to a tenth of the value of his household goods. His rank and kinship to a bishop required a lavish appearance. The well-to-do freeholder, William Bower (51), possessed clothing worth a sixth of his household goods. However, the clothes of the tanners, Thomas Catherick (22) and Michael Jeffreyson (32), were worth only 7% and 3% of their household goods. They each possessed clothes worth twenty shillings.

Toby Colling's (7) clothes were worthy of specific bequest. He left his jerkin and a doublet to Cuthbert Middleton, his best hose to John

Simpson, and to William Heviside his best shoes, boots and a pair of stockings. He left his black cloak to Thomas Colling and a hat to Thomas Mason who wrote the will. After naming his executors, he remembered his brown jerkin which he then bequeathed to John Williamson. Other testators knew how grateful their legatees would be for the clothes off their backs. This was the expression used by John Hall (12) in 1606, leaving his coat, breeches and all the rest of the apparel "on my backe" to his brother-in-law, the rest of his clothes to one son and his best cloak to another. William Bower (51) left his brother Richard one half of his clothes, specifying "the meanest and coarsest sort thereof", while the other half, "of the better sort", were reserved for his nephew. John Lisle (55) bequeathed a suit of apparel to his servant and the cloak he wore, together with a piece of new cloth to make another cloak. He also left a suit of apparel to his nephew. Richard Hudlesse (14) must have been somewhat dress-conscious, for his bequests included a fustian doublet, a pair of green kersey breeches, three pairs of hose, a white frieze jerkin, as well as his best shoes and boots. Isaac Lowden's (31) clothing, with gown, bands and cuffs, suggested the minister he was, even if no true uniformity of dress yet prevailed in the profession.

In none of the eight women's wills and inventories was clothing much mentioned. Isabel Ward (5) left her best black coat and a brode red petticoat "which was our mothers" to her sister. Agnes Claxton (34) left the best of everything to her daughter Ann; coat, petticoat, hat, band, part cloth, smock, apron and a pair of silk sleeves. Ann Dent (36) bequeathed footwear, aprons and lesser items of clothing to her servant and two sisters. Her inventory lists her matching purple outfit, worth £1 15s 4d, suggesting that she was a woman with an eye for colour. Her best coat was highly appraised at 13s 4d. Ann Surtees (39) owned apparel valued at £1, a sixth of the value of her household goods. Isabel Catherick's (24) linen and woollen apparel was worth £1 10s. The inventory of John Atkinson (49), singleman, lists and values his female attire highly at £5. William Dockera (25) left a silk hat to his daughter, Margery.

Anthony Dennis's (28) stock of materials would provide everything required to dress the 17th-century woman; wool, linen, cotton and silk cloth, dyed in soft natural colours such as hare, ginger, sage, mouse, primrose, purple, yellow, orange and ash. His stock also included garters, stockings, nightcaps, whalebone and a gentlewoman's fan.

From 1600 onwards, a softer line was introduced into both men's and women's clothing; the farthingale superseded by padding worn around the hips, longer doublets and breeches and the ruff giving way to softer falling collars. Skirts were looped up to show an elaborate petticoat, shoes (alike in style for men and women) had heels for the first time, and hats and caps were worn indoors. Cloaks or shawls would be worn by women out-of-doors rather than the coats listed in the inventories of Isabel Ward (5), Agnes Claxton (34) and Ann Dent (36). These probably were loose gowns open down the front, sleeveless and falling from the shoulders. Towards mid-century, padding and the exaggerated line were phased out as fashion responded to the religious preoccupation with decency and restraint.[17]

In general, quality of attire very sharply distinguished the classes in society and impertinent emulation would be discouraged. It was not easy for people to check their appearance. Only two of the women testators, Mary Throckmorton (48) and Margery Lassells (42) possessed looking-glasses. Anthony Dennis (28) had a dozen little seeing glasses valued, together with three combs, at 1s 8d.

Of the 14 persons who owned weapons, six possessed body armour. John Lisle (55) had a corselet only. In several instances, the weapons seem to have been no more than inherited clutter. Robert Dent (19) had two "old" swords which reappeared in his widow's (36) inventory. John Fawcet (43) had a halberd, which was valued with the fire-irons, three spits and a pair of iron racks. Christopher Foster's (45) sword was valued with a tablecloth, three cheeses, a skip and two loaves at 3s. However, Richard Hudless's (14) sword was bracketed with his pitchfork not only by the appraisers, but by him himself as a bequest in his will. This suggests the pitchfork was, in truth, a weapon. Nevertheless, it too, like Thomas Johnson's (16) long bow and half sheaf of arrows, belonged to a generation of outmoded weaponry. On the other hand, seven of the 14 had firearms. Toby Colling's (7) morion, sword, case of pistols and calliver combine with his varied wardrobe and an absence of trade or tools to hint at souvenirs of a martial past. The obligation existed for every parish periodically to provide men with arms and armour for the musters, as in 1618, when about 30 men of Darlington mustered with the whole county. The parish was able to provide 15 men with muskets and 11 with corselets. At least some of these were in private possession. Calliver, headpiece, flash and touchbox came to Thomas Guy when his father Miles Guy (15) died in 1607. Laurence Catherick (56) and Thomas Hodgson (53) appeared at the 1618 muster, armed with muskets which their inventories show them to have owned. The town bailiff, William Barnes (8), and the gentleman, John Atkinson (49), possessed such quantities of arms, ancient and modern, that one supposes they kept sufficient to arm their servants.

The house and its contents

In 1585 fire had devastated Darlington, allegedly gutting 273 houses and destroying all of High Row and Skinnergate,[18] so it may be assumed that much of the domestic building within the town in 1600 was of recent construction. These houses and older ones were probably timber built and thatched. The following streets were in existence: Bondgate, Houndgate, Blackwellgate, Skinnergate, North-gate, Market Place, Head (High) Row, Behindgarths, Tubwell Row, Priestgate, Prebend Row and, after 1600, Clay Row.[19] There is little information as to where the testators' houses were sited, but there are references in the wills: Thomas Pape's (3) house on High Row with another on Clay Row, William Barnes's (8) two houses in Skinnergate and one on the Head Row, Robert Loryman's (13) house in Northgate, Miles Guy's (15) burgages in Skinnergate and Bondgate and his personal residence on High Row.

It is known that the 12th-century manor-house at Feethams, just south of the church, was stone-built and Longstaffe refers to the Elizabethan brick-built house, where the vicar lived in 1712 and of which a very little of the fabric remains. It is possible that, with an increasing scarcity of timber, bricks made from clay from the east bank of the Skerne (Clay Row) were becoming a more popular and certainly safer material for domestic construction in the early 17th century.[20]

Of the 57 inventories examined, 34 refer to property in Darlington (two in Bondgate), ten in Cockerton, six in Blackwell, one in Oxen-le-field, one in Morton and one in Archdeacon Newton. Two also refer to the property at Bedburn Park in Hamsterley parish, occupied by William Barnes (8) and John Lisle (55) until their deaths in 1605 and 1622 respectively, which appears to have been a regular perquisite of the bishops' bailiffs. Rooms were specified in 40 inventories, of which 35 mention rooms on two or more floors. It is assumed that where the term chamber is used it describes an upstairs apartment. However, Gawen Ratcliffe (18) appears to have lived in a one-roomed house and that single room is listed as a chamber. A possible explanation is that he lived on the first floor of a shared building. In William Barnes's (8) Darlington house, there is reference to the "highest chamber", perhaps indicating a second floor. Houses of five rooms or more appear in 26 inventories, although it must be stressed that these figures may not be accurate in all cases. It is probable that some rooms were permanently empty or that goods had been gathered in a few rooms for the convenience of the appraisers. For instance, John Atkinson's (49) inventory included goods from only the hall, buttery and parlour, but there was a prodigious amount of furniture there, valued at £51 16s 2d. Poorly furnished servants' rooms were frequently recorded and in most cases employees would be expected to bed down in or over out-houses, byres or stables, with little provision of comfort or warmth.

In these larger houses, the value of household goods tended, of course, to be high. Mary Throckmorton's (48) valuation heads the list at £115 13s 8d. with only five rooms and a stable. Paradoxically, Thomas Pape (3), with eight rooms, had goods worth £9 19s 2d. Of the seemingly smaller houses, Anthony Dennis's (28) four rooms (apart from his shop) contained personal furniture worth £36 19s 6d, while the contents of the shop itself read like a veritable treasure house, bringing his total wealth to £235 7s 10d, which included the silver spoons he held in pawn.

The table opposite shows that the value of furniture and household goods bore some relation to the size of house, but not invariably. The main rooms listed include the hall, parlours, kitchen, buttery, larder, and upstairs, chambers, further parlours and lofts. Four houses had a cellar and others had milkhouse, brewhouse and shop, meaning perhaps a workshop incorporated in the main structure. Where buildings were possibly separate, such as stables, byres and barns, they are indicated. Rooms appear to be multi-purpose, especially in the less wealthy houses. Clearly the hall was used for eating, storage, cooking and sleeping, as the haphazard arrangement of furniture seems to suggest. Three inventories, including affluent Mary Throckmorton's (48), list beds in the hall.

Such designations as kitchen chamber, hall or parlour chamber determine the position of an upper-floor room by reference to the room below.[21] Access to upper floors would have been by staircase, either internal or external, but in some a ladder might still have been the only and most common means of ascent.[22]

Name	Year	Minimum no. of rooms	Approx. value of household goods	% of total wealth	Total wealth except debts & credits
at Bedburn					
John Lisle	1622	12(+ milkhouse)	30 0 0	17%	178 6 8
William Barnes	1605	9(+milkhouse,brewhouse,kiln & stable)	57 8 6	20%	293 8 6
at Darlington					
John Lisle	1622	12(+ garner)	82 14 8	33%	250 14 8
William Barnes	1605	11(+ milkhouse,brewhouse & garner)	56 3 8	24%	236 0 0
Lawrence Catherick	1623	9(+milkhouse,barn & stable)	46 11 8	16%	286 8 3
John Fawcet	1617	9(+ two stables & kiln)	32 5 10	39%	82 0 0
Miles Guy	1607	9(+ oilhouse , stable & kiln)	29 5 8	27%	107 12 4
Margery Lassels	1616	9(+ brewhouse & stable)	78 18 10	100%	78 18 10
William Bower	1622	9(+ milkhouse)	52 6 0	14%	365 16 7
Michael Jeffreyson	1612	9(+ stable)	33 8 4	72%	46 8 4
Matthew Lambert	1603	8(+ stable)	15 7 4	38%	39 9 4
Robert Loryman	1606	8	40 19 4	64%	63 9 4
Thomas Pape	1603	8	9 19 10	40%	25 2 3
Anne Dent	1615	7 (+brewhouse & stable)	33 10 6	88%	37 16 10
Cuthbert Cornforth	1616	7 (+milkhouse, oxhouse & barn)	57 8 8	16%	340 2 4
Robert Dent	1609	7(+ stable)	20 9 11	57%	35 14 2
Anthony Dennis	1611	6 (+stable)	36 19 6	16%	235 7 10
John Glover	1615	6 (+stable)	16 19 4	75%	22 9 4
Thomas Johnson	1607	6 (+barkhouse)	24 3 10	38%	62 18 5
Geoffrey Raine	1605	6 (+stables)	27 4 0	61%	43 17 4
Robert Dale	1606	6	13 6 2	16%	78 14 0
John Hall	1606	5 (+kiln)	12 14 6	20%	60 15 6
George Marshall	1622	5 (+stable)	30 17 0	67%	45 14 0
Thomas Robinson	1612	5 (+barn & dove-loft)	23 0 6	15%	151 19 2
William Sober	1620	5 (+stable)	10 4 0	12%	80 19 11
Mary Throckmorton	1620	5 (+stable)	115 13 8	64%	180 3 8
Leonard Dack	1604	4	27 15 10	45%	61 5 10
Christopher Foster	1618	4	16 19 0	29%	58 4 4
Thomas Hodgson	1622	4	15 11 10	7%	209 4 6
William Robinson	1613	4	5 6 10	28%	18 12 1
John Atkinson	1622	3 (+stable & kiln)	51 8 2	43%	118 8 0
William Thompson	1603	3 (+barn & byre)	14 4 0	8%	171 10 0
Stephen Ward	1617	3 (+oxhouse & barn)	36 4 4	21%	166 0 6
Ralph Thursby	1622	3 (+barn)	11 3 0	4%	272 12 0
Thomas Catherick	1609	2 (+tanhouse)	10 16 4	18%	59 4 8
Anthony Stainsbey	1623	2 (+milkhouse)	16 4 8	12%	134 2 4
John Marshall	1609	2	13 6 8	22%	58 15 2
Christopher Fawell	1610	1 (+milkhouse)	13 0 8	33%	38 5 0
Toby Colling	1605	1	5 17 0	20%	28 17 0
Gawen Ratcliffe	1608	1	5 0 0	90%	5 8 0

It is unlikely that corridors were built into the fabric and apartments would be linked by doorways. Problems caused by this lack of privacy and warmth would be solved by the use of screens and, in sleeping quarters, by bed-hangings.[23] Buttery, larder and dairy, all rooms connected with the storage and preservation of perishable foods, would probably have been situated on the northern side of the house, away from direct sunlight, and also as far as possible from the heat of hall or oven.[24]

William Harrison, in his *Description of England* of 1577, noted among the changes in contemporary domestic life, the introduction of the chimney and the enclosed hearth in more modest houses. This allowed the insertion of an upper floor within the hall to gain extra and more private accommodation on the upper storey.[25] The chambers and upper parlours so provided influenced in turn the style and size of furniture and led to variations in the four basic items: tables, seats, chests and beds.

The hall was still the principal room of the house. Here were one or more long tables which were probably tops with frames or boards with trestles, although the latter are rarely mentioned. In addition there were tables of all shapes and sizes throughout the house. Eleven inventories do not mention a table of any kind but in a few cases the testators owned table-linen. Carpets, a rare and expensive commodity, too good to place underfoot, were a decorative covering for furniture and beds. "Dressing tables", found only in kitchens, were used in the preparation of meat. Several playing tables are listed which may simply have been boards marked out for games. Desks then were portable boxes with sloping lids.

Chairs were at this time becoming more widely used, usually one or two at the table in the hall. John Lisle's (55) house in Bedburn boasted eight, one a "little green chair". There were buffet stools, forms and long settles. Before upholstered furniture became common, cushions provided a degree of comfort, set on a rope or leather mesh. Fawcet's (43) inventory included a back stool, the farthingale chair, armless, to accommodate the voluminous skirts then worn by womenfolk of rank.

No mention is made of the materials or woods used in making furniture except for William Bower's (51) "certain peeces of oak and ashwood unwrought". Cupboards, presses and aumbries are scattered throughout the rooms, without much indication of size or shape, with the exception of several references to Flanders chest, heavily carved pieces to be found in the wealthier homes. William Bower had three in his house, with a fourth belonging to him in Robert Newton's house. The livery cupboard stood in hall and parlour alike, for food storage, its doors and panels pierced for ventilation. Nearly every home had some means of storage and four inventories of the more affluent houses list over ten such items.

Beds accounted for a large proportion of floor space. The stand bed with its four posts and tester often had truckle or trundle beds, equipped with wheels for storage underneath. Geoffrey Raine's (9) inventory lists no fewer than eleven stand beds and three truckle-beds in a six-roomed house. Robert Dent (19) had seven guest beds in his loft. There were quantities of linen; dozens of pairs of linen sheets in the grander houses, with harden (of coarser quality) for lesser mortals. Pillows, bolsters, mattresses, blankets and coverlets furnished the beds, although in the poorer homes there is little evidence of much comfort. The number of beds in Robert Dent's (19) house and the six dozen trenchers and five dozen spoons in the smith Robert Loryman's (13) house suggest that they offered accommodation or refreshment for travellers.

Signs of affluence emerge for families in the upper income bracket. Ten households had silver spoons. Three had silver bowls. Mary Throckmorton (48) had several expensive items of gilt and silverware, glassware and three china dishes. Hers was the only house to have either a clock or a sundial. She could apparently entertain on a lavish scale for she had 88 pieces of pewter valued at £3 6s 8d. At his home in Bondgate, John Atkinson (49) possessed expensive 'oversea' covers and tablecloths and silk cushions, a citheron and a recorder, and a substantial library of books, valued at £6. Michael Jeffreyson (32), tanner, was quite exceptional in his possession of three pictures.

Many homes had food in store: beef and fish, mostly salted, bacon, cheese, butter and bread, and apples, not always kept where the modern reader would expect. Thomas Hodgson (53) had cheeses in his parlour and William Bower (51) had meat salting in the chamber above his hall. Bees and beehives were listed in five inventories. Thomas Robinson (30) had four hives in the barn and William Robinson (35) had three in the loft above the chamber. Ralph Thursby's (54) inventory speaks simply of "bees". Anthony Dennis kept honey with prunes, treacle and sugar in his shop.

The values put upon household goods varied considerably, presumably on account of their quality. Beds ranged from £6 13s 4d for an elaborately furnished one, down to a trundle bed at 3s 4d, and cupboards from 40s to 10s. Blankets were valued at around 7s 6d and linen sheets at 8s per pair. Everyday tableware was of stone, brass, earthenware, wood or pewter with prices ranging accordingly: 2d for a greenstone pot, 4s for a brass one and pewter doublers at 1s 3d. A shilling was the value put upon one of a whole range of items: a spinning wheel, a chest, a clothes-press, a cradle, a washing tub, a dozen tin spoons, a chamber pot or a pair of linen pillowcases.

Items specifically for children are rarely mentioned. Five houses had cradles, one with a cradle cloth. Christopher Foster (45), the butcher, had "a little child chaire" in the hall. Anthony Dennis's (28) shop stocked two dozen little books for children.

It is likely that several homes used coal for fuel although only four inventories list it. It was probably brought down the "coal road" through Cockerton from the pits in south-west Durham. Listed in John Atkinson's (49) stable was a bay horse with "coaling furniture", pannier baskets for carrying coals. Gawen Ratcliffe (18), despite being one of the poorer testators, used coal and stored it in his chamber, "with old stuffe" valued at 5s. Fire irons, tongs and fire shovels were common. Seven houses had lanterns, all kept indoors but probably for outside use. None was valued at more than a few pence. John Atkinson was alone in having one described as made of glass. Candlesticks were, of course, an essential household commodity and they appear in pewter, brass or latten (an alloy of copper and zinc). In two houses there were candle-cases, one valued at £2 and another to be found stored appropriately in Margery Lassells's (42) "dark buttery". John Hall (12) had a stock of oil and tallow kept in the parlour, while the cordwainer Miles Guy (15) had an oilhouse, where he stored six gallons of oil and twenty stone of tallow which was used for soap-making and leather dressing as well as for candlemaking. Kitchens housed a familiar array of pots, pans, frying pans and dripping pans.

Even in the larger houses no rooms appear to have been designated as privies. Fourteen households list chamberpots and most have one or two, sometimes kept in the hall. Margery Lassells (42) had seven, and John Atkinson (49) and William Bower (51) possessed close stools.

Brewing

The consumption of ale and beer, as part of a daily diet for all levels of society, was commended by 16th- and 17th-century writers, notably Gervase Markham, the soldier and writer, and Andrew Boord, the traveller and physician termed "a lewd popish hypocrite" by Harrison.[26] Until the general introduction of tea, coffee and chocolate much later in the 17th century, they were the most widely consumed beverages, giving nutrition and sustenance to men, women and children alike. Drunkenness was probably widespread. Presentments of Darlington people for this fault at the Archdeacon's Court in Durham, over a period of just two or three years, show that the several cases were only the more outrageous or stubborn ones. In June 1600, Richard Stainton was presented as a common drunkard,

"... & in particuler for that of laite he was so drunken amongest a great company that he could not use him self as a man but moore like a beast not able to goe but was caried home by strength of men".

At the same court, William Johnson was presented,

"That he in most beastlie maner *inter pocula* in William Hunsdens of Darlington his house did loose his pointes and let downe his britches before some gentlemen and others, and ther offered to ease him self by the fire side in presence of all the company as is enformed to the Churchwardens presentinge, by the said William Hunsdens and his wife greatly therwith offended".

In April 1601, John Sober (33) was presented as a drunkard and an idle person who after several admonitions from the minister would not be reformed. A worse case was James Askerigge, presented in June 1602,

"... he is a common drunkard and a blasphemous swearer & a bawdie Talkar, who beinge admonished ... answered with blasphemous othes ... he is a common Rayler & slanderer of every man that crossethe his affection".

The vicar and churchwardens made an earnest request to the court that this man be punished for these offences. In June 1603, they presented Michael Shaw and his wife Elizabeth as common drunkards.[27]

The inventories suggest that brewing was carried out to a greater or lesser degree in many homes. Malt was produced by steeping the barley grain in water for two to three days to promote swelling. This was then drained, spread in a moderate temperature on a malting floor and left to sprout. After carefully controlled germination, the grain was spread on kiln-hairs and suspended over heat. The resulting malted grain was cooled, ground and stored. In use, the malt was boiled with water in a large cauldron, transferred to a mashvat where more malt was added, and boiling water allowed to filter through the porridge-like substance. The resulting liquid, the wort, was drawn off and fed into a large copper pan with the addition of the hops, if used. This boiling completed, the liquid was transferred to large tubs, yeast was added and when fermentation was complete, the beer was drawn off and stored in barrels.[28] William Harrison, writing in 1577, said that beer produced by a similar method in his own household, cost about 20s for 200 gallons or more.

Hops were banned in brewing by Henry VII and, although later re-introduced, their use was frowned on for a considerable time by those who favoured the hopless ale. It was not until the last years of the 16th century that hops were commonly added to the malt infusion to give flavour and colour. In only two inventories are hops mentioned. Anthony Dennis (28) had six pounds in his shop and a quantity described as "a C: hops" in his house. William Bower (51) had six pounds of hops.

Brewhouses were incorporated in the premises of only four of the testators. William Barnes (8) had two, at Bedburn and Darlington, while John Sober (33), the drunkard, and the widows Ann Dent (36) and Margery Lassells (42) had one each. Kilns are listed in five inventories and kiln-hairs, made from woven horsehair, in six. Miles Guy (15), Lawrence Catherick (56) and William Bower (51) of Oxen-le-field owned malt-lofts, Bower's being apparently in his burgage on High Row.

Twelve list quantities of malt or barley stored in lofts or outhouses. Miles Guy (15) and John Atkinson (49) clearly ran a flourishing trade in malt. They died with over £16 and £12 respectively owed to them for sales. George Marshall's (50) funeral expenses included 6s 9d for six pecks of malt, perhaps to provide a brew made for the occasion.

Only twelve inventories had no brewing equipment listed. Of the rest, some had brewing vessels and some a stock of malt which suggests that they were active in brewing for domestic use. It is likely that beer and ale were in daily use in most households. Barrels, casks, tuns and other vessels are frequently listed in the inventories but probably they were empty. Their contents would otherwise have been valued.

Wine seems to have played little part in the lives of most of the testators. There is only one reference in the inventories: two gallons were served at John Atkinson's (49) funeral, probably mulled with the half pound of sugar listed, to warm the mourners on a cold December day. A Durham Chancery complaint records that Margery Lassells (42), the vintner, bought her wine from Robert Cock of Newcastle and refused to pay the agreed price, because of its "decayed, naughtie and not merchantable" condition.[29]

Similarly, there is little mention of spirits. Anthony Dennis (28) had several pints of "aqua vite" in his shop. William Barnes (8) at Darlington, John Lisle (55) at Bedburn, John Atkinson (49) and Margery Lassells (42) all possessed distilling equipment. The latter also had an aqua vite bottle of which the contents were unrecorded.

A variety of drinking vessels would have been included in the large quantities of pewter which are mentioned. Glasses were in use in the households of John Atkinson (49), John Lisle (55), Michael Jeffreyson (32) and Mary Throckmorton (48) who also possessed glass bottles. Margery Lassells (42) had two silver cups and John Lisle (55) left two silver beer bowls to his stepson.

Occupations

The 58 individuals may be summarily described as seven gentlefolk, 18 yeomen and agriculturalists, 24 craftsmen, shopkeepers and tradesmen; and four men and five women of unknown occupation. Eight of the 58 were women, of whom one has been classed with the gentlefolk. Another was a vintner and a third appears to have been a draper. The occupations of four men were not evident. In the table on the following page, some occupations have been deduced and are therefore indicated by brackets.

The range of occupations in the table below, appears to agree with the likely distribution of activities in a principal market-town on the Great North Road, despite being determined by the random survival of testamentary documents.

The clergy

In 1548, when the church of St Cuthbert ceased to be collegiate, the stipends of its vicar and curate had been fixed at £16 and £8 per annum respectively.[30] By the third quarter of the 16th century, the value of these stipends had been eroded by inflation and the curate was supplementing his income by combining his clerical duties with those of the master of the town's grammar school. By the end of the

Total	Occupation (assumed in brackets)	No.	Value of inventory to nearest £ i.e. goods plus credits minus debts (Act book valuation in brackets)
	Gentleman	5	544, 366, 246, 126, 9
7	Minister	1	-2 (21)
	Minister's widow	1	161 (161)
	Yeoman	11	762(817),438(437),277(254),257(269), 239(266),108(168),108(108),54,44,13(16),NK
18	Husbandman	1	31(38 gross, 31 net)
	Labourer	1	9
	(Agriculturalist)	5	301(343),171(171),160(160),47,28(29)
	Tanner	4	75 (89), 75 (79), 74 (96), 46 (46)
	Cordwainer	4	148 (148), 61 (86), 52 (62), 35 (39)
	(Cordwainer)	1	-5 (25)
	(Tanner/cordwainer)	1	37 (37)
	Glover	1	38 (44)
	Weaver	3	50 (50), 19 (22), 13 (19)
	(Draper woman)	1	23 (24)
24	(Clothier)	1	29
	(Smith)	2	59 (63), -6 (3)
	Butcher	1	83 (83)
	(Crafts-/Tradesman)	1	11 (17)
	(Chapman)	2	81, 41
	Mercer	1	485
	Vintner woman	1	134
5	Women	5	38 (38), 16, 12, 5 (5), NK (27)
4	Occupation unknown	4	32 (36), 24 (30), 8 (8), NK (9)

century, the vicar, Robert Thomlinson had annexed the post of schoolmaster.[31] The contents of the library of his successor, Isaac Lowden (31), suggest strongly that he also combined the two duties. Lowden's successors, Brian Grant and Robert Hope, in their turn are known to have done so.[32]

Edward VI had permitted the clergy to marry. So did Elizabeth in her turn, although she herself did not approve of the practice. The possibility that some of her Darlington subjects shared her views is suggested by the fact that several parishioners were accused of abusing Robert Thomlinson's wife in 1598/9.[33] Maintaining a wife and family further diminished the value of the fixed stipend. There is no evidence that either Isaac Lowden or Brian Grant was married but Robert Hope certainly had a wife who added to the family income by making and washing surplices and communion table cloths.[34]

Where Darlington's clergymen lived in the early 17th century is not clear but the Deanery, which stood at the south-east corner of the market place, was no longer available to them. It had passed into the hands of the Crown in 1548 and appears subsequently to have been leased to laymen and finally sold. The evidence of Isaac Lowden's (31) inventory is that he lodged in the house of Anthony Raynold. The only other reference to a clerical residence during this period is to a house "at the church gaites" which was later inhabited by Robert Hope.[35]

The clergy had lost in income but had gained in learning. The English Reformation had changed the role of the priest fundamentally. No longer was he required to mediate between individual souls and God. The emphasis was now upon a pastoral, preaching ministry, staffed by university graduates.[36] Isaac Lowden, and his successor Brian Grant, were both graduates of Cambridge; Lowden of Christ's College and Grant of St John's.[37]

Isaac Lowden's inventory illustrates these points dramatically. The value of his books exceeded that of all his other worldly goods. He possessed just enough to furnish one room meagrely. He did not own the bed he slept on. His clothes possibly allowed him one change of attire. All these items were valued at £4 12s 3d. His debts, amounting to £19 15s 6d included £1 10s to a Mr Allondson, who may have been his doctor, and £1 18s 4d to his landlord, Anthony Raynold, who actually obtained the letters of administration to settle the estate. In addition, the court was to charge the estate with a payment to the two women who had looked after him during five weeks' illness. His assets, which included £10 in wages owed to him by the bishop through his agent, Henry Oswald, and his library valued at £5 16s, would have been just sufficient to clear his debts.

Lowden's collection of over 70 books was listed in detail. Not surprisingly, the bulk of his library consisted of religious works, many of them written by early Continental Protestant reformers: Peter Martyr, Francis Lambert, Rudolph Walther, Nicholas Hemmingsen, and Calvin, whose *Institutes* had become the text-book of Reformed non-Lutheran theology. He also possessed copies of the works of some distinguished early Church writers: extracts from the *De Essentia Divinitatis* of St Augustine of Hippo, whose writings on original sin and predestination had exercised a great influence on Calvin and his followers; Theodoret, bishop of Cyrus, (c. 393-c. 466); Theophilactus, archbishop of Achrida (d.1100), whose commentaries were noted for lucidity of thought and expression; the Dominican, Hugo Cardinalis (Hugh de St Cher, d. 1263) and James of Voragine, archbishop of Genoa (1230-98).

Lowden's Puritan sympathies are further indicated by his collection of the works of English writers: Bartlett's *Pedigree of Popish Heretics;* the sermons of Thomas Playfair, professor of Divinity at Cambridge; the Puritan, Edward Deering's *Lectures of readings upon part of the Epistle written to the Hebrews;* the pamphleteer, Philip Stubbs's *Anatomy of Abuses* which was a denunciation of the evil customs of the time; and three works of William Perkins, *The Golden Chayne , The Reformed Catholic* and *A Treatise of Christian Equitie.* It is extremely likely that Lowden came under the influence of Perkins during his years at Cambridge. A fellow of Lowden's own college, Christ's, Perkins was renowned for his preaching and teaching and his outspoken resistance to elaborate church ritual. His works were only slightly less valued by 17th-century Puritan theologians than those of Calvin himself.

Lowden's possession of two books by the Spanish Dominican, Louis de Granada (1504-1588), *Meditations* and *Dux Peccatorum* (the Sinners' Guide), might seem surprising but de Granada considered the inner life and mental prayer of greater importance than outward ceremony. Adaptations of his works, purged of Catholic doctrine, were produced for the Protestant market.

A closer study of Lowden's theological library reveals the breadth of his reading, ranging from the sermons of James of Voragine, the 13th-century Dominican friar and archbishop of Genoa to the epistles of the contemporary Joseph Hall, bishop of Exeter and later of Norwich, whose policy of goodwill and toleration later incurred the displeasure of both Archbishop Laud and puritan zealots. He also possessed the work of several poets: Petrarch's *De remediis utriusque fortunae,* William de Salluste de Bartas' *De mundi creatione* and a work called *The Shepherd's Calendar,* possibly the one by Edmund Spenser.

Another substantial section of Lowden's library consisted of books which would have been of use to him in his secondary role of schoolmaster, such as the classical Latin authors, Cicero, Caesar, Livy, and Sallust. The *Apothegmes* of Erasmus and Lycosthenes were used in grammar schools as aids to Latin composition. Also in his collection were Scapula's Greek-Latin lexicon, Clenard's Greek grammar, Homer's Iliad and works on arithmetic, rhetoric and logic, which included the "new" logic of Pierre de la Ramee (Peter Ramus), introduced at Cambridge towards the end of the 16th century. In addition, there were a children's dictionary and Angel Day's *The English Secretarie*, written "for the unlearned to whom the want thereof breedeth so diverse imperfections". It seems unlikely that the volume of poetry by the Latin poets Catullus, Tibullus and Propertius would have been shared with his pupils, dealing as it does with love, subsequent disenchantment and disgust, and, in the case of Catullus, with homosexuality.

Of the rest, Lowden's possession of a statute book and a volume on medicine, the *Treasure of Evonimus* "conteyning the wonderful hid secretes of nature touchinge the most apte formes to prepare and destyl medicines for the conservation of helth", suggest that the people of Darlington looked to their minister for medical and legal advice. Another source of everyday assistance he could have afforded them was Day's *English Secretarie* which included "a perfect method for the inditing of all manner of epistles and familiar letters, etc".[38]

It may be observed that on the evidence of the wills and inventories, early 17th-century Darlington was not a book-reading community. Of 58 people, only six can be said to have possessed books. Of these, William Barnes (8) and Robert Dent (19), left unspecified books, the former's valued at 40s and the latter's, put together with his purse, apparel and two old swords, and reckoned to be worth £3 6s 8d. Anthony Dennis's (28) appraisers found a Bible, communion book and testament (valued at 13s 4d) stored in the loft over the hall, which would not indicate frequent use, and "2 doz[en] of litle bookes for children", valued at 6s as part of the stock of his shop. William Bower (51) of Oxen-le-field owned a Bible, a copy of Fox's *Book of Martyrs* and other little books, valued at £1. John Atkinson's (49) library valued at over £6 must have been extensive but its contents were unfortunately not listed.

The land and its occupiers

The bishop of Durham was the principal landowner in Darlington and the great majority of farmers and occupiers were his tenants. They almost all held by copy of court roll and, as copyholders, they normally enjoyed considerable security, maintaining their customs in the halmote court. Collectively, they were able to enclose and divide the fields, as they did in Bondgate in about 1585, or convert them from the rig and furrow of arable to pasture, as they did in Cockerton in about 1609.[39]   Individually, they had the right to bequeath their holdings or to sell their title and interest. It was the sub-tenants of the copyholders who bore the risks of short leases, arbitrary fines and rent increases.

There were a number of freeholders. First of all, there were the burgage-holders. In that part of Darlington known as the borough, the owners of the burgages enjoyed something of the privileges of the burgesses of incorporated boroughs, namely, the right to hold markets, regulate prices, weights and measures, levy rates and discharge the responsibilities of local government by means of their court leet. There were also a number of independent freeholders in the parish, who are not all clearly identifiable. The Durham inquisitions *post mortem* have been published and, ostensibly, during the reign of James I, the estates of eleven freeholders in Darlington were the subject of such inquiries. It is known, however, that the published collection is defective,[40] omitting at least one other Darlington freeholder.   Two freeholders, Richard Gascoigne of Sadberge and George Hutton of Sunderland Bridge, lived outside the town and owned properties throughout the county. Three, William Barnes (8), William Bower (51) and Robert Garnet (52), occur in this collection and all claimed the title of gentleman. Michael Jeffreyson (32), however, was a tanner and William Cornforth, the father of Cuthbert (41), is not known to have claimed gentle status. With the exception of Robert Garnet, an impoverished Catholic, the freeholders whose inventories are known, were among the wealthier inhabitants. Yet their status and wealth appear to have little to do with antiquity. Two of the freehold estates, Oxen-le-field and Bennetfield, had been forfeited to the crown after the 1569 rising and were subsequently sold off. Over time, building and commercial development had caused the minute subdivision of various freeholdings. The instability of economic and political fortunes in this age of inflation and Reformation can be seen at work.

Thus, William Bower (51), was an incomer from an armigerous family of Lancashire, with various kin in Yorkshire. It was only in 1602 that he bought the manor of Oxen-le-field from Thomas Brickwell, probably a relative, who had acquired it from the crown in 1574. The Bower occupancy illustrates both the instability of fortunes and the tendency to sub-divide. Longstaffe says,

> "The whole family presents a pitiable declension from good to worse and worse. Gentleman - yeoman - butcher - poor gardener - labourer".

In the five years before his death, William settled his property on his family and friends, reserving some for his own use and that of his brother Richard in their lifetimes. To his nephew William Bower, Richard's son, he gave a burgage on the High Row in 1618. In 1621, he gave a burgage on the Head Row to Bulmer Prescot of Darlington, merchant, and William Rotheram of Blackwell, yeoman, kinsman and servant. During his lifetime, he also settled his "hamlet or grange" of Oxen-le-field on Roger and Francis Anderson, husband and son of his dead daughter Jane, on Sir Robert Jackson, son of his daughter Margaret, and on his nephew William Bower junior. Even after this division, there remained a substantial holding, eventually to pass to his nephew. This nephew used to sit in church in the "litle seate in the south side of the stall whereon his unckle Bower did sit", for which right he paid 12d in 1633, and asked "to be buried in the churche in my uncles grave". Described as a yeoman, he was living at Oxen-le-field in 1631. In the next generation, his son Cuthbert, a butcher, was selling properties in 1673 but in 1685 he was still named as a freeholder of Darlington. It was Cuthbert's son, William Bower, who, as a labourer, embodies the end of the family's prosperity. By 1700, Oxen-le-field had been purchased by the Milbankes. At his burial, in 1727, William Bower was described as a "poor gardener".[41]

Episcopal land in the borough, let on leases for fixed terms of years, was usually allotted for some specific purpose or service in the town, even if to successive generations of the same family. The yeoman family of Glover discharged the important office of postmaster of Darlington from the middle of the 16th century. Peter Glover (58), whose will is the last in this collection, joined with William Barnes (8), Lawrence Catherick (56) and Francis Foster in May 1596 to take a lease of the bishop's lands in the High Park, Darlington, for 21 years. A condition was that on "reasonable warning" from the constable, ten able horses were to be found to serve as post horses at the rate of one penny a mile for those with "sufficient commission for the taking of post horses". In 1582, ten post horses had been used on the 16 miles between Northallerton and Darlington at a charge of £1; and on the 18 miles between Darlington and Durham at £1 6s 8d.[42]

Peter Glover occupied a burgage on the north-east corner of Post House Wynd (once called Glover's Wynd), which he acquired from Toby and Henry Oswald in 1605/6. The house was known as the Post House or Talbot Inn. The postmaster attended to the forwarding of letters and provided horses for the purpose which were usually ridden by boys. In 1607, Glover employed a lad called Anderson, for whom he bought shoes from Miles Guy (15), the cordwainer. There are no references to any of the Glover family as postmasters after 1681, when the Talbot was sold to Robert Clifton, a saddler.

Farmers

A comparison of the Darlington and the Bedburn inventories of William Barnes (8) and John Lisle (55) shows the greater importance of arable farming in the Darlington district. At Darlington, crops were over 50% of the value of their farming inventories but at Bedburn, in the Pennine foothills, they were 12% and less. Nevertheless, the inventories, taken as a whole, reveal a mixed farming economy at Darlington, with the emphasis upon stock. Thus Cuthbert Cornforth (41), Ralph Thursby (54) and Lawrence Catherick (56) left substantial crops in store or on the ground which were balanced by almost equal or greater values in livestock. Moreover, much of what was grown was probably intended to feed the animals. At a time of slender crop yields and high stock mortality, a system of mixed farming would best spread risks.

Cattle predominated among the livestock because they were the most generally useful. They were used for haulage, for tillage, for milk, meat and skins. They must also have had one of the most favourable ratios of cash convertibility in a market town. Twenty-three inventories record the means of butter- and cheese-making. Sheep were not as numerous and in many cases were possibly kept only for manuring and folding, with wool as a by-product. Their numbers do not suggest meat or dairy production on the same scale as cattle. At Bedburn, William Barnes (8) and, after him, John Lisle (55) kept over 300 sheep. William Bower (51) at Oxen-le-field had 248 sheep but their total value was only half of that of his 79 cattle. For draught purposes, oxen were most frequently cited in the inventories. Horses occur only in small numbers, suggesting personal and not general use. Of the 18 yeomen and agriculturalists, of whom all owned horses, only three, Thomas Hodgson (53), William Barnes and John Lisle clearly appear to have used them for field-work. John

Lisle had three "draught horses" and William Barnes and Thomas Hodgson had horse- as well as ox-harrows. Horses were, of course, to be found in the inventories of non-agriculturalists. They clearly were necessary for those who traded at a distance. The cordwainer, John Hall (12) had a load saddle and John Atkinson (49) had a horse with coaling furniture. Pigs and poultry existed only in backyard numbers and for household use exclusively.

At this time, almost all independent households were involved in some kind of farming. Most of the town's tradesmen had holdings with land and grazing rights attached. Many had stock and several grew or stored crops. The cordwainers, Matthew Lambert (2) and Thomas Pape (3), had a very large part of their assets in cattle. This was a period in which dearth was still a danger to insure against, although in a market town it would have been experienced not so much as a problem of supply as of dramatic price fluctuation.

Textiles

Darlington's textile industry can be traced back at least to 1183, when the town's cloth dyers were required to render half a mark to the bishop.[43] A fulling mill existed on the Skerne, close to the Blackwell mill, from at least the end of the 14th century.[44] In the Hatfield Survey of c.1380, the dyehouse was one of the borough's common facilities, which was being leased or farmed out by the bishop for an annual payment.[45] By then England, long famed as an exporter of wool to Europe, had become a major exporter of woollen cloth, the best broadcloth being produced from fine wool of short staple. From about 1450, its export became concentrated increasingly into the hands of the Merchant Adventurers of London. The demand was for unfinished cloth, which they obtained from capitalist rural clothiers, whose prices were lower than those of the guild-controlled urban craftsmen. As a result, the town-based textile trade suffered and declined. Quite possibly it was for these reasons that, by the beginning of the 16th century, the finishing of cloth was in decline in Darlington. The timbers of the fulling mill were being used for the repair of Blackwell mill and no rent was being received for the dyehouse in 1515 "because no dyers exist there". Some cloth production did continue in the town as two of the pardoned participants in the Northern Rising of 1569 were weavers. It is, perhaps, during this period that Darlington's textile craftsmen made the decision to diversify, producing both linen and woollen cloth.

Certainly, by the end of the 16th century, at least two Darlington weavers possessed both linen and woollen looms.[46] The manufacture of linen, for which Darlington was to become renowned, was well-established by the end of the 17th century.[47] During these centuries, profound changes had occurred in the organisation and output of the textile industry which were at least, in part, mirrored in Darlington's experience. Production of a wool of a coarser, longer staple which required combing, not carding, led to the expansion of the worsted industry and the production of the so-called "New Draperies". These were lighter, cheaper, more easily tailored cloths made from coarser wool, often mixed with silk, linen or cotton. The influx of French and Flemish Protestant refugees into East Anglia in the mid-16th century is believed to have stimulated the production of New Draperies.

Production and export of unfinished cloth continued into the early 17th century, when William Cockayne, a London alderman, hopeful of breaking the Merchant Adventurers' monopoly, persuaded James I that finished cloth would provide much needed work and produce greater profit for the country and the Crown. In 1614, the king revoked the Merchant Adventurers' charter and forbade the export of unfinished cloth, without first ensuring that the country's existing dyeing and finishing industry could cope with the extra demand. The Dutch, who had been the major importers of English cloth, immediately imposed an embargo and encouraged the development of their own weaving industry. Much of the imperfectly finished cloth proved to be unsellable and the traditional English cloth trade, already severely affected by the competition from the New Draperies, went into recession. Although James I lifted the ban on the export of unfinished cloth in 1617, the damage had been done and a major economic slump ensued.

In some parts of the country, the cloth trade collapsed completely but a developing linen industry helped to cushion the blow in others. Although there was some domestic production of linen in England, the country had depended largely on foreign imports for its supplies. Attempts were made during the reigns of Henry VIII and Elizabeth I to compel farmers to set aside acreage for the growing of hemp and flax to provide the necessary raw material for the manufacture of canvas and rope for the Navy, and of fishing nets and as a source of employment for the "idle" poor.[48] Flax was apparently being grown in Darlington parish, because the inventory of Thomas Ratcliffe of Cockerton in 1593 recorded "j bushell of lynnen sede" valued at

15s.[49] However, home-grown flax and hemp were neither sufficient nor of high enough quality to satisfy the demands of the industry. Imports, mostly from the Baltic region, through the ports of London, Newcastle and Hull continued to be necessary.[50]

Although the wills and inventories of only three Darlington weavers have survived for this period, there is supporting evidence to show that the town was actively involved in the production and distribution of yarn and cloth. Nine inventories record the possession of fleeces, wool or woollen yarn. With the exception of William Bower (51) gentleman, whose stock of wool was valued at £10, the farmers Ralph Thursby (54) and Anthony Stainsby (57) who possessed wool valued at £8 and £1 respectively, and the butcher Christopher Foster (45) who owned 12 fleeces worth 18s, the quantities held seem to have been small. Eleven inventories record the possession of flax, hemp or tow, from which linen of varying qualities could be manufactured. In only two instances was the source of the raw material specified; in Edmund Fawell's (37) inventory "for hempe which he bought at Thirsk, 8s" and, listed among John Marshall's (20) debts, "at Newcastell for thre stone of lynte £1".

Of the 14 spinning wheels listed, only four were specifically designated as linen wheels. The spinning of woollen and linen yarns required different wheels, the one for linen being higher to accommodate the longer fibres and having a smaller wheel.[51] Edmund Fawell's brother, Christopher (26), possessed three wheels, of which two were for linen, and quantities of linen and harden yarn.

By far the largest stock of linen and harden yarn was held by the spinster, Isabel Catherick (24). She also had a large quantity of linen and harden cloth, both bleached and unbleached, and it seems likely that she earned her living as a small-scale clothier, putting out the yarn to be woven into cloth and then selling the finished product. The tanner, Thomas Johnson (16), may have had a secondary occupation as a clothier or draper, his stock of over 120 yards of cloth seeming somewhat excessive for purely domestic purposes. Most of the wealth of Richard Hudless (12), whose occupation as a chapman may be inferred from his possession of a mare and pack-saddle, was invested in linen cloth, of which a quantity, worth £15, was "at bleaching".

The inventory of Richard Dack (21) consisted entirely of debts owed to him, totalling almost £29, the majority of which were "for cloth". The bulk of the mercer Anthony Dennis's (28) stock consisted of a wide range of cloth, including worsteds and New Draperies; bays and says, buffines and mockadoes, grosgrains and perpetuanas. The inventory, unfortunately torn and damaged, contains no information about his sources of supply.

Of the three weavers, William Robinson (35) of Blackwell combined the production of cloth with modest pastoral farming. He owned two looms, one woollen and one linen "lait bought of Thomas Potter". The former, with its three gears (heddles), was valued at 11s, the latter was also valued at 11s, but its gears and other attachments were reckoned to be worth the relatively high figure of £1 14s 4d. He also owned a swingle and swinglestock which were used to beat and separate the hemp and flax fibres, after the plant had been retted or steeped in water. His stock of finished cloth was small and the only yarn he possessed was apparently in the process of being woven into cloth on the loom. John Glover (40) owned both a coverlet loom and a linen loom, valued together at £2 11s, which he bequeathed to his son, along with his apprentice, Richard Collin. His inventory contained no mention of cloth or yarn. He was probably the son of William Glover, webster, whose inventory of 1592 records a coverlet loom, a woollen loom and two linen looms in his workshop. John Corker (46), by far the wealthiest of the three weavers in this collection, with an estate of £50 of which £8 14s was "money in his purse", apparently did not own a loom. Two webs of harden listed in his inventory were described as "at the weavers". His stock-in-trade included heckled flax, harden and linen yarn, a considerable amount of finished cloth (mostly harden, sameron and linen) and a small amount of woollen and linen-woollen mix.

Leather workers

Darlington's leather industry which, no doubt, had developed as an off-shoot of the town's cattle market, was sufficiently important to require the supervision of four leather-searchers, appointed by the Borough Court.[52] Leather working is reckoned to have been one of the more important trades in pre-industrial England, leather being in great demand, not only for footwear, saddles and other horse furniture but also for clothing, buckets and bellows.[53]

The inventories of 11 leather workers (four tanners, six cordwainers and one glover) have survived for the period of this study, the values of their contents ranging from £25 to £148. Miles Guy's

(15) estate of £148 perhaps should not be seen as typical of the town's leatherworkers, as approximately half of its value was derived from Guy's secondary trade as a supplier of malt.

Much of the tanners' wealth was tied up in hides and in stocks of oak bark which was used in the tanning process. Leather tanning was a long, skilled and smelly process, lasting between six months and two years. After tanning, it was necessary to replace the natural oils of the hides, to render them supple and waterproof.[54] This was normally the task of the currier who also shaved the leather to the required thickness, but it is evident from the inclusion of large stocks of oil and tallow in the inventories of four of the six cordwainers that Darlington's shoemakers were accustomed to preparing their own hides.

In 1577, the "burgesses and commonalitie" of Darlington had drawn up articles for the regulation of its cordwainers, who were required to meet annually on October 25th, the feast day of St. Crispin, the patron saint of shoemakers, to elect two wardens who were empowered to inspect the wares of any of the company's members. Both John Hall (12) and John Fawcet (43) owed money to the "companie of th'occupation" at the time of their deaths.

Unless their executors had been extremely fortunate in being able to collect outstanding debts before the drawing up of the inventories, four of Darlington's shoemakers appear not to have operated a system of extending credit to their customers. The inventories of Christopher Collin (1), Matthew Lambert (2) and Thomas Pape (3) list no outstanding money owed and John Hall was apparently owed for only two pairs of boots and a pair of shoes, valued at 10s. With the exception of the latter who left no stock-in-trade, their shop stock consisted principally of shoes, in contrast to those of Miles Guy and John Fawcet, whose shops also contained a sizeable stock of boots, both finished and unfinished. This, and the credit they had extended to their customers, several of whom lived 'out-of-town', perhaps indicates that part of both Guy's and Fawcet's trade was with the more well-to-do. The former's list of debtors certainly included the names of several members of the gentry of County Durham and North Yorkshire.

Funerals

The majority of testators expressed a wish to be buried either in

St Cuthbert's church or in the churchyard. Four people asked to be buried within the church. Cuthbert Cornforth (41) willed that he should be buried there in his "fathers grave". A grave cover bearing the name of Cornforth still exists in the south aisle of the church although it may have been resited during the extensive restoration work in the Victorian period. Unfortunately, the inscription is not dated and part of it is hidden beneath a wooden plinth, but the remainder reads,

> "Buriall place of ....
> Cornforth and Iane ...
> and their success ..."

Cuthbert Cornforth's list of debts included a payment for his mortuary (a fee due to the vicar) and his layerstall or burial place in the church for which the total cost was 13s 4d. The Darlington Church Book for 1632 shows that fees for layerstalls were variable,

> "Mrs garnet for hir doughter Layrstall 10s 0d
> Wydo Scott for hir husband Layrstall 6s 0d
> John Glover for a Child Layrstall 3s 4d"[55]

There were 24 testators who requested burial in the churchyard. Stephen Ward (44) specified that he should be buried at the "South porch doore ... neare to my lait deceassed parents ..." Naturally enough, several others wished to be buried near to close relatives; in six instances the parent or parents, in three others the wife, and in the case of Ann Dent (35) her "lait deceassed Children".

Some simply left the final decision to the discretion of friends and relatives or the executors and supervisors of the will. Eight testators specified only "church or churchyard" and Mary Throckmorton (48) added the phrase "or elsewhere as it shall please myne executors". It is not known where she was buried. It has been pointed out that leaving arrangements to the discretion of others allowed some opportunity for Catholic funeral arrangements.[56]

Three testators merely committed their bodies "back to the earth from whence it came". John Lisle (55) spoke figuratively of "my bodie to the Ground my mother from whome I was first taken". Peter Glover (58) bequeathed his "soule and bodie" into the hands of God, seeming to make no definite provision for his mortal remains. William Barnes (8) likewise only stated that he should be buried with "decent funeralls". The dying plea of Ann Surtees (39), that she be taken back from Durham to Darlington for burial, was ignored.

In 18 inventories, the total funeral costs were given, ranging from 10s to £12 14s 9d. These figures may have included payments for mortuaries, layerstalls, gifts to the poor or the cost of writing the wills and inventories, although occasionally these items were listed separately. Detailed breakdowns of the funeral expenses were only given in two inventories, those of John Atkinson (49) and George Marshall (50). The £7 5s 2d spent on Atkinson's funeral included the cost of preparing the body for burial, the coffin, the service, bread and cheese for the mourners and a gift of £3 to the poor. George Marshall's arrangements were similar but mourners were also given a very expensive dinner at Peter Glover's (58), costing £4 10s 8d. He also left £3 6s 8d to the poor. His total funeral expenses of £12 14s 9d were the highest in this collection.

Notes to the Introduction

1. The parochial returns of 1563 are published in B.J.D.Harrison, "A Census of Households in County Durham, 1563" in The Cleveland and Teesside Local History Society, *Bulletin* , no.11, December 1970, pp.14-8.

2. Public Record Office (PRO), SP 12/51, ff.170-174 (musters of 1569); C.Sharp, *Memorials of the Rising of 1569* (1840:1975), p.251.

3. PRO, E179/245/27 and E179/106/28 (Hearth Tax returns, 1665 and 1666)

4. Descriptive accounts of Darlington for this period occur in W.H.D.Longstaffe, *The History and Antiquities of the Parish of Darlington* (1854); R.Surtees, *The History and Antiquities of the County Palatine of Durham* (4 vols,1816-40, reprint 1972), III, pp.350-377; N.Sunderland, *Tudor Darlington* (Durham County Library, 2 parts, 1974-76).

5. Durham University Library, Archives & Special Collections (DASC), Probate Act Books, nos.9 (1599-1606), 10 (1607-14), 11 (1614-19), and 12 (1620-25).

6. The misuse of Durham records is referred to in *Parliamentary Papers* , 1867-68, LV, p.431. See also the appendix to the *Sixteenth Report of the Deputy Keeper of the Public Records* (1855), p.54.

7. DASC, Consistory Court Depositions, Durham V/11, ff.228-30v., 244v-5.

8. Ibid., V/10a, ff.148-v.

9. Ibid., V/8, ff.128v.-9, 152-4.

10. Ibid., V/10a, ff.184-5.

11. PRO, Durham Chancery Depositions, Durham 7/11 part 2 (1613).

12. DASC, Probate Act Book 10, f.340v.

13. See C.Cross, "Wills as evidence of popular piety in the Reformation period: Leeds. and Hull, 1540-1640" in D.Loades, *The End of Strife* (Edinburgh, 1984), pp.44-51; M.L.Zell, "The use of religious preambles as a measure of religious belief in the 16th century", *Bulletin of the Institute of Historical Research* , 50, (1977), pp.246-9; and the chapter "The Impact of Reform: Wills" in E.Duffy, *The Stripping of the Altars* (Yale, 1992), pp. 504-23; also H.Bradfield, "Tracking down Puritans" in *The Local Historian*, 16, (1984), pp. 213-6; R.O'Day, *The Debate on the English Reformation* (1986), pp.155, 157; M.Spufford, "The scribes of villagers' wills in the 16th and 17th centuries and their influence" in *Local Population Studies*, 7 (1971), pp.28-43. Professor Anthony Fletcher kindly enlightened the editors on the significance of John Atkinson's preamble.

14. Sunderland, *op.cit.*, part 2, pp.22-3.

15. Surtees, *op.cit.*, III, p.413. Perhaps T.Cartwright, *A replye to An answere made of M. doctor Whitgifte* (1573) or *The second replie of Thomas*

Cartwright: agaynst master Whitgiftes second answer (1575) or later editions and compilations.

16. PRO, Durham Chancery Depositions, Durham 7/11 (1613) part 2.

17. G.Squire and P.Baines, *Observer's Book of European Costume* (London 1975), pp.78-9; I.Brooke, *English Costume of the Seventeenth Century* (London, 1934), p.32; E.Ewing, *Fashion in Underwear* (London, 1971), p.32; R.M.Green, *The Wearing of Costume* (London, 1966), p.90; N.Bradfield, *Historical Costumes in England* (1938), p.89.

18. *Lamentable News from the Towne of Darnton in the Bishopricke of Durham* (Thomas Nelson, London, 1585).

19. P.A.G.Clack and N.F.Pearson, *Darlington: a Topographical Study* (Northern Archaeological Survey, Dept of Archaeology, Univ. of Durham, 1978), pp.12-7.

20. Sunderland, *op.cit.* , part 1, pp.3, 5; Longstaffe, *op.cit* ., p.223.

21. *Devon Inventories of the 16th and 17th centuries* (Torquay, 1966). p.xiii.

22. M.Wood, *The English Mediaeval House* (London, 1966), p.328; M.A.Havinden, *Household and Farm Inventories in Oxfordshire, 1550-1590* (Historical Manuscripts Commission, 1965), p.21.

23. Wood, *op .cit* ., p.335.

24. A.Quiney, *House and Home* (BBC, 1986), p.50.

25. *Ibid* ., p.39.

26. A.Campbell, *The Book of Beer* (London. 1956), p.14.

27. DASC, Archdeacon's Book, Durham VIII/1, ff. 17, 74v, 103v and 142v; and see Sunderland, *op.cit.* , p.61.

28. F.W.Steer, ed., *Farm and Cottage Inventories of Mid-Essex, 1635-1749* (Chichester, 1965), pp.32-4.

29. PRO, Durham Chancery Complaint, Durham 2/5, 1607.

30. Longstaffe, *op. cit.*, p.201.

31. Sunderland, *op. cit.*, part 2, p.35.

32. Idem, *History of the Grammar School of Queen Elizabeth, Darlington* (1963), p.23.

33. Idem, *op. cit.*, part 2, p.13.

34. Longstaffe, *op. cit.*, p.236.

35. *Ibid* ., p.268 note.

36. R.O'Day, *The English Clergy: Emergence and Consolidation of a Profession* (1979), p.134.

37. J. and J.A.Venn, *Alumni Cantabrigienses* (Cambridge, part 1, 4 vols, 1922-7) II, p.248; III, p.109.

38. For the works consulted for this discussion of Lowden's library, see pp.x-xi above.

39. Sunderland, *op.cit.*, part 1, pp.59-62; PRO, Durham Chancery Complaint, Durham 2/6 (1609).

40. We owe this information to Mrs Linda Drury of Durham University. See Appendix to *The 44th Annual Report of the Deputy Keeper of the Public Records* (1883).

41. Longstaffe, *op. cit.*, pp.lxxxv-vi.

42. DASC, Enrolment Book, leases and patents, Church Commission, 184957b, ff.58verso-59verso; J.Courtney, *A Postal History of Darlington* (Local History publications no.6, Darlington Corporation, 1974), pp.3-4, 11-2.

43. D.Austin, ed., *The Boldon Book* (1982), p.59.

44. N.Sunderland, *op. cit.*, part 1, p.70.

45. Longstaffe, *op. cit.*, p.87.

46. Sunderland, *op. cit.*, part 1, p.70.

47. *Victoria County History, Durham* (3 vols, 1905-28), II, pp.315-6; J.P.Kenyon, *Stuart England* (1978), pp.80-1.

48. N.Evans, *The East Anglian Linen Industry* (1985), pp.50-2.

49. *Durham Wills and Inventories* (Surtees Society, vol.38, 1860), p.240.

50. Evans, *op.cit.*, p.95.

51. *Ibid.*, p.29.

52. Longstaffe, *op. cit.*, p.272.

53. L.A.Clarkson, "The origin of the leather industry in the late 16th and 17th centuries" in *Economic History Review*, 2nd series, 16, (1960), p.245.

54. *Ibid .*, p.247.

55. Darlington Churchwardens' Accounts Book (1630-40), f.47, in Durham County Record Office, EP/Da/SC 35.

56. Duffy, *op.cit.*, p.514.

BIBLIOGRAPHY

Overton, M., *A Bibliography of British Probate Inventories* (University of Newcastle, 1983)

Concise Scots Dictionary (Aberdeen, 1985)

English Dialect Dictionary

A glossary of Yorkshire words and phrases (London 1855)

Oxford English Dictionary

Atkinson, J.C., *A glossary of the Cleveland dialect* (London, 1868)

Axon, W., *English dialect words of the eighteenth century* (London, 1883)

Ayres, J., *The Shell Book of the home in Britain* (London, 1981)

Bestall, J.M., and Fowkes, D.V., "Chesterfield wills and inventories 1521-1603", *Derbyshire Record Society*, vol. 1, (1977)

Brears, P.C.D., "Yorkshire probate inventories 1542-1689", *The Yorkshire Archaeological Society*, vol. 134, (1972)

Brigg, Mary, "The Forest of Pendle in the seventeenth century, part two", *Transactions of the Historic Society of Lancashire and Cheshire*, vol. 115, (1963)

Brockett, J.T., *A glossary of north country words* (Newcastle, 1846)

Geeson, Cecil, *A Northumberland and Durham word book* (Newcastle, 1969)

Halliwell, J.O., *Dictionary of archaic and provincial words* (London, 1901)

Hartley, Marie, and Ingilby, Joan, *Life and Tradition in the Yorkshire Dales* (Lancaster, 1981)

Moore, J.S., "Clifton and Westbury probate inventories", *Avon Local History Association*, (1981)

Moore, J.S., 'The goods and chattles of Our forefathers", *Frampton Cotterell and District Historical Studies* vol. 1, (1977)

Needham, Sue, *A glossary for East Yorkshire and North Lincolnshire probate inventories* (University of Hull, Department of Adult Education, 1984)

Peacock, R.B., *A glossary of the dialect of the hundred of Londsdale* (London, 1869)

Pease, A.E., *A dictionary of the dialect of the West Riding of Yorkshire* (Whitby, 1928)

Reed, Michael (ed), "The Ipswich probate inventories", *Suffolk Records Society*, vol. 22 (1981)

Smith, A.H., *English placename elements* (2 vols, 1956)

Smith, A.H., *Placenames of the West Riding* (1961/3)

Wright, T., *Dictionary of obsolete and provincial English* (1857)

The following have been used in the elucidation of the book-titles in Isaac Lowden's inventory, see no.31 and pp.211-18.

Bennett, H.S., *English Books and Readers, 1475-1557* (1969) [Bennett [1]]

Bennett, H.S., *English Books and Readers, 1558-1603* (1965) [Bennett [2]]

Bietenholz, P.G., ed., *Contemporaries of Erasmus* (3 vols, 1985-7)

Brinsley, J., ed. E.T.Campagnac, *Ludus Literarius or, the Grammar School* (1917)

British Museum, *Catalogue of early English books to 1649* (3 vols, 1884) [B.M.C.]

Catalogue of McAlpin collection of British history and theology in the Union Theological Seminary, E.D.C.R.Gillett ed., (5 vols, 1927-30) [McA]

Dictionary of Christian Theology A.Richardson ed., [D.C.T.]

Dictionary of National Biography [D.N.B.]

Encyclopaedia Britannica [Enc.Brit.]

New Cambridge Bibliography of English Literature, G.Watson ed., (Vol.I, 1974) [N.C.B.]

New International Dictionary of the Christian Church, J.D.Douglas ed., (1974)

Oxford Companion to English Literature, P.Harvey ed., (4th ed., 1967) [O.C.E.L.]

Oxford Dictionary of the Christian Church, F.L.Cross ed., (1974) [O.D.C.C.]

Short-title Catalogue of English books, 1475-1640, A.W.Pollard & G.R.Redgrave, (1950) [S.T.C.]

Ward, R., *Bibliotheca Britannica* (2 vols, 1824) [Ward]

TEXTS

1 Christopher Collin of Darlington, 1600

In dei nomine, Amen, I, Christofer Collyn of Darnton in the county of Durham, singleman, sick in bodye but of good & perfect remembrance, do make this my last will & testament in manner & forme folowing. First, I comend my soule to Almighty God, my Creator and Redemer, hoping assuredly to be saved by the meretes & passion of his son Christ and do requier my frindes to bury my body within the church yead of Darnton as nigh unto my father & mother as they can convenyentlie. Item, I gyve & bequyth unto Robert Grey, my grandfather, xvj^{li} nowe in the hand of Henrie Wudd, my cosin. Item, I gyve & betquyth unto the said Robert Grey, my grandfather, all my interest terme of yeares & tenant right of all that my howse which Thomas Saier nowe dwelleth in, in Darnton abovesaid, with a little chamber therunto belonginge nowe in the tenure of the said Henry Woodd and also one lyme pytt on the backsyde of the said Henry Wudd's howse with a cowe gait on Brenkyn Moore, the which howse & premisses I have & hold of the church of Darnton, & I will that for the same the said Robert Grey shall pay yearlie therout iij^{s}iiij^d to the said church. Item, I will & bequyth unto Thomas Saier, one yeare next after my decease, the free use & occupacion of the howse wherein he nowe dwelleth without any rent paying for the same but that Henry Wudd shall then pay the said Thomas upholding the same. Item, I gyve & bequyth unto Christofer Lowyck, my uncle, his three children three pounds. Item, I gyve & bequyth to Robert Foster my uncle his children iiij^{li}. Item, I gyve to Richard Collyn & Henry Collyn, the sons of Rauph Collyn, my uncle, off Langnewton, thre pounds betwixt them. Item, I gyve Edward Hall of Darnton v^s. Item, I gyve ...[torn]...rden v^s. Item, I gyve John Wudd, my cosyn Henry Wudd son, the howse wherein his father nowe dwelleth & garth with tanne howse & thappurtenances except before graunted with all my terme & tennantry therein for ever, paying the rents & fines thereof & I will that, in consideracion of this legacy, the said John Wudd shall gyve & paye unto my uncle, Christofer Lowyck abovesaid, the some of ffortie & fyve shillings at Easter next ensewing the which he lent me at Martinsmesse last. Item, I gyve & bequyth unto the saime John Wudd, my cosyn, all my leather & hydes & skynnes both within & without the howse that ar myne. Item, I gyve unto Robert Ward vs. Item, I will & bequyth unto the poore people of Darnton v^s, which I will shalbe gyven presently after my decease. Item, I make & ordeyne my said cosin, Henry Wood, sole executor of this my last will & testament & if so be he refuse the executyon thereof then I will that John Wudd, his son, shall be the same my executor & to whom as shall execute the same all the surplus of my said goodes, moveable & unmoveable unbequythed, I gyve & bequyth, my funerall expences deducted & discharged. Dayted this fourth day of December, Anno Regni Elizabethae nunc Regine xlij° et Anno Domini, 1599.

Christofer [*mark*] Collyn

Wytnesses hereof, John [*mark*] Hall, Thomas Sayre, William [*mark*] Beckwith, Robert Warde

[*At the bottom of the will occurs the following note*]

6d 21s 1d 4 dossen shoues & 4ʳ paier boots

[*Paper, 1 f.*]

The inventorie of all the goodes and chattelles of Christofer Collyn, lait of Darlington, singleman, deceased, praised the fowertenth day of Januarie, Anno Regni Elizabethae Regine xlij° et Anno Domini, 1599 [1600], by John Hall, Edward Coulson, William Beckwith and Roberte Ward, in manner & forme folowing, vizᵗ,

In primis, in the custodie and handes of Henry Woodd of Darnton as part of the porcion of the said Christofer Collyn, the some of	27. 0. 0.
Item, eight hydes and fower stick leathers	5. 0. 0.
Item, the lease of a tenemente with thappurtenances holden of Darnton church or schole	5. 0. 0.

Summa totalis £37 0s 0d

[*Parchment, 1 m., indented. Will and inventory in hand similar to 2, 15, 16, 22, 24 will, 30, 32, 41, 42 and 45 wills.*]

2 Matthew Lambert of Darlington, 1603

ihs

In the name of God, Amen, I, Mathewe Lambart of Darnton in the countie of Durham, cordioner, sound in mynd and of a good & perfect remembrannce, yet neverthelesse sick in bodie (God be praised), do make this my last will and testament in manner folowing. First, I comend my soule into the handes of my mercifull God and Saviour, hoping assuredly by his meretes and holie passion to be saved, and do further requier my bodie to be buried within the parish church of Darlington, abovesaid. Item, I gyve & bequyth to the poore of this parish v^s. Item, to the mending of the carswe going to the Armytage v^s. Item, I gyve & bequyth to Margaret Aynsley, doughter to Mr Aynsley of Egglisclif, one brasse pott which I bought of John Fawcet. Item, I gyve unto the youngest doughter of Thomas Thompson of Kirklympton one other brasse pott that was my father's. Item, I gyve unto Katheryne Hodshon xij^d. Item, I gyve unto Cuthbert Hodshon my great whetstone. Item, I gyve unto Robert Ward v^s. Item, I gyve unto the dowghter of Thomas Alderson a silver spone. All the residewe of my goodes & chattelles, my debts and my funerall expences deducted & discharged, I gyve & bequyth to Margaret, nowe my wyf, whome I make sole executrix of this my last will and testament, dayted this first day of Fabruarie in the xlvth yeare of the reign of our sovereign Ladie Quene Elizabeth &c et Anno Domini 1602 [1603]

[*Mark*]

Wytnesses John [*mark*] Fawcett, Robert Warde

[*Paper, 1 f.*]

The inventorie of all the goods, moveable and unmoveable, of Mathewe Lambart, lait of Darlington, cordiner, deceased, praised the xiijth day of Aprill, 1603, by Franncis Forster, John Fawcett, Cuthbert Hodshon and Robert Ward, as foloweth, vizt,

In the hawle house

Imprimis, a cubbord at	1. 0. 0.
Item, a long table, two formes and a wyndo leaf	5. 0.
Item, two chaires, fower stooles, fower quysshons & two shelves	5. 0.
Item, xix pece of pewther, viij saucers, vj candlestickes, thre saltes, thre cupps, a possett bowle & fower pottingers	1. 3. 0.
Item, a stone morter, a grater, a chafing dish and brasse	2. 0.
Item, two reckyn crooks, two pair of tonges, two speetes, a skimmer, a rack, a broylyron, two knyves, a skimmer & a laddle	3. 0.

in buttrie

Item, xj pece of pewther, thre sawcers, fower cupps and a glasse	6. 8.
Item, a pott, a kettle, vij bordes, vj bowles & three standes	11. 0.
Item, a tubb, a skeele, a stoole, a choppyn bord & two pottes	3. 0.

in the south parlour

Item, a cubbord, fower brasse pottes, a posnet & a panne	1.16. 8.

Item, a bedstead, a bedd, a happen with a boulster & a codd	13. 4.
Item, a long table, two formes, a paier of tables, a kyrne, trenshers & reke	6. 8.

in the east parlour

Item, a bedstead, a fether bedd, a bolster, a codd, two coverletts, a blanket, a sheet, a troklebedd and clothes at	18. 0.
Item, two oyle barrells with oyle, a chist, a coffer, a lantarne & other thinges	10. 0.

in the shopp

Item, fower paier of bootes, sextene paier of shoies, lastes, formes, leather and whetstone at	1. 6. 8.

in the chamber

Item, fower bedes with their clothes	1. 0. 0.
Item, a counter, three chistes, a forme, a wyndoleaf, a stole and a quysshon	10. 0.
Item, three paier of lynnen sheetes, viij yardes of lynnen & fower codwares	1. 0. 0.
Item, fower paier of harden sheetes and two bord clothes	1. 0. 0.
Item, his apparell at	1. 6. 8.

in west chamber

Item, fower bedsteedes & clothes, a chist with other little tryfles	1. 0. 0.
Item, in garne, vessell, tubbes and other implements	10. 0.

in kytchin

Item, a boulting tunne, a cawtheron, two tubbes, a trowgh, two mells, a skeele, two standes, a busshell & a stone trough at	1. 0. 0.

in the stable

Item, a rack & manger, a cheese presse, a stee with bords & other ware	10. 0.
Item, in kyne, 7 at	9. 0. 0.
Item, ix yewes & a toope	3. 6. 8.
Item, in leases	9. 2. 0.

Summa totalis £39 9s 4d

Owen by the testator at his death for rent	1.19. 0.
& paid for funerall expenses	2. 3. 4.

sum remaynes de claro £35 7s 0d

[*Paper, 1 f., indented. Will and inventory in hand similar to* **1, 15, 16, 22, 24** *will,* **30, 32, 41, 42** *and* **45** *wills.*]

3 Thomas Pape of Darlington, 1603

In the name of God, Amen, the eleventh day of Aprill 1603, I, Thomas Pape of Darlington within the countye of Durham, sycke in body but of good and perfect remembrance, doe make this my last will and testament in manner and forme followinge. First, I bequeath my soule to Almighty God, my Creatour, trusting to be saved by the merittes of our Saviour Christ, and my body to be buryed in the church yard of Darlington aforesayd beside my father. Item, I give to Allice Pape, my wif, my house and burgage on the High Rowe in Darlington aforesayd, with all my household stuff theirin, and also all my gates in Brankinge Moore belonginge to the sayd burgage for and during her naturall lif. Item, I give to my sayd wif my house and garth on the Clay Rowe, which my father bought of John Stappleton. Item, I give to my sayd wif my tow closes of frehold called by the name of Picolls and the Longe Close, for and duringe her naturall lif. And, after the decease of my sayd wif, I give all and every the premisses and every part thereof unto my tow daughters, Allice Pape and Agnes Pape, and to their heires for ever. Item, I give to my sayd wife all my copyhold land lyinge in the towne feildes. Item, I will that the legacy, which my father gave to the poore of Darlington, shalbe yearly payd by my executours and the legacy bequeathed to my brother Francis discharged, according to the will of my sayd father, so longe as he is dutyfull to my mother, as in the sayd will is required. And I desire my mother, for God's sake, to be kind and good unto my poore wif and succourlesse children. The residew of my goodes, my debtes payd and funerall expences discharged, I give to Allice Pape and Agnes Pape, my tow daughters, whom I doe make ioynt executoures of this my last will and testament. Wittnesses hereof, Edward Colson, Robart Thomlinson.

[*Paper, 1 f.*]

An inventory of all the goodes and chattells, mooveable and unmoveable, of Thomas Pape of Darlington, deceased, praised by John Dobson, Lawrence Elgye, Thomas Bowbanck and John Chambers, the xxvij day of Aprill, Anno Domini, 1603,

Imprimis, corne on the ground	5. 6. 8.
Item, 1 plough	3. 4.
Item, tow stottes	3. 0. 0.
Item, one horse	2. 6. 8.

Item, iij Swyne	1. 2. 0.

in the parlour on the back side

Inprimis, tow stand bedes, ij fetherbedes, iiij coverlites, one blanket, iiij codes	2.10. 0.

In the loft over the shopp

Inprimis, thre paire of bedstockes, iiij coverlittes, one happing ij codes, ij fetherbedes	1.13. 4.
Item, ij paire of linnen shetes, ij pillowbers	8. 0.
Item, iij paire of harden sheetes	10. 0.
Item, a chist	8.
Item, x bushells of malt	16. 0.
Item, in the loft over the hall, iij chistes	3. 0.
Item, iij old tubbes, ij old standes, a chirne, an old spining whele	2. 0.
Item, a cradle	1. 0.
Item, ij casiers & ij skelves	6.
Item, a lanterne, ij painted cloathes, a pair of yarne windles	1. 4.
Item, a pecke and a half pecke	8.

In the parlour beneath the doores

Inprimis, a bed	4. 0.
Item, a mattresse	4. 0.
Item, ij harden sheetes	3. 0.
Item, a blanket & thre happinges	4. 0.
Item, a chist	1. 0.
Item, ij codes	6.

In the hall

Inprimis, a cubbourd	14. 0.
Item, xvij peece of pewther	6. 8.
Item, vj sawcers, ij pottingers	1. 0.
Item, viij candlestickes	3. 0.
Item, vj saltes	1. 6.
Item, iiij pewther cuppes	1. 0.
Item, a chamber pott & a chaffinge dishe	1. 0.
Item, v old pewther dublars	1. 4.
Item, pewther vessell in the buttry	5. 0.
Item, ij tables, ij formes, 3 buffet stooles, ij chaires	7. 0.
Item, a skelse in the forehouse	6.
Item, iij spittes, ij paire of rackes, ij paire of tonges, a fire shovell, a chopping knif, a flesh crooke	6. 0.
Item, ij recken crookes	1. 0.
Item, ij girlfattes, iiij standes, vj cans, a iugge, ij dozen trenchers	1.10.
Item, iiij skelves with other implements of household	1. 0.
Item, v brasse pottes, j ketle, iij pans, a dreping pan and a frying pan	16. 0.
Item, a soe, ij skeeles, a kitt, a chirne	2. 0.
Item, a mashe fat, an old ambry, a bushell, 3 old sackes	2. 0.

Item, a ladder and a horse hecke	1. 0.
Item, a bowell of grinded malt	5. 6.
Item, in the shopp, ij dozen & ix paire of shoes, iij paire of bootes	2. 1. 0.
Item, j paire of boote trees, 20 paire of lastes	3. 4.
Item, iij peces of lether, ij knives, a paire of pincers	3. 0.
Item, a stopping sticke & a prichell	3.

Suma £25 2s 3d

Debts that he oweth

to Allice Thomlinson	12. 0. 0.
to John Scott	2. 0. 0.
to Robert Fossicke	4. 0. 0.
to Bartholomew Garnet	1.18. 0.
to Thomas Findlay	2.10. 0.
to Elizabeth Pape	1.15. 0.
to Robert Thomlinson	8. 0.
to John Richardson	1. 0. 0.
to Will[ia]m Townend	2. 4. 0.
to John Law	2. 6. 8.
to Jane Pape	3. 8.

[*Paper, 1 f., indented. Will and inventory in same hand*]

4 William Thompson of Darlington, 1603

In the name of God, Amen, the xiij[th] day of October, in the yeare of our Lord God 1603, I, William Thompson of the parishe of Darlington, sick in bodie, neverthelesse of perfect remembrance praysed be God therfor, make this my last will & testament in manner & forme followinge. First, I committe my soule into the handes of the Almightie & by whose onlye marcies in the merites of Christ Jesu I do undoubtedley belive to be saved & by none other meanes & my bodie to be buried within the churche or churcheyard of Darlington. Item, I give & bequeathe to my sonne Mathew Thompson on hundrethe poundes. Item, I give & bequeathe to my sonne, William Thompson, twentie poundes. Item, I give to Allye Thompson twentie poundes. Item, I give & bequeathe to William Fewler childer fortie shillinges. Item, I give to William Marshell iiij sonnes iiij gimmer lambes. Item, I give to Robert Stainsbey on gimmer lambe. Item, I give to John Thompson twentie shillinges. Item, I give to Jene Thompson twentie shillinges. Item, I give to Christofer Staynsbey on you & on lambe. All the rest of my goodes moveable & unmoveable, my debtes, legacies & funerell expences discharged, I give & bequeathe to my sonne, Mathew Thompson, whom I make wholl executore of this my last will & testament. In witnes wherof, I have caused theis premises to be written & therto I have sette my hand & marke in the presences of theis witnesses.

William [*mark*] Thompson

Christofer Stainsbey, William Marshell, Thomas Hodgshon & Thomas Maysonn, with others.

[*Paper, 1 f.*]

A true Inventorie of all the goodes
& chattle, moveable & unmoveable,
of William Thompson of Cockerton
in the parishe of Darlington, lait
deceased, praysed the third day
of November in the yeare of our
Lord God, 1603, by iiij honest men,
Christofer Stainsbey, William Marshell,
Thomas Bowebancke &
Thomas Hodgshon

Imprimis, vj oxen	22. 0. 0.
Item, xxx^{ti} shepe	9.10. 0.
Item, viij kine	20. 0. 0.
Item, vj yong beastes	8. 0. 0.
Item, v calfes	4. 0. 0.
Item, v meares & folles	14.14.0.
Item, ij° Swine	1. 2. 0.
Item, iiij score threve of hard in the barne	16. 0. 0.
Item, iiij score of haver in the barne	6. 0. 0.
Item, on par of Iron bound whelles	2. 6. 8.
Item, on coup, ij° ploughes & iiij harrowes	1. 3. 0.
Item, vij yokes & bowes & iij plough beames	9. 0.
Item, viij teames, ij° pare of irons withe other implaymentes	1. 0. 0.
Item, on wayne & whelles & on cowpe geven to Robert	
Thompson by legacie, praysed	2.13. 4.
Item, ij° arckes, ij° Sadles & sackes & on bushell	1. 1. 0.
Item, implaymentes in the loft beneath the door	8. 0.
Item, impleaymentes in the byer	15. 0.
Item, vij potes & on cauderon	1.10. 0.
Item, on amere & on cawell	9. 0.
Item, ij° kettles, ij° panes & all the puder vessells with other	
impleaymentes	1.10. 0.
Item, on table, ij° chayres, ij° par of racking crockes with otheris	
imp[l]aymentes	11. 0.

Item, ij° beds & on presser	19. 0.
Item, iij chistes, on bultington & on kimlinge	10. 0.
Item, ij° kirnes, on butter Kette & sext stone of salt butter in it	1. 3. 0.
Item, on matterist and coverledes with other impleaymentes in the seller	1.13. 0.
Item, wollen clothe	2. 0. 0.
Item, his apparrell	2. 0. 0.
Item, on fetherbed with implaymentes in the loft over the seller	2. 9. 0.
Item, shetes & towells	1.10. 0.
Item, his purse	20. 0. 0.
Item, vj henes, ij° cockes	4. 0.
Item, corne on the earth & hay praysed	24. 0. 0.

Suma £171 10s 0d

[Paper, 2 ff., sewn. Will and inventory in same hand]

5   Isabel Ward of Blackwell, 1603

In the name of God, Amen, I, Isabell Warde of Blackwell in the countye of   Durham, wedowe, doe make this my last will & testament the first day of September 1603 in manner and forme followinge. First, I give my soule to thalmightye God, my Maker and Redemer, and my body to be buryed in the parishe church yarde of Darlington. Item, I give to the poore of Blackwell, Darlington, & Cockerton xvjˢ. Item, I give to my syster Margret Waistell viijˢ and my best black cote & a brode reede peticote which was our mother's. Item, I give to Jefferey Holme one bushell of wheate. Item, I give to Agnes Sympson iij pottes of rye. Item, I give to my daughter Margery Warde somuch housholde stuffe as my daughter Jenet Sledd hath had of me. Item, all the rest of my goodes, my debtes & funeralles discharged, I give to all my children, that is to say, to my sonne, Steven Warde, to my daughter, Elizabeth Stockdall alias Stockton, to my daughter, Jenet Sledd, and to my daughter, Margery Warde, to be equally devided amongst them, And my will is further, that if my daughter Margery Warde doe marry Marmaducke Carnell alias Carnaby, that then the rest of my foresaide children shall have all my goodes aforesaide to be equally devided amongst them and the saide Margery to have noe parte of my sayde goods with my other children aforesaide. And, in the meane tyme, untyll she be marryed to some other, or dye, I will that that parte of my goodes which I will the sayd Margerye shall have with my saide other children, shall remaine in the handes & custodye of my said sonne Steven Warde, unto the tyme limyted aforesaide. Item, I geve to William Dobson, my godsonne xij^d. Witnesses hereof, John Dobson, Robert Garnett & Stephen Ward & Mergerie Ward.

*[Paper, 1 f., indented . In hand similar to will **20, 26, 37, 38** and **39** inventories, **40, 54** and **57.**]*

6 Leonard Dack of Cockerton, 1604

In the name of God, Amen, the second day of April, in the second yeare of the reigne of our most gracious soveraigne lord James, by the grace of God, King of England, France and Ireland, Defender of the Faithe &c., and of Scotland, the seaven and thirtieth, I, Leonard Dacke, of Cockerton within the county of Durham, yeoman, sicke in bodie but in perfect remembrance, I give God most hartie thanks, do make and ordaine this my last will and testament in manner and forme following: that is to saie, first, I give and bequeathe my soull to Almighty God, my Creator and Redeemer, throughe whose death and passion I faithfully hope to be saved, and my bodie to be buried within my parishe churche yarde of Darlington as neare unto my wife lait deceassed as conveniently can be devised. Item, I give to the poorest sort of people of the towne of Darlington three shillinges fower pence, to be distributed at the discrecion of the supervisors of this my said testament. Item, I give to the poorest sort of people of Cockerton twoe shillinges. Item, I give unto Robert Tailor and John Tailor, sonnes of Blaize Tailor of Blackwell, to either of them, iij^siiij^d a peece. Item, I give unto the said Blaize Tailor one copheaded blacke why. Item, I give to Christofer Smith, sonne of Richarde Smith of Nedder Coniscliffe, iij^siiij^d. Item, I give to the said Richarde Smith one gowded why coloured read and white, now with calfe. Item, I will and bequeath the longe table and the formes standing on either side thereof in the forehowse, before the gaie window, shall continewe as heire lomes to my sonn, Mathewe Dacke, and his sequeles in jure for ever. Item, I give unto my said sonne, Mathew, all my part of the croppe of oates, being thone halfe now sowen on the ground. The rest of all my goodes and chattells, moveable and unmoveable, not yeat given nor bequeathed, my debts paid and funerall expences deducted and fullie descharged, I give unto my three daughters, Agnes Dacke, Margaret Dacke & Grace Dacke, all as yeat unmaried, whome I do make joynte executors of this my said last will and testament, earnestly entreating my good freindes and neighbors, Thomas Simpson, Lawrence Elgey, Thomas Robinson and Ralfe Blackwell to be supervisors of this my said will. Witnesses hereof, Thomas Simpson, Lawrence Elgee, Thomas Robinson, Ralph Blackwell and Richard Pickeringe and Richard Dacke.

[*Parchment, 1 m.*]

The inventorie of all and singular the goodes & chattells, moveable and unmoveable, of Leonarde Dacke of Cockerton, deceassed, praised the xixth daie of Maie, 1604, by Thomas Simpson, Lawrence Elgee, Thomas Robinson and Ralphe Blackwell, as followeth,

Inprimis, his apparrell	2. 0. 0.
Item, mony in his purse	9. 0. 0.
Item, one faire cupborde in the forehouse	2. 0. 0.
Item, one lesse cupborde in the forehouse	13. 4.
Item, fower great pewter dublers	1. 0. 0.
Item, xxiiij^{te} lesse peece of pewter	1. 2. 0.
Item, sixe brasse candlestickes	6. 0.
Item, five brasse pottes, three ketles, sixe pannes and	
one fryinge panne, price	2. 0. 0.
Item, three chaires, sixe quishings, one table and a forme	10. 0.
Item, xxx^{tie} milke bowlls with all other wood vessell	1. 6. 8.
Item, one baconn flicke with two skelves, two speetes, a paire	
of ironn rackes, a paire of tonges and two recking crookes, price	1. 0. 0.
Item, certaine other implements in the lofte above the seller	1. 0. 0.
Item, howshold stuffe in the seller, vicz., two paire of bedstockes,	
one presse and a cawle with one litle ambrye, price	1.10. 0.
Item, fower mattrisses, five coverlettes, five happens, eight coddes,	
a paire of bedd blancketes	3. 6. 8.
Item, certaine lynnen cloath, a harden webbe and a peece of	
twill, price	1.18. 0.
Item, eight paire of straking sheetes, eight lynnen sheetes	
& eleaven harden sheetes	3.16. 6.
Item, eight bowlsters or coveringes for fether and	
sixe of towells, price	1. 6. 8.
Item, more lynnen geare in kirchiffes & raills	1. 0. 0.
Item, implements of howshold in the parlour as sixe	
paire of bedstockes, one cupborde, five happens with	
other implements there	4. 0. 0.
Item, Oats sowen on the grounde, price	10. 0.
Item, sixe kyne, fower calves, a maire	19. 0. 0.
Item, two whyes, price	3. 0. 0.

Somma £61 5s 10d

Debita debentia testatoris ut sequitur

First George Stannick	13. 0.
Item, Thomas Shawe of Cockerton	4. 0.
Item, Thomas Iley	15. 8.
Item, the said Thomas more for a quarter of oates	10. 0.
Item, George Hunter, servant to Ralph Nicholson	2. 0.
Item, Thomas Simpson	1. 0. 0.
Item, William Marshall	1. 2. 6.
Item, Edwarde Marshall	2. 4. 0.
Item, Thomas Gregorie	2.13.4.
Item, John Willson of Darlington	1. 0. 0.
Item, Thomas Iley and Christofer Garthorne	11. 0. 0.
Item, Edwarde Elgee	15.10. 0.

Summa debitorum debentium in[] testat[] £36 14s 10d
Debita nulla debentia per testatorem

Summa Totalis £108 0s 8d

[*Parchment, 1 m., indented. Will and inventory in hand similar to 10, 11, 12, 14 inventory, 23, 27 will, 28, 35, 36 will, 43, 44, 46, 48 will, 49, 50, 51 and 56.*]

7 Toby Colling of Cockerton, 1605

In the name of God, Amen, the xviij^th daie of Aprill, Anno Domini, 1604, I, Tobie Collinge, of Cockerton in the parishe of Darlington, sicke in bodie, neverthelesse of good and perfect remembrance, praised be God, therefore make this my testament and last will in manner and forme followinge. First, I comit my soule into the handes of Almightie God by whose onely mercies in the merittes of Christ Jesu I doe undoubtedly believe to be saved and by no other meanes and my bodie to be buried within the church or churchyard of Darlington. Item, I give and bequeath to Thomas Aman, sonne of Oswold Aman, fortie shillinges. Item, I give to Elizabeth Collinge, daughter to Thomas Collinge, xiiij^s. Item, I give to Thomas Collinge my blacke cloake. Item, I give to my sister, Anne Lodge, my litle graie maire. Item, I give to George Lodge fortie shillinges. Item, I give to Marmaduke Willyamson v^s. Item, I give to John Marshall v^s. Item, I give to Robert Willyamson v^s. Item, I give to Thomas Raine v^s. Item, I give to John Simpson v^s. Item, I give to Rauffe Smurfett vs. Item, I give to Wedowe Bellingbey iij^s. Item, I give to theldest sonne of Elizabeth Waker x^s. Item, I give to Cuthbert Middleton my jerken and a dublett. Item, I give to Thomas

Maison my hatt. Item, I give to John Simpson my best hose. Item, I give to Willyam Glover v^s. Item, I give to Margerie Applebie v^s. Item, I give to Richard Stealley v^s. Item, I give to Willyam Heviside my boots and my shoes and a paire of stockinges. Item, I give to the poore people in Darlington parishe iij^{li} vj^s viij^d by yeare, for the tearme of three whole yeares and to be paid out of my lease at Cockefeild. Item, I give to Thomas Collinge fortie shillinges yearelye, for the tearme of five yeares, and to be paid out of my lease att Cockefeild. Item, I give to Margarett Lodge fortie shillinges to be paid out of my lease also. Item, my will is that my brother Gregorie Lodge have the occupacion of my lease att Cockefeild, paieinge these legacies abovesaid (that is to the poore people, Thomas Collinge and Margarett Lodge, above written). Item, I give George Lodge halfe a oxgange right in the Grange Close or, for the want of the said halfe oxgange, vij^{li}. Item, I give to my sister, Susan Collinge, my oversea coverlett. And all the rest of my goodes and chattle, my debtes, legacies and funerall expences discharged, I give and bequeath to Gregorie Lodge and Susan Collinge, whome I ordeine and make whole executors of this my last will and testament. In witnes whereof I have caused these presentes to be written. Item, to John Willyamson my browne jerkinge. Testes, Thomas Simpson, Thomas Hodshon, John Simpson and Thomas Maison with others.

[*Paper, 1 f.*]

An inventarie of all the goodes and chattles of Tobie Collinge of Cockerton, late deceased, praised the xxiiijth of August, 1604, by these fower men, Christofer Stainesbie, Thomas Hodshon, Raiph Blackwell and Thomas Maison

In the hall

Inprimis, one longe table and a square table and a buffett stoole	16. 0.
Item, one stand bedd with all that belongeth to it	2. 0. 0.
Item, ij stocke bedds	3. 0.
Item, one chaire	1. 0.
Item, one chist	3. 0.
Item, one washinge tubb	1. 0.
Item, a sworde, a case of pistolls	15. 0.
Item, a callever and a morean	15. 0.
Item, ij leedes	1. 0. 0.
Item, iij stees	3. 0.
Item, his lease in Cockfeild for thre yeares to come	22. 0. 0.
Item, his apparell	1. 0. 0.

Debtes owne to the testator

Item, John Warkupp	3. 3. 0.
Item, John Simpson	2.10. 0.
Item, Christofer Bainbridge	1. 0. 0.
Item, Christofer Warkupp	6. 0.
Item, Christofer Arthur	5. 0.
Item, Willyam Marshall	4. 0.
Item, Thomas Raine	2. 3. 4.

Summa £38 13s 4d

Debts that the testator oweth

Inprimis, Richard Stealley	3.17. 0.
Item, to John Simpson	2.13. 4.
Item, to John Warkopp	1. 0. 0.
Item, to Raiphe Blackwell [*from here page torn*]	...xjˢ..
Item, to Mathew Thompson	.....ˢ..
Item, to Thomas Or....	.xxiiijˢiiijᵈ
Item, to Robert Waide	..ijˢ..
Item, to Jane Willyamson	.iiijˢvjᵈ.
Item, to Christofer Maugham	....
Item, to Robert Willyamson	....vˢ

S[um]ma .....xv[ˡⁱ] vijˢ ixᵈ

[*Paper, 1 f. Will and inventory in different hands.*]

8   William Barnes of Darlington and Bedburn Park, 1605

In the name of God, Amen, I, William Barnes, of Bedburne Parke in the countie of Durham, gentleman, now sick in bodie but of perfect remembrance for which I thank Almightie God, doe make this my last will and testament in manner following. First, I comitt my soule into the handes of Almightie God, from whom I receyved the same, and I will that my bodie shalbe buried with decent funeralls at the sight of my executors, with certeine hope of a ioyfull resurrection and future glorie with the elect of God through the onelie merrittes of our Lord and saviour Christ Jesus, who hath redeemed us with his precious bloud and in whom I have assured confidence laid up to be made partaker of those blessinges procurable by him soe dearelie purchased for his Church, of which I professe my selfe to be a member and most humblie, hartelie, freelie and constantlie, doe make profession of my faith in him according to those articles of doctrine and faith now publicklye professed by ...[*ill egible*]... through his divine mercye by this Church of England, as the same is nowe generallie receyved and taught, and was sett forth by aucthoritie in the ...[illegible]... of the Raigne of our late, most gratious Soveraigne Ladie, Queene Elizabeth, of most blessed memorye. I will that Barbarie, my welbeloved wife, shall, together with the free houses and burgages in Darnton beinge her owne inheritance which I latelie builded and with my coppieholde landes which after my death by custome doth come to her in her widowe right, have and enioye for the better bringing up of my yongest children the full moytie and halfe part of my leases of the towles of Darnton withall other thinges therein demised and alsoe the moytie and full halfe of my lease of Bedburne parke with thappurtenances, and alsoe the thirds of my freehold land in Darnton during her life, and one hundred poundes in satisfaction of her dower and widowes part; and all other rights of in and to my landes and goodes. Item, I will that my sonne Christofer shall have my freeholde landes in Darnton which I purchased of Thomas Denham, William Corker and Robert Darnton, after my decease, according to the intent and true meaninge of a deede of feoffament by me thereof made and executed to my welbeloved cosine, John Barnes of Durham, Esquier, and Robert Ward of Darnton, draper, yf he will performe this my will and testament in the clauses underwritten, otherwise the same to passe according to the said deed & also the other moyties of my said leases of the Towles of Darnton and Bedburne Parke aforesaid. And my will is that my said sonne, Christofer, shall have the benefitt and preferment for the renewing of the said leases, from time to time, to his owne use any uses estate ...[illegible]... the moyties of the said leases as aforesaid to my said wife ever reserved during her life. And if it fortune that my said sonne, Christofer, doe die before the said leases happen to be renewed, soe that the whole interest thereof doe come to my said wife, then my will is, and I hartelie intreate my said wife, that the said leases maie be renewed to theuse and behoofe of his next brother and heire who, at that time, shall happen to be livinge, her whole interest in the severall moyties thereof to her duringe her life ever reserved. Item, I give and bequeath unto Thomas Barnes, my seacond sonne, all my estate, title, right, interest and terme of yeares, which I have yet to come unexpired in the lease made to me and others by the nowe Lord Bushopp of Durham, of the High park in Darnton together with the said lease. Item, I give and bequeath unto my sonne, Henry Barnes, and his heires, my houses in Darnton which I bought of one Mr Dixon Clark, now in the occupacion of Richard Pickering and Richard Boswell. Item, I give to my sonne, William Barnes, and to his heires, my twoo houses in Skinnergate in Darnton, which I bought of Thomas Denham and now in the tenure of Anthonye Short, together with the rent of five poundes issueing out of the house wherein Richard Elstobb nowe dwelleth, scituate on the headraw in Darnton aforesaid, during the terme which I have therein of the demise of Richard Stainton, and alsoe the rent of fortie shillinges issuinge out of the milnedam close there, and also the yearelie rent of vs issueing out of Denhams house there, duringe all the terme to me demised by the said Richard Stainton, and also xiiij^s yearlie rent of Robert S...[illegible]...'s house. And for the further advancement of my three younger sonnes and all my daughters, Bridgett, Anne, Margaret, Elizabeth, Jane and Dorothee, for and towardes their education and to make them stocks and better porcions for theyre preferment, I will that out of my sonne Christofer's part of the severall leases of the Towles of Darnton &c and Bedburne Parke, and out of my said freehold land in Darnton which I purchased of Thomas Denham and William Corker, per Robert Darneton, the some of fiftie poundes shall be yearlie raised during the space of seaven yeares next ensueinge & the some to be putt forward & employed for ther benefits till they come to full age. The residue of the proffitts to be raised of the said land & ...[illegible]... of my severall leases to be for the mayntenance and education of my said sonne, Christofer, duringe the said yeares, and afterwardes to be whollie to his owne use as is aforesaid, and my said landes to be to him and his heires for ever, if he consent thereunto, and doe not offer to hinder his said brethren of their porcions, intended by this my will to be soe raised and levied, and whereunto I doe charg him of my blessinge to consent when he cometh to full age. Otherwise, if he will not consent thereunto, my will is that my cosine, Mr John Barnes, and Robert Ward shall be seized of my saide landes to them and their heires and to theire onelie use and behoofe to the end that they maie sell the same at the uttermost value and the money to be levied of the price thereof to be presentlie paied to the said Thomas Barnes, Henry Barnes and William Barnes or soe manie of them as shall be then livinge, equallie. Item, I give and bequeath to my daughters, Bridgett, Anne, Elizabeth, Dorothee, Jane and Margaret, to everie of them, xl^{li} for their porcions out of my goodes, to be likewise presentlie imployed & putt forward for their benefitt untill they shall be ...[illegible]... or come to the age of xxj yeares. Item, I give and bequeath unto the Right Honorable, my verie good lord, the Lord Bushopp of Duresme, as a poore token of remembrance & of my dutiefull and good will, one dubble soveraigne in gould. Item, I give and bequeath to the poore of the parish of Hamsterley xx^s, to the poore of Darnton iiij^{li}, to my brother John Barnes xs in gould, and to Richard Barnes and James Barnes, my brethren, x^s in goulde. Item, I give and bequeath unto my sonne, Christofer, a bed with the furniture belonginge unto it, now standing in my house at Bedburne Park. And also my will and intent is, that if my wife Barbara doe marrie and take another husband after my decease, That then such porcions as I have given unto all my children, shall be governed and disposed by my supervisor as he shall thinke most fitt for the increase of their said porcion forward thereof for their best proffitts, if that she the said Barbara or her husband, if she chance to marrie, doe make wast thereof. The rest of my goodes and chattells, my debtes and funerall expenses discharged, I give and bequeath to my wife and my said sonnes, Thomas Barnes, Henry Barnes & William Barnes, Bridgett, Anne, Elizabeth, Dorothee, Jane and Margaret Barnes, equallie to be devided amongst them. And I make my said welbeloved wife, Barbara Barnes, sole executor of this my last will and testament, and doe make and constitute and hereby doe declare it to be my full will and pleasure that my said wife shall have the tuicion of all my said Children and their landes, rentes & porcions duringe their minorities for their best commoditys and the education of them during all the said time, by and with the advise of my said welbeloved cosine, John Barnes, whom I intreat make & nominate to be supervisor of my will, and to take care of, and to be helping to my said wife and children, in anie their iust occasions, and to foresee as much as in him is, that they receyve noe losse for want of sufficient surties upon anie of their tuicions to be grannted in the spirituall Court. And, lastlie, I praie my said wife to be advised from time to time by my said supervisor, touchinge the education of my said children and the goverment of their severall porcions, And them alsoe to be advised by his godlie counsell, and I praie God to blesse them all. In witnes whereof I have hereunto sett my hand and seale, the xxvjth daie of September, 1605.

William Barnes

[*Paper, 1 f.*]

A trew inventarie of all &
singuler the goodes and chattells, moveable and
unmoveable, of William Barnes of Darlington, gentleman, lait
deceased, and first of his said goodes and chattells at
Bedburne, taken and praised the xiiijth daie of December,
1605, by William Hutton, gentleman, Henrie Folansbie, Peter
Hodgson and Thomas Young, yeoman, as followeth,

Implements of houshold stuff in the hall

First, a long table, a long settle, one buffett forme with another
forme, one new presse and an olde presse, five staffes, two bagges
of arrowes and one chist   2.13. 4.

In the parlour

Item, two truckes, xxiiij paire of shetes, xx^{tie} yeardes of harden,
xxvth linnen shetes, ten pillows   9. 0. 0.
Item, one long bowe, a crosse bowe   5. 0.
Item, one speare staff and a steele capp   3. 4.
Item, one case of pistolls and a touch boxe   5. 0.
Item, one square table and a long settle, six buffet stooles, a
liverey cupbord, one other cupbord and two ioyned chaires   2. 0. 0.
Item, five mappes and a dozen of quishinges   13. 4.

In the greene chamber

Item, one stand bed, one fether bed and greene curtaines, one
greene rugg, two coverlettes, two blanckettes, two bolsters and
two pillows   5. 0. 0.
Item, one trindle bed and a fether bed, one bolster and two
coverlettes   1. 0. 0.
Item, one cubbord and a cubbord cloth, one silke quishing, one
table & a ioyned chare   1. 0. 0.

In the chamber over the parlour

Item, one stand bed, a fetherbed, one rugg, a double blanckett, one
single blanckett, a bolster, two pillows & greene curtinges   5. 0. 0.
Item, one trundlebed & a fetherbedd, a bolster, two coverlettes,
2 tables & 2 mappes, one liverey cupbord and a chist, one truncke,
a chare, one chist with a hammer staff   2. 0. 0.

In the chamber over the hall

Item, one canabie bed with a fether bed, one bolster, 2 pillowes, 2
blanckettes, one stand bed, fower coverlettes, one mattresse, a
blankett, two pillowes, a chare, one table, one cupbord and a chist   2. 0. 0.

In the chamber over the kitching

Item, two bedes, two mattrisses, 4 coverlett and two bolsters   1. 0. 0.

In the chamber over the buttrie

Item, two dozen of napkins, iiij table cloathes, one presse, vij bear
barrells, one paire of gaintreis, iij skelves   1.13. 4.
Item, one bazen and eewer & xxvj pece of pewter   1.13. 4.
Item, vij candlestickes, iij saltes   5. 0.
Item, iij dozen of trenshers and vj plates   2. 6.
Item, six sawcers   1. 0.

Item, fower flower pottes, a quarte pot, one pynte pott, a liverey pott
   & two tunnes   3. 4.

In the milkhouse

One chirne, two butter tubbs and two kittes and xxij stone of butter 4. 0. 0.
Item, xxiiij^{tie} cheses, xx^{tie} milk bowles   1.13. 4.
Item, one dozen of chesfattes and three skeles   6. 8.

In the brewhouse

Item, one masking tubb, a cooling tubb, one guylefat, a stone strough,
   one wood troughe, a chese presse, a winding cloth, iiij sackes, v
   sives and riddles, ij skeeles and a soae   1. 0. 0.

In the kitching

Item, one cupbord and a cawell with vj brasse pottes, 2 tables, 2
   spetes & iij kettles   2. 0. 0.
Item, one chaffing dish, x pannes, 2 dropping pannes, a girdle, two
   broyling irons, 2 bread grates, 2 great knives, iij paire of pott kilpes,
   2 baisting ladles, a scummer, one latten ladle, a paire of rackes,
   2 skelves, a paire of tonges, iij recking crookes, a frying panne, 2
   knopp tubbs, a morter and a pestill   1. 0. 0.

In the kilne

Item, one great tub & a kilne heare   1. 0. 0.

In the stable

Item, one materesse, 2 coverlettes   10 0.
Item, one bolster and a paire of sheetes and two horses   10. 0. 0.
Item, one helme of Rye   4. 0. 0.
Item, two helmes of oates   5. 0. 0.

In the feildes

Item, two horses, three mayres & one fole   14. 0. 0.
Item, five fatt hogges and iiij other swyne, one dozen of geese, viij
   turkeys, viij capons, one dozen of hennes and a cock   4. 0. 0.
Item, xvj kyne and a bull, with a ruck of haye   40. 0. 0.
Item, ten score olde sheepe   60. 0. 0.
Item, six score and xviij hogges   28. 0. 0.
Item, two trees in the wood, standing uncutt   13. 4.
Item, corne on the earth   6.16. 8.
Item, in the medow, Brearfeild, xiiij calves and a ruck of haie 8. 0. 0
Item, fower fat oxen   13. 6 8.
Item, six oxen and a long waine   21. 0. 0.
Item, at home, one ruck of haie   3. 6. 8.
Item, in the Brearfeild one ruck of haie, in the meadowfeild two
   ruckes, in Shipley hill one ruck   6. 0. 0.

Item, at home iiij sheepe hackes and two on the feild, one sock & a
coulter and fower teames, 2 boltes, a shackle, a lowze crooke, 2
coopes, two ladders and a pitchfork, one oxe harrow, 2 horse
harrowes, one gavelock, a mattock, 2 dungforkes, one spade and two
ploughes, with other woodgeare in the woodhouse   2. 0. 0.

Sume 293. 8. 6d.

The like inventorie of
all his goodes and chattells, moveable
and unmoveable, of Darlington, taken praised the
xvjth daie of Januarie, Anno predicto, 1606, by Tobie
Oswold, Francis Forster & Robert Ward, yeoman,
as followeth,

In the hall house
ffirst, one square table with a carpett, two ioyned chaires
one long table with a carpett, iij buffett formes   2. 0. 0.
Item, one cupbord, one presse, one liverey table with a carpett
thereon and xvj quishinges   3.10. 0.
Item, one iron chimney, a paire of tonges, a porr   10. 0.
Item, three halbartes, a bow & a quiver with a dozen arrowes
& a pike   8. 0.
Item, a paire of tables   2. 0.
In the buttrey
Item, xij beare barrells   18. 0.
Item, xliiij pece of pewter   1.12. 0.
Item, a dozen sawcers, two saltes, iiij pottingdishes   6. 0.
Item, eight candlestickes, halfe a dozen brasse measures, with a
brasse yeardwand, a pewter cann   8. 0.
Item, three dozen of trenshers   1. 0.
Item, one sylver guilt bowle, with a cover, and another silver
tunne, parcell guilt, with ten silver spones   5.10. 0.
Item, six skelves & a bord, 2 paire of gauntreis   5. 0.

In the little parlour adioyning upon the butterie
Item, a table, one langsettle, a buffett forme, one cupbord with a
carpett thereon, 2 chistes and a long skelfe   1. 0.0.

In the kitching
Item, two brasse pottes, a possnet, 2 great caldrons, three kettles, xij
pannes, one litle brasse morter with a pestell, 2 ladles, three
baisting ladles, a scummer and a chaffing dish   3.10. 0.
Item, one paire of iron rackes, a pare of lesse called cobberons, 2
spettes, one dreeping panne, 2 broyling irons, one frying panne, 2
paire of pottkilpes, 2 recking rookes and a bread grate and a paire
of tonges   1. 0. 0.
Item, one dressing bord, one cawell & a skelffe   6. 8.

In the milkehouse
Item, one table, fower skelves, halfe a score of milke bowles, vj
chesfattes, fower wood doublers, one chirne and a stand and two
   kittes of butter   1.10. 0.

In the larder house
Item, one dressing bord, 2 tubbs, a stand and a kitt   3. 4.

In the brewhouse
Item, iij tubbes, a stone trough, iiij sackes, one window cloath, a
   bowle, skepps, iij sives and a riddle & 2 scuttles   10. 0.

In the little low parlour
Item, one stand bedd, a trindle bedd, tow mattresses, iij coverlettes,
   2 bolsters   1. 0. 0.
Item, one little table, a hopper, a leape, a haie spade   2. 0.
Item, certaine webbs of lead   3. 0. 0.

In the chamber over the parlour
Item, one faire stand bed, a fether bedd, one bolster, 2 pillowbers, a
   paire of blanckettes & a rugg, a trindle bedd, a fether bedd, one
   coverled, with their furniture   8. 0. 0.
Item, one chist, one table, 2 chaires, one trunck, 2 coffers, a still, a
   quishing   2. 0. 0.
Item, his apparell   10. 0. 0.
Item, his bookes   2. 0. 0.
Item, iiij paire of fyne lynnen sheetes, vj paire of courser, tenn
   pillowbers, 2 table clothes, three dozen of napkins, item, three
   cubbord clothes   8. 0. 0.
Item, two swordes & a dagger   1. 0. 0.

In the great chamber over the hall
Item, two tables with carpettes, xvj buffett stooles, one liverey table
   with a carpett and a quishing   4. 6. 8.
Item, one iron chimney   10. 0.
Item, corne windowed in the said chamber   2.13. 4.

In the chamber over the parloure adioyning
upon the butterie
Item, two great chists, a trindle bed with furniture on the same, a
   chare and an iron chimney   2. 0. 0.

In the maides chamber
Item, one bed and a forme   5. 0.

In the highest chamber
Item, two bedstedes and a boulting tunne   10. 0.

In the garner

Item, xxxij bushells of malt	3. 4. 0.

on the feild

Item, xviij head of younge cattell	27. 0. 0.
Item, xxix gimmers	6. 0. 0.
Item, vj oxen furnished	22. 0. 0.
Item, 2 longe wanes, iij cowpes, iiij paire of cowpe stangs, ij paire of unbound wheeles & a paire of iron bound wheles	3. 6. 8.
Item, corne on the grounde	20. 0. 0.
Item, corne in the barne & in stakes	50. 0. 0.
Item, one ruck of hay in Mr Skepper feild, another in the holme with other haie at home & abroad	6. 0. 0.
Item, the lease of six gaites in the High Park for six horses	15. 0. 0.
Item, the lease of Milnedame Close, Richard Elstobbs howse and other parcells of Deanehames landes	6. 0. 0.
Item, fower swyne	1. 0. 0.
Item, oates wyndowed at marie garthornes thirtie and eight bushells	2. 0. 0.
Certaine implementes in Richard Elstobbes contayned in an Inventarie made thereof praised worth	2. 0. 0.
Item, for certaine implementes omitted & forgotten	12. 4.

Summe bonorum apud darlington £236 0s 0d

Debts owen to the said William Barnes
at the houre of his death as followeth

Mr Doctor Emanuell Barnes	23. 0. 0.
Oswold Thomson	19. 6.
Coroner Oates	4. 0. 0.
Fees for the Coroner office	6.13. 4.
Fees for the balliwick	5. 0. 0.
Raph Gibbon, Robert Wilburne, Henrie Nattrisse & Raph Wilburne	15. 0. 0.
Robert Wilburne	15. 0.
John Dowson the yonger	13. 0.
John Nattrisse	1.15. 0.
Raph Gibbon	3. 6. 8.
Robert Wilburne of old debt	7. 0.
John Dawson thelder	12. 0.
Henrie Nattresse more	16. 0.
Christofer Wilburne	12. 6.
Thomas Husband	6. 8.
...[name illegible]... Gelder	10. 0.
William Wilburne	15. 0.

Summa debitorum £65 1s 8d

Summa totalis £594 10s 2d

For tythe	15. 0.
To my Lord	13. 0. 0.
Servantes wages	5.14. 0.
To Christofer Nicholson	3. 7.
To William Stock	20. 0. 0.
To Mr Skepper	3.15. 0.
To William Townesend	3. 6. 8.
To Harbatt Day	1.10. 0.

Summe £48 4s 3d

Charges about the probacion of the will   2. 3. 4.

[*Parchment, 3 mm., sewn, indented. Will and first inventory in same hand.*]

9 Geoffrey Raine of Darlington, 1605

Memorandum that Giffray Raine, late of Darneton, sicke in bodie but
of good & perfect memorie, did nuncupativeley declare his last will
as ffolloweth, about the iiij^th of ...[*torn*]... bre 1605, vidzt, he did give
& bequieth ...[*torn*]... & Ch ...[*torn*]... daugh ...[*torn*]... st Isabell Joan
& Elizabeth and to his sonn Thomas a bedd ...[*torn*]... its stede
behynd the parlour doore & he did give his howse to his two sonnes,
Henrie Raine & Thomas Raine, in the presence of Robert White,
Robert Howseden, Thomas Raine & others

[*Paper, 1 f.*]

An inventorie of all the goodes
and chattles, moveable and unmoveable, of Geffray Rayne,
late of Darneton in the countie
of Durham, glover, deceased, sene
and praised by Lawrence Catte-
ricke, Thomas Nawton, Henrye
Rayne, and Anthonye Claxton,
the xvij° day of Januarie, Anno
Domini, 1605 [1606]

In primis, his gyrdle and his purse & the money in yt & his
  apparell   1.13. 4.

In the hall

Item, one cupborde	1. 0. 0.
Item, ij tables, ij formes and 2 seates	13. 4.
Item, one chaire	1. 8.

Item, xxix° peice of pewther & one basinge	1. 13. 4.
Item, vj candlestickes	3. 4.
Item, vj saltes, 2 tunnes and 2 potingdishes	3. 4.
Item, one chaffingdishe	8.
Item, one paire of tables & a lyttle shelffe	2. 0.
Item, one brushe	1. 0.

Summa £5 12s 0d

In the buttrye

Item, one old amerye, iiij°ʳ stands, ij barrelles, j kirne, 3 shelves, j wood dishe and 3 skeales	11. 0.
Item, 3 dozen trenchers & iiij°ʳ	1. 0.
Item, 7 cannes & a cuppe	2. 0.
Item, 2 lyttle furmes, j old table & an old chist	3. 0.

Summa 17s 0d

In the little chamber

Item, one standbedd, j trucle bedd, 2 chistes, j shelfe, one fetherbedd, fyve coddes, one coverlett, 2 happinges and 2 blanckettes	1. 10. 0.

Summa £1 10s 0d

In the lowe parlour

Item, one table, j furme, j seat and 2 chaires	10. 0.
Item, 4 standbeddes and j trucle bedd	1. 10. 0.
Item, 3 fetherbeddes, j matteresse, 9 bolsters & coddes, 4 coverlettes, 4 happinges & 4 blanckettes	6. 13. 4.
Item, xiij quishions	4. 0.

Summa £8 17s 4d

In the lofte

Item, 6 stand bedds & one trucle bedd	13. 4.
Item, 6 matteresses, 7 codds, one coverlet and x happinges	3. 6. 8.
Item, one arke price	5. 0.
Item, one boulting tunn, with other houselments	5. 0.

Summa £4 10s 0d

In the kitching

Item, 2 pottes and 2 pannes	17. 0.
Item, 2 fryeing pannes and one drepinge panne	6. 0.
Item, 4 kettles price	1. 10. 0.
Item, 2 pare of rackes, 3 spettes, 2 pare of tonnges, one fier showle, 2 pare of pottkilpes, 4 reckinge crookes, one fleshe crooke, one shering knyfe, one laddle and 2 skimmers	1. 3. 0.
Item, one old cawell, j maskingfatt, one gilefatt, one old tubbe, fyve kym- linges, one stone troughe, one kneding tubbe, one brake, j soe, one chesepresse, and j lyttle swawle price	1. 12. 0.

Summa £5 8s 0d

In the stables

Item, xiij heckes, 3 manngers, one stee, one spade, one g.....pe, 2 showles, xij^{th.}.....with other houselment	13. 4.
Item, his market stawle & furmes	1. 8.

Summa 15s 0d

Item, eight score calff lether	6. 0. 0.
Item, the lease of a close	4. 0. 0.
Item, one cowe price	3. 0. 0.

Summa £13 0s 0d

Napperie

Item, 3 paire of lynnen sheetes, 4 paire of harden sheetes, fyve pillowbeers, 2 table clothes, one towell, half a dozen napkinges	2. 3. 0.

Goods abrode in the towne

Item, in Henrie Raines house, j cupboord	10. 0.
Item, one cupbord in Anthony Glovers house	15. 0.

Summa totalis £43 17s 4d

debttes owing by the deceased

Item, to Robert Whyt	6. 0. 0.
Item, to Edward Clark	2. 4.

Summe [blank]

[*Paper, 2 ff., sewn, indented. Will and inventory in different hands.*]

10 Ralph Hugill of Darlington, 1605

In the name of God, Amen, the seconde daie of November, in the thirde yeare of the reigne of our most gracious soveraigne, Lorde James, by the grace of God, kinge of England, France & Irelande, defender of the faith, &c., and of Scotlande, the xxxixth, 1605, I, Ralphe Hagill, of Bongait in Darlington, in the County of Durham, labourer, sicke in body, but of good and perfect remembrance I give God most hartie thanckes, do make and ordaine this my last will and testament in manner and forme followinge, that is to saie, first, I give my soulle to almightie God, my Creator and Redemer, and my body to be buried within the parish churchyarde of Darlington aforesaide. Also, I doe committ and referre the full trust of tuicion and governement of my sonne Richarde, during his minoritie, to my brother, Henry Hugill, and my howse, keping the same in good reparacion untill my said sonne shalbe of full age. Also, I doe give and bequeath the yearelie profit and benefit, arising of the sheepe standes, to be kept and imployed to some use for to helpe to put my said sonne to an occupacion. Also, I give to my said brother, Henrie, my cloke: and the rest of myne apparrell. The rest of all my goodes, not given nor bequeathed, I doe give unto my said sonne Richerd whome I make my whole executor, provided that, if he dye, then I do give all my said goodes to my brethren, Thomas Hugill, James Hugill and Henry Hugill, (myne apparrell and howse onely excepted) which I do give to Henry whome I then make my whole executor. Witnesses hereof, Lawrence Hewitson, Lyonell Claxton and Phillipp Sadler, with others.

[*Paper, 1 f.*]

A true inventorie of all and singular the goodes and chattells, moveable and unmoveable, of Ralph hugill of Bongait in Darlington, lait deceassed, taken and praised the xxjth daie of December, 1605, by Symon Giffarde, gentleman, Christofer Nicholson ,William Burdon and Cuthbert Carre, as followeth,

Inprimis, his apparrell	13.4
Item, tenn pewter dublers, three sawcers, thre saltes, two candlestickes, two litle pannes, one brasse pott, one speet, a stand, one kimling or knack tubbe, one litle tubbe, with other trifeles	7. 8.
Item, his wife hatt, one raill, one pillowbere, an appron, with other old napprie waire	2. 6.
Item, flaxe and towe	2. 6.
Item, one old ambrie, a cawell, three bed steades, one chist, one borde, thre litle formes, one chaire, two stooles, a coverlet, thre litle coddes, with some other trifeles	10.0
Item, one close at Cockerton, taken and paid for, beforehand, for one whole yeare yeat to come	4. 0. 0
Item, corne in the howse, with a bushell and a pecke	4. 0
Item, tenn old fleakes	2. 6
Item, one rucke of haye	15. 0
Item, one horse, a mayre, sadles and sackes, with a cowe	6. 3. 4

Some £13 5s 10d

Debtes owing to the said Ralph Hugill

first, Robert Dawson	2.10. 8
Item, the said Robert more	2. 4. 0
Item, John Simpson	2.19. 0
Item, Edmunde Favell	1.19. 0
Item, George Stannicke	6. 8

Somma debitorum debentium £9 19s 4d
Summa totallis £23 5s 2d

Debtes owing by the said Ralph Hugill

First, to William Stoddart	2. 6. 8
Item, to William Lee	2.10. 0
Item, to Richard Smith	1. 4. 0
Item, to John Dobson	2.12. 0
Item, to Cuthbert Carre	5. 0
Item, to Barnarde Langestaffe	3. 0. 0
Item, more to Cuthbert Carre	6. 8
Item, to Lawrence Cathericke	5. 6
Item, to Agnes Dossye	1. 0

Summa debitorum debentium per ipsum defunctum £12 10s 10d

Summa de Claro Debitis deductis £8 13s 4d

[*Parchment, 1 m., indented. Will and inventory in hand similar to 6, 11, 12, 14 inventory, 23, 27 will, 28, 35, 36 will, 43, 44, 46, 48 will, 49, 50, 51 and 56.*]

11 Robert Dale of Darlington, 1606

In the name of God, Amen, the xxxth daie of Januarie, in the third yeare of the reigne of our moste gracious soveraigne, Lord James, by the grace of God, Kinge of England, France and Irelande, Deffender of the faithe, &c., and of Scotlande, the xxxixth, 1605 [1606], I, Robert Daill, of Darlingtonn, in the countie of Durham, Tanner, sicke in bodie, but of good and perfect memorie, I yeald God most hartie thankes, do make and ordaine this my last will and testament in maner and forme following, that is to saie, first I give and bequeath my soull into the handes of Almightie God, my Creator and Redeemer, faithfullie belevinge through the merites of Christe his deathe and passion to be saved, committing my bodie (if it shall please God to call me to his mercy) to be buried within the parish Churchyearde of Darlington and as neare unto my father, Anthony Daill, lait deceassed, as can convenientlie be devised. Item, I give unto the poore people of the parishe of Darlington three poundes, to be distributed at the oversight of my supervisores hereafter nominated. Item, I give unto my sonne, Johnn Daill, five markes. Item, I give unto the child, which my wife is nowe with and as yeat undelivered, if it please God it shall live and accomplish full age, five poundes, and, if it chance to die and departe this liefe before it shall accomplish full age, then I do will give and absolutelie bequeath the saide five poundes to my sonne, Johnn. Furthermore, I will (the lawe permittinge) that if either of my childrenn shall die before their accomplishment of their full ages, that then the survivor of them twoe shall have and enioy bothe the said legacies of five markes and five poundes. Also, I give to my sister, Meriole Wadley, twentie shillinges. Also, I give to Agnes Wadley and Katherine Wadley, her daughters, to either of them, tenn shillinges, to be paid them at the feast of St John Baptist next after my deceasse. The rest of all my goodes and chattells, moveable and unmoveable, not given nor bequeathed, I give unto my wife, my sonne, John, and the child yett unborne, whom I do make and ordaine my ioynt coexecutores of this my said last will and testament, desyring my father-in-lawe, John Garthorne, James Daill, my brother, Christofer Richardson and Gregory Lawe to be supervisores thereof. In witnes of James Daill, John Garthorne, Christofer Richardson, Gregorie Lawe and Lawrence Elgee, with others.

[*Parchment, 1 m., indented*]

The inventorie of all and singular the goodes and chattells of Robert Daill, deceassed, as well moveable as unmoveable, praised the xxvjt^h daie of Marche, 1606, by John Fleminge, Thomas Johnnson, Lawrence Stainesbie and Henry Allonson, as followeth, viz.

First howshold stuffe in the lawe parlour

Inprimis, all his apparrell	1.13. 4
Item, one standbedd, a fether bedd, a bolster, two coddes, two happinges and a coverlet	2. 3. 4
Item, five pillowberes, two paire of lynnen sheets, two towells, two table cloathes and three table napkynnes	1. 6. 8
Item, one table withe a frame, a longe buffet forme, iiij^er chistes, one other forme and a chaire	19. 0
Item, lyne spunne and unspunne, with a pounde of jarsey	11. 0

Implementes in the butterie

First, a great arke, three skelves, a choppinge borde, a chirne & a chirnestaffe, a drincke barrell, two standes, three milke bowlles, an old chaire, a buffet stoole, two stone pottes, with some other small trifles	18. 0
Item, two brasse pottes, a fryinge panne, a litle caldronn, a litle panne, withe fower litle pewter dublers	1.10. 0
Item, a paire of beddstockes in the chamber over the butterie, with some woollenn yarne for a happine	6. 0

Implementes in the hallhowse

First, a cupborde, tenne peece of pewter, iiij^er candlestickes, three saltes, a pottell pott, a sawcer, halfe a dozen tynne spones	3. 0. 0
Item, a square table, another litle longe table with a forme, a joyned chaire & iiij^er quishinges and a cradle	11. 6

Item, a paire of woollenn cards, a new sacke & an old barke sacke	3. 4
Item, a trundle bedd with an old mattrisse, a paire of sheetes, three happinges and an old codde	13. 4
Item, a paire of litle ironn rackes, a speet, a paire of tonges, two reckingcrookes, a litle brasse pott and a panne	9. 0
Item, a tubbe, a spynninge wheele, two skeeles, two ironn forkes, a mashinge bowlle and thre litle stooles	5. 0
Item, two kyne and a calfe	4. 6. 8
Item, a why and a stotte	3. 3. 4
Item, tenne ewes	3.10. 0
Item, two swine	12. 0

Implementes in the workehowse

Inprimis, eight barke tubbes and a stone troughe	6. 0. 0
Item, a soe, an apronn, two workinge knifes, a barckhowse bowlle, two stooles, a pannyer, three thralles, a ridle, a workinge tree and two powlles and a croke	6. 8
Item, a dozen gyrthes for tubbes	6. 8
Item, a troughe stone in the kitchinge	10. 0
Item, in haye and ann olde syle	4. 0
Item, a swine troughe and pearkes for lether	2. 6
Item, in barke chopt and unchopt and lether tanned and untanned	45. 2. 8

Somma £78 14s 0d
Debts owing by the testator

First, to Christofer Richardsonn	2. 0. 0
Item, to Thomas Thuresbie	5. 6. 8
Item, to John Fleminge	1. 6. 8
Item, more to my sister Richarson	15. 0
Item, to my sister Daill	5. 0

Som £9 13s 4d

Somma declaro debitis deductis £69 0s 8d

Certaine desperate debtes owen to the testator as followeth, vicz.,

Inprimis, John Stephenson	15. 0
Item, John Reethe	13. 0
Item, John Wilkinson	5. 0
Item, Francis Wadley, deceassed	4.10. 0

Som £6 4s 0d

[*Parchment, 1 m., indented. Will and inventory in hand similar to 6, 10, 12, 14 inventory, 23, 27 will, 28, 35, 36 will, 43, 44, 46, 48 will, 49, 50, 51 and 56.*]

12 John Hall of Darlington, 1606

In the name of God, Amen, the xij[th] daie of September, in the fourthe yeare of the reigne of our most gracious soveraigne Lorde James, by the grace of God, kinge of Englande, France and Irelande, defender of the faithe, &c., and of Scotland, the xl[th], 1606. I, John Hall, of Darlington, in the countie of Durham, cordiner, sicke in bodie but of good and perfect remembrance, I give God most hartie thanckes, do make and ordaine this my last will and testament in maner and forme followinge, that is to saie, first of all, I give and bequeath my soull into the handes of Almighty God, my Creator, through whose precious bloudshedding I faithfullie trust to be saved. Item, I will and bequeath my bodie to be buryed in the parish churchyeard of Darlington, aforesaid, and as neare unto my wife, lait deceassed, as possiblie cann be divised. Item, I give to the poore of the towne of Darlington, aforesaid, three shillinges and fower pence. Item, I give unto my sonne, Cuthbert Hall, my shopp, during all my lease, with all my shoppgeare. Also, I give and bequeath to my sister, Elizabeth, my litle parlour on the backside, likewise during all my lease, if she live so longe. Item, I give unto my nephewe, Edwarde Hall, a gymmer lambe. Item, I give to my brother, Richard Riggmaide, my coate and my britches, with the rest of myne apparrell, nowe on my backe. Also, I give all the rest of myne apparrell unto my said sonne, Cuthbert, my best cloake excepted, which I give unto my sonne, Christofer Hall. Item, I give and bequeath to my wife, Elizabeth, my cupborde and my best cowe. Also, I give to my sister, Isabell, one ewe. Also, I give unto my sister, Elizabeth, aforesaid, a gymner lambe. The rest of all my goodes, not given nor bequeathed, my debtes paid, I give unto my wife, Elizabeth, my sonne, Cuthbert Hall and my sonne, Christofer Hall, if he returne into the cuntry alive, whome I make Joynt executores of this my said last will and testament. In witnes of John glover, Edwarde Hall, George Marshall and Richarde Pickeringe.

[Paper, 1 f.]

A true inventarie of all and singular the goodes and chattells, moveable and unmoveable, of John hall of Darlington, cordiner, lait deceassed, taken and praised the vj[th] daie of November, 1606, by Richard Wheatley, Christofer Nicholson, John Glover and William Townend, as followeth, vicz.

In the hall house

First, a cuppborde   1. 0. 0

Item, xxiij pece of pewter & vij sawcers	1. 3. 4
Item, two pewter candlestickes, two brasse candlestickes, thre saltes with covers and one without a cover & a drincking tunne	6. 8
Item, a litle brazen morter, a pestell and a brasse chafing dishe	3. 4
Item, two long setles, two formes and a table with a frame	6. 8
Item, two speetes, two cobbirons, two reckin crokes, two paire of tonges and two paire of pot kelpes	10. 0
Item, a chopping knife, a shearing knife, a brasse ladle, a scummer, an iron scummer, a fleshe croke	3. 4
Item, an old chaire, a litle buffet stoole, a bread grate with a lanthorne	1. 2.
Item, iiijor silver spones	1. 0. 0.

In the butterie

Item, iiijor brasse pottes	13. 4.
Item, a great caldron, two litle ketles and two pannes	10. 0.
Item, a frying panne and a dreping panne	3. 0.
Item, a guylinge tubb, another tubb with iiijor standes, three skeeles, a washing bowlle, a kitt and other implementes of wood in the buttery	10. 0.

In the parlour adioyning upon the hallhowse

Item, a table and a frame with a forme	4. 0.
Item, two stand beddes, two fetherbeddes, a paire of blancketes, iiijor coverlettes, two bowlsters	2.13. 4.
Item, a trindle bedde, two mattrisses, two happins and a bowlster	6. 8.
Item, two chistes	1. 0.
Item, three lynnen sheetes, iiijor harden sheetes, iiijor pillowberes and a frindge	1. 0. 0.
Item, in oyle and tallowe	1.16. 8.
Item, a trough stone and a masking tubb	2. 0.

In the kilne

Item, a steepe leade and a kilne haire	5. 0. 0.
Item, three riding sadles an two loade sadles, with their furniture belonging theim	15. 0.
Item, three sackes, a poke and a windowcloth	8. 0.
Item, an iron forke and rakes, with a hay spade and a diking spade	5. 0.
Item, an Ironbound carte, with furniture	1. 6. 8.
Item, xxj yeardes of woollen clothe	1.10. 0.
Item, the leasse of the howse, with appurtenances, the litle parlour and shopp given by legacie except	12. 6. 8.
Item, two maires	7. 0. 0.
Item, a branded cowe	3. 0. 0.
Item, three gymmer hogges and a gymmer	15. 0.

Item, two calves	1.16. 8.
Item, tenn ewes with a ramme	3. 6. 8.
Item, thre gymmer hogges more	9. 0.
Item, the haie and harbadge of the Bennetfeild untill Sainct Hellen daie next coming	2.15. 0.
Item, another branded cowe	3. 0. 0.
Item, the leasse of a gait in the High Parke	2.13. 4.
Item, a pigg, a bushell and a pecke	4. 0.
Item, the shopp and shoppgeare, with the litle parlor on the backside	10. 0.

Debtes owen to the testator as followeth

First, Anthonie Howpe for two paire of boates and a paire of shoes	10. 0.
Item, Robert Kelley	2. 0.
Item, Johnn hodgshonn	4. 6.
Item, Jane Sanderson, my lait servannt	3. 0.
Item, Christofer Hall of Worsall	2. 6.

Somma £1. 2. 0.

Somma Totallis £61.17. 6.

Debtes owing by the testator as followeth

First, to William Townende	2. 8. 6.
Item, more to the saide William for John Williamson	14. 0.
Item, to the cordiners of Darlingtonn	1. 2.10.
Item, to Henry Collinge	8. 0.
Item, to Agnes Johnsonn	18. 0.
Item, to John Newton	16. 0.
Item, to the clenser	19. 6.
Item, for the scholehowse rent	4. 1.
Item, to John Fawcet for Bennetfeild rent	1. 7. 6.
Item, to John Glover	7. 0.
Item, for coales	2. 8.

Summa debitorum £9 8s 1d

Summa de Claro debitis deductis £52 9s 5d

[*Paper, 1 f., indented. Will and inventory in hand similar to 6, 10, 11, 14 inventory, 23, 27 will, 28, 35, 36 will, 43, 44, 46, 48 will, 49, 50, 51 and 56.*]

13   Robert Loryman of Darlington, 1606

In dei nomine, Amen, 29º Augusti, Anno domini, 1606, I, Robert Loryman, of the parish of Darlington, sicke in bodie, but whole in minde and in good and perfect memorie, doe make and ordaine this my last will and testament, in manner and forme followinge. First, I give my soule unto Almightie God my Creator (of whom all thinges are), which hath reconciled me unto Himself by Jesus Christ, my Redeamer, who hath geaven Himself for me to be an offeringe and a sacryfice, of a sweete smellinge savoure, to God, His father; and my bodye to be buried within the church yard of Darlington, aforesaid, with an assured hope of Resurreccion to immortalitie when Christ, our head, shall come to Judgement. Item, I give unto the poore people, to be distributed at the discretion of my wiffe, vjˢ viijᵈ. Item, I give unto my sonne, Matthew Loryman, all such instrumentes as belonge to the shopp and one stande bedd in the further part of the parlill, with all furniture therto belonginge, & the great table in the parlill. Item, I give unto my said sonne, Matthew, my house in Northegate, with all profitts or appurtenannces therto belonginge, always provyded that my wiffe, Jane Loryman, shall inhabite the same duringe her liffe naturall, and, if please God that my said sonne, Matthew Loryman, shall dye without issue, I will that my said house shall come to my three daughters, Elizabeth, Isabell and Margrett Loryman, after the decease of my said wiffe. Item, I give unto my wiffe, Jane Loryman, one blacke Cow. Item, I will that my said sonne, Matthew, shall pay unto my daughter, Isabell Loryman, five poundes of currant money of Englande, at such times as my said sonne, Matthew, and my daughter, Isabell, shall agree upon. Item, I give unto my daughter, Margrett Loryman, one whye of a year old. Item, I give unto my daughter, Wedoo Nicholson, and her two sonnes, xxˢ amongest them. Item, I give unto my sonne-in-law, Bryan Coates, one read why of halfe-a-yeres old, to the use of his first child which god shall give unto him by my daughter Annas, his wiffe. The rest of all my goodes, moveble and unmoveble, my debtes first paid and legacyes discharged, I give unto my wiffe, Jane Loryman, and my three daughters, Elizabeth, Isabell and Margrett Loryman, whom I doe make and constitute full and whole executrices of this my last will and testament. Witnesses hereof, Isaac Lowden, Clerk, Lawrence Dobson and Matthew Loryman.

[*Two copies, parchment, 1 m., and paper, 1 f.*]

A true inventorie of all the goodes and
cattels, moveble and unmoveble, which Robert
Loriman, late of Darlington, deceased,
dyed possessed of, prysed by fower honest men:
William Scurfield, Lawrens Catherick,
James Dale and Christopher Richardson:
the xvj^th of November, Anno Domini, 1606,

Imprimis his apperrell, 2 bowes and arrowes	2. 0. 0.
Item, a cuppord in the hall with 10 peece of pewther vessell, candlestickes, with other furniture therof & a morter	2. 6. 8.
Item, 2 tables, 2 chares, 4 buffett stoles, 2 formes, 6 old quishions	10. 0.
Item, 2 reckinge crookes, 2 rackes & a speate	3. 4.
Item, 6 litle cheases and a stone of butter	6. 8.
Item, in the parlour, 2 stannd beddes, 2 feather beddes with all ther furniture	6.13. 4.
Item, a long table, 2 formes, 2 buffett stoles, 2 chares, 7 quishions, a litle cupporde with some pewther vessell, one chist & a crooke	3. 0. 0.
Item, 7 paire of linnen sheates, 6 pair of sammeringe sheates, xj pillivers, 2 linninge table clothes & 2 of sammeringe, 2 short table clothes, 4 towells, 3 dozen of table napkines, 8 hand towells	8. 0. 0.
Item, in the buttrie, 2 litle cuppordes, 2 litle boordes, 36 peece of old pewther dishes, 8 pottingers, 10 saucers, 4 saltes, 4 pinte pottes, 4 candlestickes, a litle botle, a morter, a chafin dish, 6 dozen & a half of trenchers, 5 dozen of spoones, 20 drinkinge cuppes & cannes, 10 barrells & standes, a kerne with other implementes	4. 0. 0.
Item, in the loft, a stannd bedd, a fether bedd with some furniture, a table, a chist, 2 buffett stoles, a lanterne & 2 quishiones	2.13. 4.
In a litle loft, 12 bushells of bigg	1. 8. 0.
Item, a servannts bedd, a mattress, an old chist, a bushell measure, with other old implementes	12. 0.
Item, in another loft, 2 stand beddes, 3 law beddes, 3 feather beddes, 2 mattresses, with ther furniture wantinge linninge, an old table, an old counter, 2 buffett formes and an old linen wheele	8. 0. 0.
Item, in the kitchine, 2 cawdrones, 2 ketles, 2 pottes, one possenett, 4 pannes, a fryinge pann, a drippinge pann, 2 speates, a paire of iron rackes, a pair of tonges, 2 pair of broyling irons, a coolerack, a reckinge crook, 4 skeales, a boule, a knock tubb, a say, a guyle fatt, a mass fatt, a bread brake, an iron forke, a fash tubb with 2 litle bordes, with all other small implementes	2.10. 0.
A quarter of malt	16. 0.
Item, 3 kine, a why and a stirke	9. 0. 0.

Item, a sow and five shotts	16. 0.
Item, 8 hennes and a cock, 3 turkes, 2 duckes and a drake, a layd sadle, an old stee, a grinstone, a buckitt, some coales with some trash wood	14. 0.
Item, in hay and a fogg of a close	3. 6. 8.
Item, in the shopp, 3 stiddyes, 2 vices, a pair of bellowes with hammers and fyles, 2 gunnes and other iron instrumentes	6.13. 4.

Summa totalis Inventarii

Debtes owinge to the said Robert Loryman

Mr Robert Talboys	2. 0. 0.
Mr Thomas Norton and Mr. William Talboys for ther father Ralfe Talboys	1. 3. 0.
Mr George Bainbrigg	1. 5. 6.
Mr Francis Storie	18. 0.
Edward Bratt of Preston	3. 4.
Thomas Blenkinsopp	2. 0.
William Sayre of Haughton	17. 0.

Summa Debitorum

Debtes which the said Robert Loryman oweth

To Mr John Lyons	10. 0.
To Mr Symon Giffarde	12. 0.
To Christopher Wilkinson	3. 6. 8.
To Richard Wheatley	1.10. 0.
To my daughter Isabell Loryman by the gift of John Cupberde	5. 0. 0.

Summa Totalis [blank]

[*Paper, 1 f., indented. Will and inventory in hand similar to 14 will, 18 and 19.*]

14 Richard Hudless of Darlington, 1606/7

[*filed under 1606*]

In dei nomine, Amen, vicesimo primo die februarij, Anno domini, 1606 [1607], I, Richerd Hudlesse, of Darlingtonne, sicke in bodie but whole in minde and in good and perfect memorie, doe make and ordaine this my last will and testament in manner and forme followinge. First, I give and bequeath my soule unto Almightie God, my Creator and my Redeamer, and my bodie to be buryed within the churcheyard of Darlingtonne, with a livelie hope of resurrection by vertue of the resurrection of Jesus Christ, whose pretious bloode shedd upon the Crosse hath purged me from all my sinnes. Item, I give to the poore people of Darlingtonn, xx^s. Item, I give to my wiffe, Dorithie Hudlesse, xx^{li}. Item, I will that my said wiffe (if she think goode) shall give unto Thomas Jennyson, gentleman, viij^{li} x^s, for the house we now dwell in, and that shee enioy it for her liffe naturall, and after her decease, I give it to Thomas, the sonne of John Lumley of Darlingtonne, my god sonne, for ever. Item, I give to Thomas Eyanson, of Kirbiethure in Westmerlande, my brother-in-law, one fushion dublett, a paire of grene kersey britches, three paire of hose, a white freyse Jerkine, my best shoes and my bootes. Item, I give unto his wiffe, Barbarie Eyansone, my sister, vj^{li}. Item, I give unto the two sonnes of the said Thomas and Barbarie Eyanson, to eyther of them, iiij^{li}. Item, I give to Symon Giffarde one sworde and one pitcheforke. Item, I give to Meryall Giffard, his wiffe, v^s. Item, I give to John Giffard, his sonne, xxs. Item, I give to Isaac Lowden iij^{s}iiij^d. Item, I give unto my wiffe, Dorithie Hudlesse, one gate in the parke. The rest of all my goodes and cattells, moveble and unmoveble, my debtes first paid and legacyes discharged, I give unto my wiffe, Dorithie Hudless, whom I make my full and whole executrix of this my last will and testament. In witnes wherof, Symon Giffard, gentleman, and Isaac Lowden, Clerk.

[*Paper, 1f, in hand similar to* **13, 18** *and* **19.**]

A tru inventorie of all the goodes and chattells,
moveable and unmoveable, which Richard
Hoodlesse of Darlington, deceassed, died
possessed of, prised by fower honest men.
Thomas Emmerson, William Lawson,
Edwarde Ward and Anthonie Rainton, the xjth
daie of March, Anno Domini, 1606 [1607], as followeth,

Imprimis his apparrell and purse	3. 0. 0.
Item, one maire and a pack sadle	2.10. 0.
Item, fower score and tenn yardes of unbleacht harden	2. 5. 0.
Item, nyne remnantes of cloath	9. 0.
Item, fiftene scoore yardes of course linne and stralines	11. 0. 0.
Item, in cloath at bleaching	15. 0. 0.
Item, in brasse and pewter	1.10. 0.
Item, a bushell of rye and the poke	3. 4.
Item, a score of yarne	1. 0.

Item, one cupbord, one cawll with dishes and other implementes	13. 4.
Item, one old table, two chistes, one chaire, twoe buffet stooles,	
tonges, rackincrokes, a paire of rackes, with old formes & bordes	6. 0.
Item, in beife	1. 6.
Item, an old ambrie a badderhaie and old implementes	3. 0.
Item, a gait in the High Park	13. 4.
Item, a sword and a pitchforcke	2. 0.
Item, in cloth sold	8. 0.

Summa totalis Inventarii £38 5s 6d

Debtes owinge to the said Richard Hudless

of John Harrison of Blackewell for a gray maire and a foale	3. 3. 4.
of Anthonie Shorte	1. 0. 0.
of Anthonie Raynerd	11. 0.

Summa totalis £4 14s 4d

Debtes which he oweth

To George kidder	18. 4.
For funerall charges	1. 0. 0.

[*Parchment, 1 m., indented. In different hand to will, similar to 6, 10, 11, 12, 23, 27 will, 28, 35, 36 will, 43, 44, 46, 48 will, 49, 50, 51 and 56.*]

15 Miles Guy of Darlington, 1607

In the name of God, Amen, I, Myles Guy, of Darlington in the countie of Durham, cordyner, sick in body but sound in memorie, god be praised, do make this my last will and testament in manner and forme folowinge. First, I bequyth my sowle into the handes of Almighty God, my Creator and Redeemer, and my bodie to be buryed in the parish church of Darlington, at the discretyon of my executor. And, of my temporall goodes, I thus dispose. First, I gyve & bequyth to the poore people of Darnton, xˢ. Item, I gyve & bequyth to Thomas Guy, my eldest son, his heires & assignes for ever, as well my freehold land as copyhold which I have lying at norgait end, next to the land of the kinges Majesties on the south syd & on the landes of Mr Calverley on the north. Item, I gyve and bequyth to John Guy, my eldest son by this my nowe being wyf, his heires & assignes for ever, in full satisfaction & payment of his lait brother Cockfeild porcion, which to him befell by lawe & I hadd for his use, all that my

Burgaig garth & kilne with thappurtenances, scytuate in skynnergait
in the said Darlington, next adyoyning to a burgaige of George
Randsons ther. Item, I gyve & bequyth to my son, Robert Guy, his
heires & assignes for ever, my burgaige lying & being at Bondlegait
end, next adyoyning to the landes of Edmond Bland. Item, I gyve &
bequyth to my said sons, Thomas Guy and John Guy, their heires &
assignes for ever, all my burgag with thappurtenances, scytuate in
Darnton upon the Hy Rowe wherin I nowe dwell, paying out of the
same to my said son, Robert Guy, during his lyf naturall, yearlie ten
shillinges at the feastes of Penthecost & St Martin in winter byshopp,
by equall porcions. Item, I gyve more unto every of my said three
sons viz., Thomas, Roberte and John, the some of vj^li xiij^s iiij^d. Item, I
gyve unto my doughter, Marie Guy, xx^li, my Cubbard in my
haulehowse & fower great dublers therupon withall. Item, I gyve &
bequyth of seaven poundes that John Sober, my son-in-lawe, owes to
the said John & his wyf iiij^li and to Georg Rogerson thereof xxx^s and
to Robert Lambart thother xxx^s. Item, I gyf & bequyth to my brother,
William Guy, one rayment of my clothes and fyve shillinges yearlie,
during his lyf, to be paid at Whit & Martinmas by equall porcions.
Item, I gyve to my sister, Elisabeth, during her naturall lyf, v^s at lyke
tymes to be paid yearlie. Item, I do requyer Robert Ward, my
neighbour, to be supervisor of this my last will & testament and to
do his best to cause this my will to be dewlie executed & trewlie, my
goodes destributed as is aforesaid, & I do gyve unto him for his
paynes therein to be susteyned, x^s. Item, I will that the yron
chymbney in my chamber shalbe an heir lome to the said howse
wherin it standes and thereto belonginge. Item, I gyve & bequyth to
my son, John Guy, all my shopgeare. Item, to my son, Thomas, my
callover, flask & tutchbox & headpece. Item, the residewe of all my
goodes (my debtes paid, my funerall expences deducted & discharged), of what nature & kynd soever, as well reall as personall they
be, I gyve & bequyth unto Margaret Guy, nowe my wyf, whome I do
make my sole executor of this my last will & testament, dayted this
seacond day of May, Anno Domini, 1607. Miles Guy [mark]
Wytnesses hereof William Guy John Redding   Robert Warde

[Paper, 1 f.]

The inventorie of all the goodes, moveable & unmoveable, quyck & dead, of
Myles Guy of Darlington, deceased, praised by Richard Bradock, John Fawcet,
Henry Elstobb and
Robert Ward, the xvj^th day of May, Anno Domini, 1607, vizt,

Inprimis, in the hall, a cubbard, a long table, a little table with two
  firmes & sex quysshinges, ij chaiers, 2 stooles, a morter & a braike   1. 8. 4.
Item, 24 dublers, 6 candlestickes, sex saltes, a brasen morter,
  a chafindish, a pewther bottle, a canne, 2 chamber pottes, 2 dossen
  & a half of spoones & 4^r sawcers   2. 0. 0.
Item, a callever, a head pece, flask & tutchbox, a drypping panne,
  a frying panne, 2 paier of tonges, 2 paier of potkilpes, 2 laddles,
  a speet, 2 recking crookes, a fyer shovell, a shelf, 5 score garne   1. 7. 4.
Item, a kytt, a stand, 2 shelves, a dish case   2. 0.

Item, in little buttery, 3 kettles, 4^r pottes, 3 pannes, a cawle, 2 tubbes,
  2 saaes, a trough, a barrell, 4^r earthen pottes, cannes, trenshers, wudd
  dublers, bowles, shelves, 2 seates, 3 seckes, a pook, a grape, a spade,
  a moldraik & other little trifles   2. 2. 0.

Item, in the kytchin, a masking tubb with a shovell   1. 0.

Item, in the stable, 4^r bordes, a stee, 5 jeastes, a firme   5. 0.

Item, in the oyle howse, 6 gallons of oyle, 20 stones of tallowe, rosell
  pyck j dossen & a half, 4^r tubbes & costrelles, a lecker panne & chist
  with a fleak & tresses   3.18. 0.

Item, in the lawe howse, 2 bedstockes, a flocked bedd, 2 coverlettes,
  2 wheeles, 2 paier cards & chist   11. 6.

Item, in the farre lofte, 5 beddes & bedsteades & a saddle   3. 6. 8.
Item, in the little chamber, a bedd & bedstead, halfe a stone of
  hemp, a salt tubb & bord   10. 0.
Item, in the fore chamber, his apparell, his purse money & gold   6.17. 6.
Item, 2 beddes & bedsteades, a trunke, a chist, 4^r quyshinges, 5^{li} garne
  & lyne, 6 quyshinges more, a shelf, a paier of tables, a squair table,
  firmes, chistes, a chaier with a iron chimbney   3.15. 0.
Item, 5 silver spoones, 4^r paier of lynne sheetes, 4 paier of harden,
  2 table cloothes, a dossen napkyns, 10 codwars & wullen cloth & a
  score of harden garne   4.10. 6.
Item, leather, a stand, a kyrne, a stoole & a shelf   5. 8. 8.

Item, in the shopp, 2 dossen & 5 paier shoies, 17 paier of bootes,
  11 paier of boot legges, shopp geare with a cowe & a calf at   9. 0. 0.

Item, in the malt loft, 3^{xx} quarters of malt &, in the garth, a stamp
  of hay; in the kylne, ootes, a tubb, a peck & busshell, a cubbard at
  the curriers & other trifles   60.13. 0.

Item, the cropp on the earth & a scoore of harden cloth   1.16. 8.

Debtes owen to him by

Anthony Elge by bondes	6.13. 4.
Thomas Howme of Yngleton	3. 0. 0.
John Sympson of Cockerton against malt	19. 0.
Ralph Nicholeson for malt	12. 0.
John Glover against malt	19. 0.
Wydo Wadley for malt	1.12. 0.
John Wyldman of Apleby for malt	10. 0.
Thomas Kewe for 2 busshels malt	5. 0.
Andrewe Moore for malt	12. 6.
Mark Shawe for malt	10. 0.
William Beckwith a quarter malt	1. 4. 0.
Richard Branson for malt remainder	1.12. 6.
John Spenc a quarter & lood malt	2. 9. 0.
Isabell Startfurth 3 busshels malt	7. 6.
Richard Elstobb 21 busshels malt	2.12. 6.
Christofer Naytby a quarter malt	18. 6.
John Acrigg of Pearsbrig a quarter	19. 0.
Wydow Stockdaile remainder	1. 5. 6.
John Stephenson remainder	15. 0.
John Sober	7. 0. 0.
Mr Errington of Cleasby for bootes & shoes	16. 0.
Mr Chilcoat of same a paier shoies	2. 8.
Mr Lancloot Hilton of Dyons 2 par shoes	4. 6.
Bowbank of Pearsbrigg a pair shoes	1.10.
Francis Castle a paier of shoes	1.10.
Georg Emmerson of Eriholme a pair shoes	2. 4
Paycock of Sadbury remainder	1. 4.
Mr Care of Mydelton 2 pair shoes	3. 4.
Sir John Maltyn of Dinsdall a pair botes	6. 0.
Mr Henry Killinghall a pair shoes btho:	2. 4.
Robert Dakers for 6 pair shoies	9. 8.
Peter Glover a pair boots to	5. 0.
& more for a paier Botes & shoes to post boy Anderson	4. 0.
Richard Wheatley a pair bootes to John Darnton	5. 0.
John Wudd for a close rent remainder	10. 0.
& that his wyfe ought for malt	8. 0.
John Wilkinson for malt	7. 6.
Bryan Threakeld 1 busshel ry & 12d	4. 0.
Robert Wrenne of Walworth	10. 0.
Thomas Kewe a pair shoues	1.10.
John Watson a pair shoes to Thomazin	1. 4.
William Ward of Hurworth for shoes	4. 0.

Summa totalis of goodes & debtes [blank]

he ought for hemp & rosell   8. 0.

Summa remaynes 147.15. 0d.

funerall expences to be deducted & for chadges at the ordynary

[Parchment, 1 m., indented. Will and inventory in hand similar to 1, 2, 16, 22, 24 will, 30, 32, 41, 42 will and 45 will.]

16 Thomas Johnson of Darlington, 1607

The inventory of all the goods and chattells of Thomas Johnson, lait of Darlington in the Countie of Durham, tanner, deceased, praised the xxth day of November, Anno Domini, 1606 by Lawrence Catherick, Lawrence Stainsbie, John Harreson and Robert Warde, as foloweth viz..,

in the hall howse

Imprimis, a cubbard xxvj^s viij^d, a long table with a frame & twoo firmes viij^s, a counter with twoo firmes & a frame, twoo chaires, sex quysshings, a buffett stoole, two seats and a little shelf viiij^s, in toto 2. 2. 8.
Item, seaven pece of pewther, eight candlesticks, fower sawcers, fower salts, a tunne, a chafyndish, a pynt pott and a chamber pott   1. 6. 2.
Item, two reckyn crooks, two potts, one potkylpe, a fyer showle, a paier of tongs, a choppyn knyf, a scommer, a flesh crooke, a latten laddle & a paier sheers   16. 0.
Item, happen garne xij^d, a long bowe with halfe a shafe of arrowes iij^s iiij^d, two percers, a brace, a brush, a kyrnestaf vj^d, three skeeles & dishes xij^d, a brasen Morter & pestle iij^s iij^d, in all   9. 2.

in the parlour

Item, a stand bedd with the fether bedd & furnyshment xlvj^s viij^d, two chists ij^s vj^d, a counter, a forme, a cradle, a bushell, sex bowles, a bradrith, a bordshelf, a tempts, trenshers with a speet ix^s, three potts, a cawtheron, twoo kettles, twoo pannes, a broyl yron xxxv^s, a pound of towe, a pound of lyne, a tubb, a cawell, a seth, a poke iij^s iiij^d   4.16. 6.
Item, 50 yards of harden & eight yeards of lynne xlij^s, seaven yards of huswyfe cloth & 38 yards of lynne l^s, xx^{tie} yards of harden xiij^s iiij^d, wudd vessell & pewther in the little buttery viij^s, in all   5.13. 4.

in the hy chamber

Item, a bedstead with furnyture & a shelf x^s, a syde sadle & a beef flick iij^s iiij^d   13. 4.

in the lowe parlour

Item, a bedstead with furnyture xiij^s iiij^d, a trunk & two chists
vij^s vj^d, his apparell xl^s, three paier of lynne sheets & 3 paier of
harden sheets xl^s, three towells, seaven napkynnes, a bordcloth &
fower pyllyvers xvj^s, in his purse in money xxx^s & a sword
iij^s iiij^d 7. 9. 2.

Item, in the kytchin divers little parcells of furnyture there
iij^s iiij^d, in bark howse in bark v^{li}, in all   5. 3. 4.

Item, more in bark howse, twoo dakers of leather & three clowt
hyds   12. 0. 0.

Item, two daker of dry leather xiij^{li}, tubbs & girthes v^{li}, twoo kyne
& a why vij^{li} x^s, two fillyes iiij^{li}, in beanes xx^s, bend leather, dry
pullen xx^d, the cropp of corn in the ground xiij^s iiij^d and fower
silver spoones xiij^s iiij^d, in all   36.17. 4.

debts owen to him

By one of Newcastle, Sotheron	7. 0. 0.
Cuthbert Hodshon of Darlington	2. 9. 0.
Cuthbert Cornfurth	1. 0. 0.
John Stephenson	16. 0.
William Dobson of Burrell	15. 0.
and in bark a quarter & fyve busshels	3. 9.

Summa total £89 7s 2d

debts which he did owe

To Marke Johnson his brother	12. 0. 0.
paid for his funerall expenses	2. 6. 8.

So remaynes de claro £75 0s 8d

[*Parchment, 1 m., indented. In hand similar to* 1, 2, 15, 22, 24 *will,* 30, 32, 41,
42 *and* 45 *wills.*]

17 Thomas Nawton of Darlington, 1607

xxvjth Martij, Anno Domini, 1607

A trewe inventorie of all such goodes, chattells and credittes
of Thomas Nawton, late of the parishe of Darlington,
deceased, which came to the handes of Thomas Hull, his administrator,
and praysed by Symon Gifford, gentleman, Richard Braddock,
Cuthbert Hodshon and Percyvell Trewhett, as foloweth:

Imprimis, a turne, a scammer and a dropping pann	4. 3.
Item, a paire of olde blankettes	9. 0.
Item, ij olde coverlettes and an olde blankett	8. 0.

Item, iij olde lynen sheetes & a coverlett and ij harden sheetes	1. 5. 0.
Item, lynn, harden yarne and woole	14. 1.
Item, a bolster, a codd, 4 olde quisshions and one kettlee	17. 5.
Item, ij stooles, a spence of wood, a cooling tubb, a tun and a bushell	10. 5.
Item, iij pack saddles	9. 0.
Item, 1 stand bedd, a long settlee, one littlee round table, 3 sithes &	
j paire of playing tables	1.14. 0.
Item, a dung hill	5. 0.
Item, his apparell	10. 0.
Item, iiij kyne and iiij calves with a horss and certen haie &	
harbage	11.13. 4.

Suma Bonorum £19 0s 6d besides a maire
which Robert Hodes wyfe tooke away and as yett deteyneth
from the said administrator

Debtes dewe to the said deceased and secoured by his said administrator as
foloweth:

Imprimis, of Michaell Jeffrason	8. 5. 4.
Item, of Peter Glover	1. 9. 0.
Item, of John Thompson of Elton	2.16. 8.
Item, of John Woode of Darlington	3.15. 0.

Summa £16 6s 0d
Some Totallis of goodes & debtes recovered £35 6s 6d

A note of such debtes as the said Thomas Nawton caused
to be sett downe at his deathe as dewe unto him which
as yet are not recovered nor comed to the
said administrators handes as foloweth:

Mr Brian Thaddie thelder	1.16. 0.
Lawrence Stell of Berwick super Twed	2. 8. 0.
John Turner of the same	8. 8.
Thomas Hernebie of Danbie	2.10. 0.
Richard Baystane and Edward Baystane of Shipdon nere Hallyfax	
and Elizabeth Roper for woole	14. 0. 0.
William Shutt of Askequith for a ferme	5. 0. 0.
And more of lent money to him	3. 0. 0.
Mr Marmaduke Wairick of Rippon of lent money 10s whereof he is	
to have back for shipp rent 4s	6. 0.
Richard Atkinson of Rippon of lent money	1. 0. 0.
Thomas hamerton of Hornecastell in Lincolnsher for a horss grass	
for ij yeares	1.10. 0.
Richard Mawer paid for him for a wayne 1s & for cariages of	
woole to Hallifax 3s	4. 0.
George Wells of lent money iiij^{li} and about xx^s more, v^{li} which 4^{li}	
he paid Arthur Happ...[illegible]...	

Allan Barker	2. 0. 0.
Thomas Robinson of Aclam for a sythe	3. 0.
John Spence of Darneton	1. 0. 0.
Thomas Bailes of Pearcebridge	1. 0. 0.
John Bailes of the same ·	1. 6. 0.
Roland Bell of the same	5. 0.
Sir Maior Vavicec Knight for a horss	4. 6. 8.
George Stead of Burley for a whye	1. 7. 0.
Rowland Sarre	16. 0.
Anthonne Glover	2. 8. 0.

[Parchment, 1 m., indented]

18   Gawen Ratcliffe of Darlington, 1608/9

[filed under 1608]

A true inventorie of all the
goodes and cattells, moveble and
unmoveble, which did appertaine unto
Gawin Ratcliffe of Darneton,
deceased, prysed by fower honest
men, Symon Giffard, Richard
Braddocke, Cuthbert Carr and
William Bell, 28º Februarij, 1608,

Inprimis, his purse and his apperrell	8. 0.
Item, an old trindle bedd with a torne coveringe & an old bolster	2. 0.
Item, an old table with stooles & an old chiste	2. 0.
Item, an ambre and dish binke	3. 0.
Item, an old pott, iij litle pannes, a fryan pann with some pewther	6. 0.
Item, wood vessell with shelves, crooks & other implements	2. 0.
Item, some coales with old stuffe in the chamber	5. 0.
Item, his stocke in new wood vessell at home, with some abroade	4. 0. 0.

Summa totalis £5 8s 0d

Debtes owinge unto the said Gawen Ratcliffe	
of Richard Robinson of Bonegate in Darneton	2. 0. 0.
of a man dwellinge near Railie	10. 0.
of a woman in Winston	1. 0.
of a woman in Chester, thre dozen of cuppes	9.

Summa debitorum £2 11s 9d

Summa totius Inventarii £7 19s 9d
Funerall charges 10s

[Paper, 1 f. In hand similar to 13, 14 will and 19.]

19 Robert Dent of Darlington, 1609

A true inventorie of all the goodes and
cattells of Robert Dent of Darneton, deceased,
prysed by fower honest men, Christofer Sayer,
Christofer Nicholson, John Scott and Thomas
Sober, the tuelfe day of June, 1609

Imprimis, his apperrell, purse, some books with two old swordes	3. 6. 8.
Item, a lease of one house in Darneton	3. 6. 8.
Item, a part of one lease with John Scott of two grasse closes	
taken of Bryan Thaddy, gentleman, with one horse gate in the parke	1.10. 0.
Item, one horse	1.13. 4.
Item, two kine and a stott	5. 0. 0.
Item, 2 beddes with furniture, 3 litle chistes & one table in the	
upper parlour	4. 0. 0.
Item, in the low parlour, one bedd with furniture, 2 chares, one	
table, a forme and a buffett stole, 2 quissions, an iron chimney, a	
pair of belowes with 2 chamber pottes	2. 0. 0.
Item, in the hall, 2 tables, one cupporde, one chist, 2 chares, 3 formes,	
one stole, olde quissions and a pair of playinge tables	1.15. 0.
Item, 20 peases of pewther, 4 candlesticks, 4 saltes, 4 pewther pottes	
with 2 pottingers	2. 0. 0.
Item, 3 morters, 2 lattin candlesticks, one chaffindyshe with a grate	5. 0.
Item, 3 speetes, 3 pair of tonges, pott kilps, 2 choppin knives with	
other implementes	10. 0.
Item, in the larder, 7 pottes, 4 pannes, one droppinge panne with a	
kaule, an old bedd, a fryan pann with other implementes	1.13. 4.
Item, in the buttrye, in wood vessell with other implementes	1. 0. 0.
Item, in the loft, 7 guest beddes with one chist, a truckle bedd	
with other implementes	6. 6. 8.
Item, in the kitchine, one ketle, one panne, a pair of rackes, massfatt	
with other inplementes	1. 0. 0.
Item, in the stable, one heck & one manger	2. 6.
Item, one litle shotte	5. 0.

Summa totalis Inventarii £35 14s 2d

Debtes which the said Robert Dent, deceased, aught

To Christofer Sayer	1. 5. 0.
To John Scott	1. 5. 0.
To Robert Warde	17. 6.
Funerall expences	1. 0. 0.

Summa Debitorum £4 7s 6d

[Parchment, 1m., indented. In hand similar to 13, 14 will, and 18]

20 John Marshall of Cockerton, 1609

In the name of God, Amen, the xxij^the^ day of Aprill, in the yeare of our Lord God, 1609, I, John marshell, of Cockerton in the parishe of Darlington, sicke in bodie neverthelesse of god & perfecte remembrance, praysed be God therfor, make this my testement & last will in maner & forme ffollowinge. First, I comende my soull into the hands of thallmightie God, in whose onlye marcies in the merits of Christe Jesu I do undoubtedlye beleve to be saved, & by no other means, & my bodye to be buryed within the church or churchyard of Darlington. Item, I give & bequeath to my brother, Frauncies Marshell, on ewe & on lame. Item, I give to my brother, Henry Marshell, on gimmer lame. Item, I give to my sister, Isable Marshell, on gimmer lame. Item, I give to my sister, Margreat Marshell, on gimmer lame. Item, I give to my sister, An Marshell, ten shillings in money. Item, I geve to my brother, Richard Marshell, 13s. 4d. in money. All the residewe of my goods & chattle, moveable & unmoveable, unbequeathe, my debts, legacies & funerall expences discharged, I give & bequeath to my wife, Katheron Marshell, & Dorytye marshell, my daughter, whom I make & ordeane wholl executors of this my last will & testament, conteyninge herin my last will, & I utterlye revoke all & every other former will, testement legacie, bequeath, executor or overseer by me in any wise befor this time maid, named, willed or bequeathed, & therefor I have caused theis premises to be written, befor theis witnesses, Christopher Staynsbey, William Marshell, Edward Marshell, Thomas Robinson & Thomas Mayson.

John marshell [mark]

[*Paper, 1 f. In hand similar to 5, 26, 37, 38 and 39 inventories, 40, 54 and 57.*]

A trew inventorye of all the goods and chattels, moviable and unmoviable, of the late, disceased, Jhon Marshell of Cockerton, priced the nynthe daye of May, 1609, by these foure honest men, viz., Christofer Staynesby, Thomas Simpson, Lawrence Elgye & Edward Marshell.

Imprimis, wynter corne and ware corne in the fields growinge	12. 0. 0.
Item, fyve styrkes and one calfe	5. 0. 0.
Item, in sheepe	5. 0. 0.
Item, one oxe and one horse	6. 0. 0.
Item, one mare	3. 0. 0.

Item, fyve kyne	11.10. 0.
Item, his purse and his apparell	2. 0. 0.
Item, in the hall and seller, all the householde stuffe	13. 6. 8.
Item, one swyne	8. 0.
Item, two saddles, one spade, and two sackes	8. 0.
Item, fyve hennes and one cocke	2. 6.

Suma totalis £58 15s 2d

Debts which the saide disceased Jhon Marshell did owe at the
tyme of his deathe

Imprimis, to Wylliam Marshell	3.13. 4.
Item, to Wylliam Marshell for wheate	9. 8.
Item, to George Stanyne	15. 0.
Item, to Thomas Bowbanke	2. 0. 0.
Item, to Roberte Leadam	12. 0.
Item, at Newcastell for thre stone of lynte	1. 0. 0.
Item, to Anthony Gilpin his father in lawe	2. 6. 8.
Item, to Cuthbert Cornforth for haver	10. 0.
Item, for funerall expences	16. 0.

Suma £12 2s 8d

[Parchment, 1 m., indented . In different hand to will.]

21 Richard Dack of Darlington, 1609

A true & perfect
inventory of suche debts
& creditts as wer owing
to Richard Dack at the tyme
of his death, 1609

Imprimis, George Lonsdale for cloth	11.
Item, Anthony Blenkinsopp for cloth	6. 2.
Item, Eliz. Clerkson for cloth	4. 8.
Item, Cuthbert Eastgate for cloth	2. 9.
Item, Abraham Taylor for cloth	5. 4.
Item, the said Abraham for cloth	2. 4.
Item, lentt to Cuthbert Harwod	2. 6.
Item, Margery Bell for cloth	4. 8.
Item, Margaret Allanson for cloth	3. 3.
Item, Widow Allanson	8.
Item, Robert Brass wif	4
Item, Wyllyam Garnett wife	9.
Item, Eden Walker for clothe	6.
Item, Raphe Robson	3.
Item, Robert Emerson, senior, for cloth	2. 8.

Item, Robert Tompson	1. 0.
Item, Thomas Tyndall for cloth	2. 0.
Item, lentt to Reynold Morton wif	2. 0.
Item, James Shaw for clothe	1.10.
Item, Bartholomew Kipling for cloth	3. 8.
Item, Anthony Pearson	3. 4.
Item, George Allanson & his wif	1. 7.11.
Item, Anne Huganson	1. 4.
Item, Launcelot Longstaffe for cloth	1. 4.
Item, Thomas Baxter for cloth	8. 8.
Item, William Mitchell wife	8.
Item, John Naitbye	1.10. 0.
Item, Margaret Langstaffe	17. 5.
Item, William Bigland wif	6. 0.
Item, Richard Bell wif for cloth	1.10.
Item, Mrs Thursby for cloth	1.10.
Item, Edward Dixon wif	5.
Item, Janet Laydman for cloth	9.
Item, Thomas Sanderson	8. 8.
Item, Henry Lonsdale for cloth	10.
Item, Cuthbert Lonsdale for cloth	8.
Item, Thomas Tompson for cloth	2. 0.
Item, George Arthur for cloth	2. 0.
Item, Laurence Rayn wife	1. 3.
Item, Anne Jackson for cloth	2. 0.
Item, William Herrison for cloth	2. 2.
Item, great Anne Cotes for cloth	1. 0.
Item, Anne Horne for cloth	2. 4.
Item, Thomas Herrison for cloth	10. 0.
Item, Thomas Johnson	10.
Item, William Dodsworth	2. 0.
Item, the wife of the said William	4. 3.
Item, Thomas Allanson for cloth	5. 0.
Item, Francis Atkinson & his wife	4. 0.
Item, Henry Tompson for cloth	1. 1.
Ambrose Vyntt for clothe	9. 0.
Item, Richard Preston for cloth	8.
Item, Widow Hunter for cloth	2. 1.
Item, Dorithy Gillott	1. 6.
Item, William Paycok	3. 6.
Item, his wif	1. 9.
Item, Gyles Fothergill wif	2. 9.
John Buxter & his wif	19. 0.
Item, Reynold Brecking wif	4.
Item, Mrs Allan for ...[*illegible*]... cloth	4. 8.
Item, Jane Tompson for cloth	4. 2.
Item, Dorithy Hildreth	5.

Item, Raphe Crawforth for cloth	10.
Item, Henry Mason for cloth	3. 5.
And more to his wif for cloth	10.
Item, William Davison	1.14. 6.
Item, Anne Tompson	2. 8.
Item, Umphrid Robinson for cloth	6. 0.
Cuthbert Greene wif for cloth	1. 2
Item, Cuthbert Stobbes	2.13. 4.
Item, William Smyth	17. 6.
Item, Francis Topias wif for cloth	2. 1.
Richard Cowherd alias Norman for cloth	1. 8.
Item, Dame Carnibye	5. 4.
Item, Thomas Todd	3. 0.
Item, Henry Gybson	12. 4.
Item, Widow Dixon	4. 0.
Item, Alexander Crawforth	3. 6. 8.
Item, Robert Colson	3. 6. 8.
Item, John Hackforth and his sonne	1. 5. 4.
Item, George Goundry for cloth	4. 6.
Item, John Nicholson for cloth	7. 0.
Item, Widow Graynger	1. 6.
John Shawe for cloth	1. 5.
Item, Mrs Eden for cloth	8.
Item, Widow Thorpe made	4.
George Cotsworth	8. 0.
Item, Thomas Claton	1. 1. 0.
Item, Christopher Natby for rentt	16. 0.

Summa £28.19. 7d.

[Parchment, 2 mm., glued, indented .]

22 Thomas Catherick of Darlington, 1609

In dei nomine, Amen, I, Thomas Catherick, of Darlington in the county of Durham, tanner, sick in bodie but sound in mynd and of good & perfect remembrance, do make this my last will & testament in manner & forme folowing. First, I bequyth my soule into the handes of Almightie God, my Maker and Redeemer, and my bodie to be buried within the parish church yeard of Darlington aforesaid, and of my temporall goodes, I thus dispose. First, I gyve & bequyth unto Elizabeth, nowe my wyf, my black cowe. Item, I gyve & bequyth unto Isabell, my dowghter, my branded cowe. Item, I gyve & bequyth to John Catherick, my son, my bay meare. Item, I gyve & bequyth unto my said doughter, Isabell, my cubbord in my hall howse. Item, all the rest of my howshold stuff, I will & bequyth unto

my said wyf, Elizabeth, and Isabell, my doughter, to be equallie
devyded betwixt them, saving that I gyve & bequyth unto the said
Elizabeth, my wyf, out of the said howshold stuff one feather bedd &
a call...[*abbreviation?*].., which standes in Agnes Nicholson's howse,
& also that I gyve of the said howshold stuff unto Isabell, my
doughter, one fether bedd. Item, I gyve & bequyth unto Thomas
Catherick, son to my said son John, an angell of gold for a
remembrance. Item, I gyve & bequyth unto the children of my
brother & sister, to ich of them, xij^d. Item, I gyve unto every child of
my said wyfe, xij^d a pece. Item, the rest of all my goodes
unbequested, the moyitie thereof I gyve & bequith unto Elizabeth,
my said wyf, & thother moytie unto the said John and Isabell, my
children. And I will they shall gyve unto Thomas Coolson, my
servant, ij^s vj^d, and unto Joan, my son's wyf, to buy her lyne with, x^s.
Item, whereas I have hertofore covenanted the purchase of the nowe
dwelling howses wherein I am, and am to pay xjli xs, being the
moytie of the spurchace of the said howse, & my said son, John,
thother, I will & bequyth that the some of xj^{li} x^s, parcell of my said
goodes, shalbe paid unto the said John Catherick for the performance
of the payment and that, in consideracion thereof, he, my said son,
John, shall fynd upon his proper costes & chardges, one competent
howse for the said Elizabeth, my wyf, to dwell in & inhabit, during
her lyf naturall, and one other howse for the said Isabell, my
doughter, so long as she shall kepe her self unmaryed, & no longer,
and I do ordeyne & make executors of this my will, John Catherick,
my son aforesaid, & Isabell, my doughter, and I do make supervisors
of this, my said will, my brother, Lawrence Catherick, & John
Fawcett and I do gyve either of them for their paynes, one bushell of
wheat. Item, I do gyve unto Robert Ward v^s. And unto Agnes
Nicholdson, my sister-in-lawe, j bushell wheat. Dated this 25 day of
October, 1608.

Debtes which I owe

to Agnes Nicholdson	1. 0. 0.
to John Catherick	5. 3. 4.
to Lawrence Cathrick [*crossed out*]	1. 5.10.
to John Fawcett [*crossed out*]	

Debtes owed me

John Wetherelt of Eavenwudd	7. 0.

Wytnesses: Lawrence Catryck, John Fawcet [*mark*], George Marshall,
Robert Warde

[*Paper, 1 f.*]

The inventory of all the goodes and
chattells, moveable and unmoveable, quick and
dead, of Thomas Catherick, lait of Darlington,
tanner, deceased, praised by Lawrence Catherick,
John Fawcett, Lawrence Stainsbie and John
Herreson, the xjth day of Aprill, Anno Domini, 1609

Inprimis, in the hawle howse, a cubbord	1. 0. 0.
Item, a cawle and an old ambry	10. 0.
Item, ij tables, 2 firmes, a chaier and stooles	4. 0.
Item, x brasse pottes	2. 0. 0.
Item, 5 kettles, 6 panns, a frying panne, a speet & rackes	1.10. 0.
Item, 8 candlestickes of brasse, 26 pece of pewther, 14 sawcers,	
3 saltes and a pewther tunne	1.13. 4.
Item, a shelf, 2 skeeles, a kytt, 3 quysshinges, a morter of stone	2. 0.
Item, 2 paier of tonges and a reckyncrooke, with painted cloothes	2. 8.
Item, an ax and twoo spaides	1. 0.

in the parlour

Item, his apparell	1. 0. 0.
Item, in his purse	2. 0. 0.
Item, 2 bedsteades, a feather bedd, 6 coveringes, 3 happens and	
5 coddes	1.10. 0.
Item, 3 chistes, 2 standes, a firme, 2 paier of lynen sheetes, 2 paier of	
samaron sheetes, 7 harden sheetes, 3 beddcloothes, 5 codwars and 6	
towelles	2.13. 4.
Item, 9 milk bowles, 3 shelves & other trifles	3. 4.
Item, a cubbord in Marget Nicholdson howse	6. 8.
	7. 13. 4.

in tanne howse

Item, vj daycars of untanned hydes and 4^r odd ones	37. 0. 0.
Item, unburyed corne in the laith	2. 0. 0.
Item, his cropp of sowen corne upon the ground	6.13. 4.
Item, 2 kyne & a meare	8. 0. 0.
Item, 2 saddles	5. 0.
	53.18. 3

Debtes owen to him

Lawrence Catherick	10. 6.
John Catherick	5. 5. 0.
Henry Elstobb & Christopher Robinson	7. 3. 4.
Thomas Stephenson	3. 8. 0.
Thomas Davyson	10. 0.
John Wetherelt of Evenwudd	7. 0.
	17. 3.10

Summa totallis £95 18s 6d

Owen by him to

To John Catherick   5. 3. 4.

[Parchment, 1 m., indented. Will and inventory in hand similar to 1, 2, 15, 16, 24 will, 30, 32, 41, 42 and 45.]

23   Anthony Claxton of Darlington, 1609

A true inventorie of all and singular the goodes and chattelles, mo=
veable and unmoveable, of Anthonie Claxton of Darlington
in the countie of Durham, lait deceassed intestate, praised
the xvth daie of Julie, 1609, in the vijth yeare of the reigne
of our most gracious soveraigne, Lord James, by the grace
of God, King of England, France and Ireland, defender
of the faith, etc., and of Scotland, the xliijth, by John
Gill, Edward Atkinson, John Harrison and Lawrence
Dobson, as followeth

First, his apparrell	10. 0.
Item, a cupborde and eleven peece of pewter, seaven litle sawcers and one pottinger, iiij^{or} saltes and two candlestickes of pewter	1.13. 4.
Item, a brasse pott and two pannes	5. 0.
Item, a chair, with two tables and two frames belonging them, and two formes with two stooles and three quishinges	11. 0.
Item, a reckingcroke, a speet, a broyle iron and a paire of tonges	2. 6.
Item, a mattrisse, two happines and a coverlet	10. 0.
Item, a paire of harden sheetes, a paire of lynnen, two coddes and two pillowbers	13. 4.
Item, vj bowlles, a chaire, a stand, a little barrell and two old skeeles	2. 6.
Item, one trundle bedd	3. 4.
Item, xx^{tie} cutts of yarne and an old table cloath with an old chist	2. 6.
Item, iiij^{or} sawes, two iron squares, with other his working tooles	10. 0.
Item, one maire, sacke, sadle and furniture	3. 0. 0.
Item, two kine and two whyes	6.13. 4.

Some £14 15s 10d

Debtes owing to the deceassed as followeth

Edward Elgee   3. 0. 0.

Somma totalis 17.16.10.

Debtes owing by the deceassed as followeth

First to Adam Harrison	4. 0. 0.
Item, to Henrie Oswald for a parcell of his rent	1. 7. 4.
Item, to John Clarke	7. 4.
Item, to William Townend	5. 0.
Item, to Lawerence Catherick	4. 0.
Item, to Grace Placket	6. 0.
Item, to Jennet Placket	2. 0.
Item, for the landlordes rent	4. 0.
Item, to John Atkinson	12. 0.
Item, to Anthony Stainsbie	2. 6.
Item, to Christofer Sayde	3. 0.
Item, to Agnes Claxton childe	2. 0. 0.

Summa debitorum £9 13s 2d

Summa de Claro debitis deductis £8 3s 8d

Desperate debt

Item, Robart Hoode	3. 0. 0.

[*Parchment, 1 m., indented. Inventory in hand similar to 6, 10, 11, 12, 14 inventory, 27 will, 28, 35, 36 will, 43, 44, 46, 48 will , 49, 50, 51 and 56.*]

24 Isabell Catherick of Darlington, 1610

Memorandum that Isabell Cathrike, of Darlington, being sicke in bodie, yet in good and perfect memorie, did ordaine hir last will and testament, in manner and forme following. First, she did give hir soule to Almightie God and hir bodie to be buried in the churchyard at Darlington. Item, she willed that Jenett Russell and Allison Hodgson, who weare then present with hir, should deliver the keyes, which she before had delivered them, to John Cathrike, hir brother, and willed them, if she did not speake with him hir selfe, they should tell him that he should find that which she had, either in money or moneyworth. And, moreover, she said that, if it should please God to lend hir liffe till she spake with hir brother, that then the said Jenett Russell and Allison Hodgson should not in any case make it knowne.

Witnesses hearof Jennett Russells Allison Hodgson

[*Paper, 1 f. In hand similar to 1, 2, 15, 16, 22, 30, 32, 41, 42 and 45 wills.*]

The true inventorie of Isabell
Cattrickes of Darlington, deceased,
prassed the eight daie of Aprill, Anno Domini, 1610,
by these men whose names are under
writen, John Fawcett, Laurance Catericke,
Laurance Stainsbie and John Harrison

Imprimis, tow kie	5. 0. 0.
Item, one cubbert, a cauell with a bord and a little forme	
& tow stoles	1. 6. 8.
Item, fowerteen dublers, 4 sawcers, 3 saltes, 4 candlestickes, a puther	
pott and a little porraige dish	1. 0. 0.
Item, six brasse potts, 3 kettles, a fish skamer, 2 pans and a plate pan	1. 6. 8.
Item, tow skelles, 7 bolies, a pudding pie pott, 3 trenchers and a scuttle	3. 0.
Item, one chare and a stand	1. 4.
Item, one paire of rackes, a paire of tonges and a reckon crooke	
with a paire of pott kilps	2. 4.
Item, one skell with halfe a stone of butter	2. 3.
Item, one bedsteed, a fether bed, 4 cods, 3 coverlitts, 2 happins	
and a old blanckett	1. 0. 0.
Item, sevenscore & ten cuttes of lin yarne and five score of harden	
yarne	16. 0.
Item, three bushells of wheet	13. 4.
Item, all hir apperrell, linen and wollen which she used to weare	1.10. 0.
Item, one paire of sameron sheets & 2 paire of harden sheetes, 3	
coodwaires & 3 towelles	16. 0.
Item, tow chists & a coffer, a firme, a teamce and 3 little bordes	4. 0.
Item, thirtie five yeardes of unblecht harden	15. 0.
Item, seven and twentie yeardes of unblecht lin	1. 1. 0.
Item, thirtie five yeardes of blecht harden	1. 0. 0.
Item, threescore & ten yeardes of round blecht lin	3. 6. 8.
Item, eight yeardes of wollen cloth and a yeard and a halfe of quell	10. 6.
Item, money in hir purse	2.10. 0.
Item, fower hennes	2. 0.

The whole some comes to £23 6s 8d

Debtes owing unto the said Isabell
Cattricke, deceased

Imprimis Christopher Robinson of Darlington, cordiner	13. 4.
Item, Thomas Hewgh, of the said towne, wright	2. 0.
Item, Cuthbert Hall de eadem	10.
Item, John Trotter of Northallerton	3. 0.

The some is 19s 2d

Debtes which the said
Isabell Cattricke deceased
owith

Imprimis, to John Cattricke for tow kie wintringe	1. 8. 0.
Item, to Elizabeth Browne	7. 0.

The some is 35s

John Fawcet [*mark*]
Lawrence Cateryck
John Harryson
Lawerence Stayesbye [*mark*]

[*Paper, 1 f. In different hand to will.*]

25   William Dockera of Blackwell, 1610

23 Aprilis 1610

Legasses geven by William Dockera unto his children

The youge gray meare to be kept whell Martinmas and then sold, and iij^{li} to be geven to my iij yongest children, and the rest I give to my eldest sonne. I give to my daughter, Anerill, a read why calf, about a yeare olde. I give to my sonne, John, a yonge black calfe, to be brong up a bout house whel saint tillinmas, com a twelmunth. I give to my daughter, Margere, a cubbert, a brace pot and a great chiste and a silke hat. I give to my two yonge daughters and my wiffe daughter, to everrie one of them, a gimer hogge. I give to my sonne, Robert, my daughter, Margere and Brigat and Anerill, and John, to everrie one of them, a ewe and a lame, and all the rest of my goods to be equally devided amongst all my children. Witnesses hereof, Thomas Bowbank & Stephen Ward.

[*Paper, 1 f.*]

a trewe inventore of William Dockera goods praised the [torn] day of
May, 1610

A horse and twoe meares, praiste to, with the furneture,	8. 0. 0.
Two kine and a calfe, praiste to	5. 0. 0.
and a why stirk, praiste to	16. 0.
Five hogges, praiste to	1. 5. 0.
A one wether, praiste to	6. 0.
Five ewes and lames, praiste to	1.10. 0.
One rome of hay and one pike of blonglemear, praiste to	3. 0. 0.
One swine, praiste to	10. 0.

One goosse and eleven gosslinges, praiste to	5. 0.
One coke and fower henes ...[*illegible*]...	vij grots
Gesstes and bordes, praist to	10. 0.
Hard corne growing upon the earth, praist to	12. 0.
Ware corne growinge upon the earth, praiste to	9. 0.
Donnge praist to	1. 4.
One stoddie, ij hamers, iiij paire of tonges, iiij naile toulles	1. 6. 8.
Thre brace pots and a frinn pane, praiste to	14. 0.
Twoe ketels and fower panes, praiste to	10. 0.
Thre kandell stickes, ij salts with other puder vessell	10. 0.
One cubert and a calle, praist to	12. 0.
iiij standes, ij skeles and a kimlinge	3. 8.
Thre tubes with other wood vessell, praiste to	6. 0.
One kirne with a kirnstaf	1. 0.
One whele with a whelestole	1. 0.
One table, ij formes, ij stoules	1. 4.
Thre linin shetes, ij harden shetes and a towel	11. 0.
Five pounde of hekelte line	5. 0.
Thre hapins, one blanked, ij kodes, ij quisons	10. 0.
Seven sekes and one poke	6. 0.
Thre haire ropes, praiste to	1. 0.
Linin yarne, praist to	2. 6.
His aparell, praiste to	7. 0.
One reken croke, a paire of tonges and a spete, ij pair of pot kilpes	2. 6.

£29. 2. 4d.

depts owinge

Imprimis, Christofer Wethrelt	4. 0.
George [*torn*]yler	1. 0.
Edward Harison	3.
Robert Harrison	4.
Ringin [*torn*]awbreth	1. 6.

7s. 1d.

Summa bonorum et debitorum 29 9s 5d.

depts that I owe

Imprimis, to Rowlan Browne	6.10.
To Kathren Kaperwhit	5. 0.
To Cuthbert Cornforth	5. 0.
To Steven Ward	5. 7.
For rent	10. 0.
To Easebell Wrene	6.

32s 11d.

remanet £27 16s 6d.

[*Paper, 1 f. Will and inventory in hand similar to 53.*]

26 Christopher Fawell of Cockerton, 1610

In the name of God, Amen, the xxiijth day of February, in the yeare of
Lord God,1609 [1610], I, Christopher Fawell, of Cockerton in the
parrishe of Darlington, husbandman, sicke in my bodye, neverthelesse of wholl mynd & in good & perfite remembrance, praysed be
God therfor, I make & ordeyne this my last will & testement, in
manner & forme followinge. First, I comende my soule unto the
Allmightye God, Maker & Redemer, by whose marcies, in the
merittes of Jesu Christe, I doe undoubtedlye belive to be saved & by
none other meanes, & my bodye to be buried within the church or
churche yard of Darlington. Item, I will & charge my executores to
pay all my debts to these, whose names hereafter followeth, viz.,
first, to John Busbey, iij^l v^s. Item, to Richard Busbey, xxij^s. Item, to
Richard Pattinson, iij^s. Item, Rapht Smurfite, xiij^s. Item, to my mother,
Jene Surties, for rent, xiij^s iiij^d. Item, I give & bequeth to my son,
Robert Fawell, by legacie twentye marke of lawfull Englishe money,
to be payd to him when he cometh to the full age of xxj yeares, if he
be then liveinge, & if he be not then liveinge, my will is, the sayd
some of xx^{ti} marke shall then remayne to my executoures, Item, all
the residewe of my goodes & chattles, moveable & unmoveable, my
debtes, legacies & funerall expence discharged, I give & bequethe to
my wife, Margreat Fawell, & to my daughter, Isable Fawell, whom I
make joyntley executoures of this my last will & testement, in maner
& forme aforsayd, & therfor I have caused theis premises to be
writen, befor theis witnesses, Thomas Hodgshon, Laurance Elgie,
Edward Marshell, Thomas Robinson & Thomas Mason, Christofer
Fawell [*mark*].

[*Paper, 1 f.*]

A trew inventory of all the goodes
& chattles of Christopher Fawell, lait
of Cockerton, deceased, praysed by theis
men, Thomas Richardson, Laurance
Elgie, Edward Marshell, Thomas
Robinson & Thomas Hodgshon, the eight
day of March, 1609

Inprimis, his aparrell, his purse & fornitor	1.10. 0.
Item, on cobbord	2. 0. 0.
Item, ix peece of pewther, v sawsers, five candlestickes, on tyn pot	
& on salt	18. 0.

Item, on kettle, v panes	1. 4. 0.
Item, on brasse pote	2. 0.
Item, on friing pane, on raken crocke & on pare of tonges	2. 4.
Item, iiij earthen potes	1. 0.
Item, ij° cheese fates, ij° sinckers, on dosen of trenchers	1. 0.
Item, ij° kayser & ij° shelves	1. 0.
Item, ij° hinge lockes	8.
Item, on forme, on stoll, iiij quishens	2. 8.
Item, ij° pick staffes	1. 0.
Item, iiij spades	1. 4.
Item, on ax, on eache, on hack	2. 0.
Item, on hay crock, an hand sawe, on hammer with other od implementes	1. 0.
Item, ij° sith & on racke	1. 4.

Items in the chamber

Item, on bed stead fornished	2. 0. 0.
Item, ij° coverledes, on blanckete, on happen, iij codes	1. 6. 8.
Item, iij chestes, on coffer	5. 0.
Item, iij bridles	1. 0.
Item, on spininge whell, ij° par of cardes	1. 0.

Items in the milke house

Item, ij° lyne whelles	3. 0.
Item, 12 bowles	4. 0.
Item, on kirne, on kirne staffe	2. 0.
Item, iiij sith snedes, on flayll	6.
Item, on stand	1. 0.
Item, iij skelles	1. 6.
Item, iij sadles, sackes & girthes	8. 0.
Item, iiij pare of lynen sheetes	1.12. 0.
Item, vj lynen pyllyners	8. 0.
Item, on parr of harden sheetes	5. 0.
Item, xiij yardes of lynen cloth	13. 0.
Item, lynen yarne	8. 0.
Item, harden yarne	5. 0.
Item, ij° table clothes, ij° brushes	3. 4.
Item, ij° kyne & iij whyes	11. 0. 0.
Item, iij mears & on stage	10. 6. 8.
Item, hay in the field	1. 0. 0.
Item, iij old shep & on lambe	1. 0. 0.

Sume £38 5s.

debtes owinge by the testator

Fyrst to John Busbye	3. 5. 0.
Item, to Rychard Busby	1. 2. 0.

Item, to Rychard Patteson	3. 0.
Item, to Ralfe Smurfyte	14. 0.
Item, to Jane Surtyes, his mother	13. 4.
Item, the funerall expensis	13. 4.
Item, the mortuary	6. 8.

Some £6 17s 4d

Summa declaro £31 7s 8d

[*Paper, 2 ff., sewn. Will and inventory in similar hand to 5, 20 will, 27, 37, 38 and 39 inventories, 40, 54 and 57.*]

27 Ralph Wrenn of Blackwell, 1610

In the name of God, Amen, the xxiij^th daie of Maie, 1610, I, Ralfe Wren, of Blackwell in the countie of Durham, yeoman, sicke in bodie, but in good and perfect remembrance I give god most hartie thanckes, do make this my last will and testament, in maner and forme following. First, and principallie, I bequeath my soull into the handes of Almighty God, my Creator and Redemer, by and throughe whome I faithfully beleve to be saved, and my body to be buryed in the parish church yard of Darlington, in such place there as to my wife in her discrecion, shalbe thought most convenient. Also, I give to the poore people of Blackwell, ij^s, to be distributed at my said wife, her discrecion. Item, I give to my brother, Rowland Wren, his sonne, lyonell Wren my Godsonn, five shillinges. Item, I give to Richard Pickering, the parish clark of Darlington, xijd. The rest of all my goodes and chattelles, moveable and unmoveable whatsoever, my debtes and funerall expences paid and deducted, I frely give and bequeath to Rosamond Wren, my loving wiff, who best deserveth the same, whome I make my sole and whole executrix of this my said last will and testament, humbly praying and entreating my good freind, Richard Wheatley, to be assisting her in her right and not to suffer her to be wronged, either by myne owne freindes or anie other. In witnes hereof, I, the said Ralf Wren, have hereunto set my hand, the daie and yeare abovesaid.

Ralf Wren [*mark*]

witnesses hereof Rychard Wheattlay Christofer Wetherelt [*mark*] Richard Pickeringe

[*Paper, 1 f. Will in hand similar to 6, 10, 11, 12, 14 inventory, 23, 28, 35, 36 will, 43, 44, 46, 48 will, 49, 50, 51 and 56.*]

The inventory of the goods
and chattell of Rayphe Wrennes, lait of Blackwell
within the parish of Darlington, deceased, praised
by fower honest men, vidt, Richard Wheatley, Johnn
Chamber, Christofer Wetherellt and John Martinfield,
the xv° of June, Anno Domini, 1610, as followeth

Item, towe covbords & a amrye	3. 0. 0.
Item, xxvj pese of puwder	1. 0. 0.
Item, iij candellstyckes	1. 0.
Item, v salltes	1. 3.
Item, ij pouder coupes, for to drynck in	1. 0.
Item, one slomber	3.
Item, one bronzene kaddrene	16. 0.
Item, one brese pott	4. 0.
Item, one pann & ij lyttell ons	2. 0.
Item, iij spetts & a payer of cobe irones	4. 0.
Item, on rackencrook, on payer of tonges & browl irons	2. 0.
Item, skells	1. 0.
Item, on maske fatt, on gyll fatt, on cowllyer	6. 0.
Item, one barell, on stand and a kyrne	3. 0.
Item, one grene stone pott	2.
Item, one taybell & towe ffourmes	5. 0.
Item, on cowntter	4. 0.
Item, towe chayers	1. 0.
Item, on chest & on coffer	2. 6.
Item, hyse aparerell	1.10. 0.
Item, on payer of lene shettes	6. 0.
Item, iij payer harden shettes	10. 0.
Item, ij codwoorars, iij towelles, xiij nattkens	6. 8.
Item, vj queshens	2. 0.
Item, vj happens, one cowerled and the beddsted	1.10. 0.
Item, on sowe & v shottes	1. 3. 0.
Item, viij hens, v duckes, one dracke	7. 0.
Item, ij dowsen leathers	6.
Item, xx boushell of hydg maryll	4. 0. 0.

£16 8s 4d

Debtes which the deceased did owe

to Rychard Wheattley	5. 0. 0.
to lorancer Cattryck	1.12. 0.
to Thomas wren	12. 0.

£7 4s 0d

Debtes owen to the deceased

Item, Mr Robert Garnatt	2. 8. 0.
Mychell Garnatt	4. 4.
John Arkes	2. 0.
Symon Roberson	2. 8.
Christopher Pyborn	4. 0.
John Langstaf	9. 0.

Some £3 9s 4d

Rescat de claro
debitis deductis £12 14s 0d

[*Paper, 1 f. In hand similar to 5, 20 will, 26, 37, 38 and 39 inventories, 40, 54 and 57.*]

28 Anthony Dennis of Darlington, 1611

The inventorie of all and ...[*faded*]...
moveable and unmoveable, ...[*faded*]...
in the countie of Durham, ...[*faded*]...
daie of August, 1610, by Peter Glover, John ...[*faded*]... John
Oswold and Richard Morley as followeth

The waires in the shopp

First, tenn yardes of ginger coloured fustaine and ten yardes of haire coloured fustaine	2. 6. 8.
Item, two peces of white fustaine of 20 yardes	2.10. 0.
Item, one peece of white fustaine of 12 yardes	1. 6. 0.
Item, another peece of fustaine of 10 yardes	1. 3. 4.
Item, another peece of white fustaine of 12 yardes	1. 0. 0.
Item, 2 remnantes of white fustaine, thone 2 yardes, thother two yardes and a halfe	5. 6.
Item, 10 yardes more of sage coloured fustaine	1. 0. 0.
Item, another of the same of tenn yardes	16. 8.
Item, a remnant of ginger coloured fustaine of sixe yardes and another of white of 5 yardes	1. 2. 0.
Item, a remnant of xj yardes sadd hayre coloured	18. 0.
Item, 10 yardes of primerose coloured fustaine	18. 0.
Item, another remnant of iiij^{er} yardes	6. 0.
Item, 2 remnantes contayinge 10 yardes	15. 0.
Item, 10 yardes of coloured fustaine	13. 4.
Item, 8 yardes of stript fustaine	15. 0.
Item, more in two severall peeces	1. 0. 0.
Item, 7 yardes of coloured fustaine	9. 0.
Item, 9 yardes of mouse coloured fustaine	17. 0.

Item, 11 yardes of white holme fustaine	16. 0.
Item, 8 yardes of deare coloured fustaine	13. 4.
Item, 5 yardes of ginger coloured fustaine	6. 0.
Item, severall remnantes contayning 7 yardes	7. 0.
Item, 10 yardes of blacke fustaine	1. 7. 6.
Item, 2 hole peeces of fustaine, thone holmes, thother jeanes	1. 6. 0.
Item, a whole peece of holmes of 14^{en} yardes	1. 0. 0.
Item, another contayninge the like measure	18. 8.
Item, a whole peece of course millaine sage colour	1.10. 0.
Item, 2 whole peeces of course millaine	3. 0. 0.
Item, another peece contayning xv^{ene} yeardes	1.10. 0.
Item, iiij^{er} whole peeces	6. 0. 0.
Item, another whole peece of fustaine	1. 5. 0.
Item, 7 whole peeces of seckine	1. 8. 0.
Item, 14 yardes of rawed seckine	8. 0.
Item, 14 yardes of yallow seckine	15. 6.
Item, 2 other remnantes contayning 12 yardes	7. 0.
Item, 9 yardes of tuft canvisse & 7 yardes of stript seckine	5.10.
Item, a french bodie and a dozen of longraces	1.10.
Item, 2 peeces of buccram contayning 22 yardes	15. 0.
Item, 2 dozen of litle bookes for children	6. 0.
Item, 9 dozen of trenshers & 4 rowlles of whalebone	6. 3.
Item, 2 dozen of girdles and a dozen of brushes	10. 0.
Item, 4 dozen of bowstrings & 4er bridleraines for women	8. 8.
Item, 12 dozens of blacke buttons and three purses	7. 0.
Item, 3 ...[torn]... combes and a dozen little seinge glasses	1. 8.
Item, 2 ...[torn]... knottes of pack threed	1. 5.
Item, 2 ...[torn]... of blacke ...[torn]... grograin & a peece of dans ...[torn]... with 13 yardes of stuff called Phillip and ...[torn]... and 7 yardes of fryons rashe	7.17. 0.
Item, v ...[torn]... of bullaines rash & 10 yardes of threed grograin	...[faded]...
Item, 18 ...[torn]... of Spanish sciac & 12 yardes of bullaine Rash	...[faded]...
Item, 3 ...[torn]... vallens & ...[torn]... of blacke silk rash	4.10. 0.
Item, 11 yards ...[torn]... blacke ...[torn]... stuffe & 9 yardes of ...[torn]... stuffe with 9 yardes of purple buffaine	2.13. 0.
Item, 10 yardes of brackotilloe and 8 yardes of maiden haire coloured searge with 16 yardes of grene searge	3. 7. 0.
Item, 8 yardes of blacke searge 6 yardes of grene wadnell	15. 8.
Item, 12 yardes of double buffine & 8 yardes of stript buffaine	1.10. 0.
Item, 23 yardes of stript say and 18 yardes of single stript say and 20 yardes of stript buffine	4. 9. 8.
Item, 10 yardes of orenge coloured buffine	8. 4.
Item, 4 yardes of moccadoe and 15 yardes of perpetuan in 2 peeces	2.10. 0.
Item, 11 yardes of phillisselloes & 10 yardes of perpetuan	3. 0. 0.

Item, 9 yardes of coloured sparke of velvet	1. 7. 0.
Item, another of 10 yardes and another of 7 yardes	2.11. 0.
Item, 7 yardes of bustaine and 10 yardes of browne canvisse	1. 4. 0.
Item, 6 yardes of cushing canvis & 8 yardes of browne	5. 4.
Item, 5 yardes of browne canvisse & 3 coloured skines	13. 3.
Item, 29 yardes of white cotton in 2 peeces	17. 0.
Item, 2 yardes of blacke freze & 12 yardes of blacke cotton	6. 8.
Item, 12^{li} of fringe, 10 yardes of boutcloath & 18 dozen of poyntes, sixe dozen of round poyntes and 7^{li} of crooles	3.17. 8.
Item, 9 paire of gloves & 46 dozen of threed poyntes	12. 3.
Item, 5 dozen of lether poyntes and j^{li} and 3 quarterns and a halffe of threed with 23 groze of buttons	2. 1.10.
Item, 28 groze more of buttons	5.17. 0.
Item, 9 groze more, with 14 groze of hayre buttons	2. 7. 4.
Item, 6 groze of threed buttons, with 2 reeme of paper	11. 0.
Item, 2 dozen and a half of cards, with pynnes	6. 6.
Item, 10 remnantes of stuffes, with some other peeces	1. 3. 4.
Item, 3^{li} and a quarterne of black silke lace	4.16. 0.
Item, in ashe coloured silke lace, with 2^{li} & 2 ounce of black silke lace	4.15. 4.
Item, more a pound lack 2 ounce and 9 dozen of small lace	2.13. 4.
Item, in stript ribbine and velvet lace	2.10. 8.
Item, in tuft silke lace and bobbinge lace	1. 5. 0.
Item, 3^{li} and two ounces of coloured silk	5. 0. 0.
Item, 2^{li} and a quarterne of blacke silk and 15 ounces of Spanish silke & 11 paire of silke garters	5. 6. 6.
Item, in statine lace and 2 paire of knit stockines	2. 4. 0.
Item, in ribbine of mixt coloures and blacke pirled ribbyne and pirled velvett lace	1.16. 8.
Item, 9 long buttons of silke & 2 dozen & a half of short buttons, with silk lace of mixt coloures	2.14. 6.
Item, 2 purses and buttons for clokes	2. 6.
Item, 4 girdles and a paire of garters	15. 0.
Item, black and white threed & j^{li} of coloured threed and 2 night cappes	5. 4.
Item, in inkle 2 peeces of statine lace, white Skene threed and silke and gold lace	9. 0.
Item, in small laces & 2 dozen of black silk ribbine	1. 0. 4.
Item, in small ribbine and 9 yardes a quarter and a halfe of taftay & a gentlewomans fanne	5. 4. 8.
Item, a yeard and a half of velvett	1. 6. 8.
Item, a yarde and a halfe of tuft taftay	12. 0.
Item, a remnant of tuft stuffe	2. 6.
Item, in copweb lawne & 18 yardes of white tiffany	1. 1. 0.
Item, 8 yardes more of copweb lawne & 2 dozen and a halfe of pepper & 7^{li} of powder blewe	3.10. 0.
Item, j^{li} of judice and 50 bone combes	8. 4.

Item, in nedles and 6 ounce of silver and gold twist	1.14. 4.
Item, 3^{li} ...[*torn*]... pynts of aqua vite and a lytle fringe with	
...[*torn*]... trifling things	7. 0.
Item, ...[*torn*]... quicksilver & ...[*torn*]... of ginger	...[*torn*]...
...[*torn*]...	7. 0.
...[*torn*]... li	...[*torn*]...
...[*torn*]... quarter of prunes with hony and triakle	...[*torn*]...
Item, 30^{li} of sugar	2. 0. 0.
Item, half a dozen pound of hoppes & a dozen rozell	6. 0.
Item, ... quarters of a C. of pitch, 3 boxes, half a C razines, a little	
chair & 2 chists	2. 3. 0.
Item, 5 pair of scales with balkes and weights and skelses in the	
shopp and other implements	15. 0.

Somma £177 13s 4d

Houshold stuffe and some
other merchantdiz therein

First, his apparell and mony in his purse	4. 0. 0.
Item, a cupbord, 14 cushinges & a litle cupbord cloath	2.10. 8.
Item, 2 chaires, half a dozen of buffit stooles	12. 8.
Item, 2 dreping pannes, a speet, a paire of tonges, a paire of iron	
rackes, a chafing dish, a pair of bellies, 2 reckines, a chopping knife	
& a cradle	17. 0.
Item, in yarne and paire of woollen cardes	1. 0.10.
Item, j^{li} of flax, 2 jugges and a glasse and a paire of playing tables	.5. 2.

In the butterie

Item, 30 peece of pewter, more and lesse	1.10. 0.
Item, half a dozen candlestickes	6. 0.
Item, 5 silver spones and a little silver goblet	1.13. 4.
Item, wood vessell and other implementes there	2. 6.

In the parlor kitchinge and stable

Item, a stand bedd, with the furniture	2. 0. 0.
Item, a litle table & iiij^{er} firkines of sweet sope	2. 2. 6.
Item, a kimline, an old Tubb and a chaire	5. 8.
Item, a C: hoppes and 9 firkines more of sope	5.16. 8.
Item, halfe a dozen of silver spones being pawned	1.13. 0.
Item, a tablecloath & 6 paire of course sheetes	17. 0.
Item, 3 lynnen sheetes, 4 pilloberes, a course harden shete	1.10. 0.
Item, 6 course harden towelles, thre pilloberes and a harden	
borde cloath	2. 6.
Item, a dozen napkines, a lynnen table cloth, two drincking	
napkines & a cupbord cloathe	1.10. 0.
Item, 5 sweet bagges, a peece of old tastar & a trunck with thre	
chistes and a cradlecloath	1.16. 0.

Item, 2 ketles, 3 brasse pottes, 3 pannes, a frijng panne and a ladle	1. 6. 8.
Item, a kitching plancke with tresseles, 2 formes & a planck, 3 barrelles, a guylfat, a kimline with 2 skelses and a chamber pott	8. 8.
Item, 16 firdailes, with certaine old wood and some old hayr	2. 6. 8.

In the loft above the hall

Item, a table, a trundle bed, 3 happines & furniture	1. 3. 4.
Item, a stand bed, with furniture & a spynning whele	15. 0.
Item, 17 shovelles	6. 8,
Item, a syde sadle with furniture	3. 6. 8.
Item, a Bible, communion book and testament	13. 4.
Item, a case of trenshers & a dozen other	1. 0.
Item, 2 kyne	4.10. 0.
Item, oates on the grounde	4.10. 0.
Item, one horse and a mayre	7. 0. 0.

Som Totallis £235 7s 10d

debtes owing to the deceassed

First, Sir George Conyers, knight	27.15.11.
Item, my Ladie Conyers, his wife	1. 5. 9.
Item, Mr John Conyers	7. 7. 0.
Item, Mrs Marie Conyers	6.19. 7.
Item, Michaell Forewood for Ralph Conyers	7.16. 6.
Item, Elinor Cathericke	24. 0. 0.
Item, William Lancaster	4. 8. 0.
Item, Mr Marmaduke Vincent [crossed out]	2. 4.10.
Item, John Burnet	3. 0. 0.
Item, Sir Richard Colmeley, knight [crossed out]	3.11.10.
Item, Mr John heron [crossed out]	9. 1. 6.
Item, Mr Richard Samforth [crossed out]	1.14. 0.
Item, Ralfe Harvie [crossed out]	1. 4. 0.
Item, George Husband	5.17. 3.
Item, Parcivall Bell	13.10.
Item, Vincent Freare	2.13. 7.
Item, Robert Wormeldy	3.11. 8.
Item, Thomas Tonstall	9.
Item, James Clement	8. 6.
Item, William Rippon	14. 5.
Item, Robert Brasse	1. 6.
Item, henrie Wilkinson [crossed out]	17. 0.
Item, Edwarde Atkinson	1. 3.
Item, John Vaux	2.11. 5.
Item, George Grainge [crossed out]	2. 9. 9.
Item, Margaret Bell [crossed out]	5. 0.
Item, Thomas Norton	12. 3.

Item, Robert Hutton, clarke	1. 2. 0.
Item, Mr William Hutton	2. 0.
Item, John Braidley	1. 1. 6.
Item, Alexander Westwood	12. 9.
Item, John Shawter [crossed out]	2. 6.
Item, Richard Braddocke	8. 8.
Item, Olliver Brakenbury	14. 6.
Item, William harrison [crossed out]	8.
Item, Ralf Coatesworth Junior	1.14. 6.
Item, George Emmerson	9.
Item, ffrancis Storie [crossed out]	1.14. 0.
Item, William Killinghall	3. 2.
Item, Thomas Clement	3.16. 4.
Item, Nicholas Pudsey	2.13.10.
Item, George hodgshon	3. 4.
Item, Ralf Coatesworth	2. 3.11.
Item, Isaac Lowden	9. 4.
Item, Toby Tonstall	14. 6.
Item, William foreman	14. 2.
Item, Robert Sigiswicke [crossed out]	1. 9.
Item, John Wood [crossed out]	1.15.1.
Item, John Cathericke gent [crossed out]	...[illegible]...
Item, John Burnet Junior for Richard Gower	2. 1. 5.
Item, Thomas Coward [crossed out]	...[illegible]...
Item, William Thomlinson of Midleton Tias	4. 0.
...[torn]... Garthorne	4. 4.

[nine lines torn and damaged]

Sum of the debts ...[torn]... said £123 11s 10d

Debt ...[torn]... bylls and obligacions

First Mr fairfax	3. 3. 4.
Item, Mr William Savill	
Item, Mr John Errington [crossed out]	5. 0. 0.
Item, John Peele Schoolmaster	2. 1. 6.
Item, Marmaduke Vincent [crossed out]	3. 8. 0.
Item, Brian Daniell [crossed out]	7. 0. 0.
Item, Charles Slingsbie [crossed out]	8. 0. 0.
Item, Marmaduke Vincent more	8.16. 0.
Item, Robert Norton	6.12. 3.
Item, Robert Davill	4. 0. 0.
Item, George huthwait and William bewen-ley [crossed out]	4. 7. 2.
Item, Ralfe Aizelabie by bond [crossed out]	7.18. 2.
Item, Robert hardy [crossed out]	1. 2. 0.

Somma of the last recited debtes £25 12s 10d

Some Totallis is £384 12s 6d

Desperate owing to the said deceassed

First, Richard Bee	8. 0.
Item, William Soppeth	19.10.
Item, Robert Dawson	3. 3.
Item, Brian Metcalfe	1.14. 6.
Item, Elizabeth Stockton, vidua	6. 0.
Item, Jeffray holme	7. 0.
Item, Christofer Rearton	4.10.
Item, Christofer Warcoppe	7. 7.
Item, Lawrence Huitson	10. 9.
Item, Francis Lazinby	1. 4.
Item, Ralfe Thompson	3. 6.
Item, William Shawe	2. 4. 0.
Item, Katherine Edeson	1.10.
Item, Mr Marmaduke Cholmeley	8. 1. 4.
Item, William Chamberlaine	9. 3. 4.
Item, George Dent	2. 4. 3.
Item, Mr William Harrison	9. 1. 0.
Item, William Hock	1. 1. 2.
Item, Mr Chomeley, more	3.11.10.
Item, Robert Readhead	1.14. 4.
Item, John Hixon	1. 6.
Item, Margerie Rey	2. 2.
Item, William Gower	1.13.11.
Item, William Simpson	1.10. 4.
Item, Christofer Busby	1. 0.
Item, John Topliffe	7.11.
Item, Robert Parkinson	9. 0. 0.
Item, Mr Marmaduke Vincent	2. 4.10.
Item, Sr Richard Chomeley knight	3.11.10.
Item, Mr John Heron of Bockenfield	9. 1. 4.
Item, Richard Samforth	1.14. 0.
Item, Raufe Harvey	1. 4. 0.
Item, henry Wilkinson	16. 0.
Item, George Grange	2. 9. 9.
Item, Margaret Bell	5. 0.
...[torn]... John	2. 6.
	8.
	1.14. 0.
	1. 0.
[six lines torn and damaged]	1.15. 1.
	10.10.
	3. 0.

[Parchment, 3 mm., sewn, indented. In hand similar to 6, 10, 11, 12, 14
inventory, 23, 27 will, 35, 36 will, 43, 44, 46, 48 will, 49, 50, 51 and 56.]

29 John Lomley of Darlington, 1611

1610

Invatory of all the goodes
of Johne Lomly of Darlyngton,
lattly desesed, praysed by
theis fowre men, Anton Ruton,
Henry Becrofte, Barnat
Lessheman, Gilbart
Lowton

In prymyse, on stiddye, on payre of belloes & one tewe iryron	1. 6. 8.
Item, on gret hamer, thre lettell hammeres & towe payre of tonges & on pare of pensharies & on butter, on crester, on hewe iron & fowerten new horisshowes, on punche & on bascat & on budgett	6. 6.
Item, on flakit, thre canis, on lettel puder dubler	8.
Item, on chare	10.
Item, on lettell old counter	8.
Item, all his apperill	8. 0.
Item, honge flesshe	1. 6.
Item, on yard of whyt carssae	1. 6.
Item, tow lettell pesses lensy wolsey	1. 0.
Item, tew remlanes of corse len	9. 0.
Item, sartan remlandes	1. 0.

Summa Bonorum £3 2s 8d

Dettis owen to Johne Lomle, desessed,

Dettis ownge by Johne Lomlye

Item, to Johne Watson	1.13. 4.
Item, to William Sherwod	17. 0.
Item, to william tonnend	9. 0.
Item, to Jeanet Wilson	1.10. 0.
Item, to John Stott	8. 0.
Item, to John Stanrupe	8. 6.
Item, to Raffe Grene	15. 0.
Item, to Christofer Wilkenson	2. 0.
Item, to William Collen	2. 0.
Item, to Henry Branson	7. 0.
Item, to Tibe Sadler	1.12. 0.
Item, to Tidd Sadler	16. 0.

[Paper, 1 f.]

In the name of God, Amen, I, Thomas Robinson, of Cockerton within the County of Durham, yoman, being sicke in body but of sound and perfect memory, thankes be unto Almightie God, do make this my last will and testament, in manner and forme followinge. First, I bequeath my soule into the handes of my Saviour and Redemer, Jesu Christ, who I besech of his great goodnes to pardon my sinnes and offences, and my body to be buryed in the churchyard of Darneton. Item, I give & bequeath to my two daughters, Isabell Robinson and Jennett Robinson, all my household stuffe whatsoever, within my now dwelling house in Cockerton. Item, I give and bequeath to Cutberte Robinson, my eldest sonne, my mare and hir fole. Item, I give and bequeathe to Peter Robinson, my second sonne, a gouldin cowe which was John Newbye's, with the land which I bought of John Dent in full satisfaction of his childes porcion. Item, I give to the poore of Darneton parish, xiij^s iiij^d. Item, whereas I did promise Jennett Dent, if she did survive hir brother, John Dent, to pay hir vj^s viiij^d, during hir life, I do charge my sonne, Peter Robinson, to pay hir the said vj^s viij^d, during hir lyfe naturall, in regard I purchased the land for hir. Item, I do give and bequeath to Henry Robinson, Christofer Robinson, Anthony Robinson, Thomas Robinson, Isabell Robinson and Jennet Robinson. my children, all my debtes and goodes, moveable and unmoveable, my funerall chargs and expenses onely to be deducted, to be equally dedived[sic] among them. Item, I do make Raphe Blackwell my executor of this my last will and testament, to whom I do comitt the tuicyon of Henrie Robinson, Christofer Robinson, Anthony Robinson, Thomas Robinson, Isabell Robinson and Jennett Robinson, my said children. In wittnes wherof, I, the said Thomas Robinson, have sette my hand, the xvj^o day of October, in the tenth yeare of his highenes rigne that now ys. Thomas Robinson, his marke, Debtes owing to Thomas Robinson, without specialty, H. Raine, in lent money, xl^s. More, for my sonne's, Peter's, wages, xlviij^s. John Scott, viij^l Wittnesses herof, Lawrence Catryck, William Marshall, Lawrence Elgye [mark], H. Oswolde.

[Paper, 1f.]

An inventory of all the goodes, chattels, debtes & credittes whereof
Thomas Robinson of Cockerton, within the parishe of Darneton, dyed
possessed & which, now, by a deed of gifte bearing daite with the
last will & testament of the said Thomas, intended or mencioned to
be granted to the same partyes as appeareth the same to be devised
unto by the said will, the xvijth day of October, 1612. Praysed
by Thomas Emmerson, Lawrence Elgy, Lawrence Kathericke,
William Marshall & John Simpson as followeth

Inprimis, his purse with his apparrell   6.13. 4.

In the haule
Item, ij° cubbordes, ij° buffett stooles   2.13. 4.
Item, iiij° queshions, ij° tables, j fourme & ij° chaires   12. 0.
Item, xxvij° peece of pewder, iiij° sawcers, j chamber pott, ij°
   pottindiches, iij° saltes, iij° brasse candlestickes, ij° pewder tunes 3. 0. 0.
Item, j reckin crooke, j loose crooke, j fireshovel, j pair of tonnges   3. 4.
Item, a broling iron, one frying pann, one speett, one dreping pann,
   one paire of iron rackes   2. 6.

In the chamber
Item, iiij° skeales, xxviij° boulles, iij° standes, j gallond pott, j chearne
& staffe, iij° kannes, vj° diches, vj° chesfattes, j cinkar, iij° wood
   dublers   12. 0.
Item, one chaldron, ij° brasse pottes, j fishe pann, iiij° other pannes, j
   chaffing dishe, a scimmer & a laddle   2. 0. 0.
Item, one ould aumbrey, j chest, v^{li} of lyne, ij shelfes   10. 0.
Item, j bedsteed with a featherbed, ij° coodes & a boulster, ij°
   happins and a coverlett   2. 1. 0.

In the lofte over the haule
Item, j paire of bedstoockes, j matteresse, a cod, j blankett, ij° happins   7. 0.

In the low parlour
Item, reckin crook   2. 0.
Item, j new cubbord   1.10. 0.
Item, j standbed with a featherbed & matteresse, j boulster, ij coodes,
   ij coverlettes & a blankett   4. 0. 0.
Item, j chest & a foorm   3. 4.
Item, iij° paire of lynnen sheettes, j paire of samoring sheetes, vj° paire
   of hardin sheettes, iiij° coodwardes, ij° long towels, x° table napkins 4.10. 0.

In the lofte over the parlour
Item, j bedsteed and a happin   10. 0.
Item, a trindlebed and a chest   4. 0.

In the barne

Item, xxxº threves of ry	7.10. 0.
Item, xxxº threves of oottes	5. 0. 0.
Item, corne on the ground	10. 0. 0.
Item, the 4 parte of the tyth corne of Cockerton	5. 0. 0.
Item, vº loades of hay	3. 6. 8.
Item, lynnen yarne	5. 0.
Item, j iron coulter	2. 0.
Item, j cheespresse, j tubb, iiijº iron steakes, j iron teame, ij heckes, ij stupes, ij iron nailes	13. 4.
Item, ij queshions	5. 0.
Item, j pair of wood wheeles	13. 4.
Item, iiijº bee hyves	1.13. 4.
Item, vijº hennes, j cocke, vº checkins	3. 0.
Item, j swyne hogg	13. 4.
Item, one butter kitt with butter	1.12. 0.
Item, xxiijº cheases with iron geare in the dove lofte	2. 3. 0.
Item, iij hay racks, ij mould racks, ij peecks, j sheve, ij riddles, j hay spade	4. 0.
Item, ij seckes, j iijº[sic] pooks	1. 4.
Item, waine geare and plowe gear att Raphe Blackwels	3. 0. 0.
Item, j mare & foole, with saddle & bridle	4. 0. 0.
Item, j gouldin cowe	2.10. 0.
Item, xiiijº kine and a bull	34. 0. 0.
Item, vj sturkes	6. 0. 0.
Item, ix calves	4. 6. 8.
Item, xvjº yewes & xxiiijº hogges	8.17. 4.
Item, one hay stack	5. 6. 8.
Item, one lease of a close	15. 0. 0.
Suma Bonorum £151 19s 2d	

Debtes owing to Thomas Robinson

Raphe Blackwell	22.10. 0.
Robert Parkinson	13.11. 0.
Edward Elgy	22. 2. 0.
Edward Marshall	9. 0. 0.
Thomas Simpson & John Simpson	3. 4. 0.
William Story	1. 0. 0.
Robert Key & Raphe Fawdon	2. 0. 0.
John Simpson & Nychollas Smith	6.13. 4.
Edward Marshall	2.16. 8.
Lawrence Elgy	1. 0. 0.
John Skott	9. 0. 0.
Henry Raine	2. 0. 0.
more for Peter Robinson clothing	2. 8. 0.

Anthony Sotheron	3. 0. 0.
George Stanicke	5. 0.
Henry Oswald	6. 0. 0.

Suma debitorum £104 10s 0d

Suma totalis Bonorum et debitorum £256 9s 2d

Debtes owing by Thomas Robinson

To Anthony Sotheron	4. 6. 8.
To Henry Raine for a stone of wooll & iiij° sheepe skinnes	5. 4.
To my Lord of Durham for rent	1. 6. 4.
To Thomas Heddon	2. 4. 0.
To Raphe Blackwell	13. 8.
For hird wages	5. 8.
For the children waiges to the schoolemaster	2. 0.
To Cutbert Robinson	4. 0.
Item, spent about his funerall	4. 0. 0.
Item, given to the poore	1. 2. 0.
Item, to Mr Gifford for his mortuary	10. 0.
Item, paid for the charges of provinge of the will & lettres of tuicion of the children & the charges of vj men and thre horses for one daie and night	2. 6. 8.

Wittnesses herof Lawrence Caterick Thomas Emerson William Marshall
   [mark] Lawrence Elgy [mark] John Simpson

Item, paid to Mr Calverley for passinge of a lease of a copiehold and for the cesse dewe to my Lord of Durham	13. 4.

Suma debitorum £17 19s 8d

Suma declaro debitis deductis £238 9s 6d

[Paper, 1 f. Will and inventory in same hand as 1, 2, 15, 16, 22, 24 will, 32, 41, 42 and 45 wills.]

31   Isaac Lowden of Darlington, 1612

An inventorie of the goodes of Mr Isaac
Lowden, praysed by Mr Brian Grant,
Mr Simon Giffard, Richard Braddoke
& Robert Warde, the xvth of Julie, 1612

Apparell

Imprimis one gowne	13. 4.
Item, a cloke	10. 0.
Item, dublett, Jerkin, breeches & stockinges	10. 0.
Item, a hatt & band	2. 6.

Item, a shirt, two bandes, two payre of custes, a payre of boote hose & an handkercher	4. 0.
Item, a sleeved cloke	1. 0. 0.
Item, dublett & breeches	4. 0.
Item, a payre of bootes	1. 4.
Item, scarfe	3. 4.
Item, a yard of stuffe	2. 0.
Item, a chaire & cushion	3. 0.
Item, a chest	10. 0.
Item, a trunke	2. 0.
Item, a chest	2. 6.
Item, a payre of tables	2. 0.
Item, a candlesticke, a payre of tonges, fire shovle & a raster	3. 4.

Summe £4 12s 4d

Bookes [see pp. 215-22 below]

Item, Gualthe uppon Luke	8. 0.
Item, Peter Martir uppon the Rom:	4. 0.
Item, Lambert uppon Luke	1. 0.
Item, Erasmus paraphrase uppon matt:	2.
Item, Jacobus de voragne	4.
Item, Urstitius Arethmeticke	6.
Item, Cesars Comentarie	1. 0.
Item, Hermanus Bodins	1. 0.
Item, Theodorettus	1. 0.
Item, Titlemans physickes	6.
Item, xx^{tie} small bookes	5. 0.
Item, Erasmus Apothegmes	4.
Item, a scapula	14. 0.
Item, Gualthers homilies	6. 8.
Item, Hugo Cardinalis uppon the whole Bible	7. 0.
Item, Homers Illiades	1. 8.
Item, Brittaynes resurrection	1.
Item, French & Italian Testament	4.
Item, Direction to death	8.
Item, Simon de Cassia	2. 6.
Item, The Reformed Catholicke	4.
Item, a Childrens dictionare	2.
Item, Chemnisius 4^{or} tom:	10. 0.
Item, Theophilactus uppon the fower Evangelistes	1. 6.
Item, Calvins institution	3. 4.
Item, Christes Triumph	2.
Item, Granadoes meditacions	1. 0.
Item, Mr Deeringes lectures	1. 6.
Item, Dux peccatorum	2. 0.
Item, Sheppardes Callender	4.

Item, Setons log:	4.
Item, Mr Estie workes	2. 0.
Item, Bartasias de mundi creatione	8.
Item, Aulus Gellius	1. 8.
Item, Comedia sacra	2.
Item, Petrarch de remedijs utriusque fortunae	6.
Item, Quintilians Institutions	2. 6.
Item, Brittaynes deliverance	2.
Item, Directions to the holy land	2.
Item, King uppon Jonas	2. 0.
Item, Bilsons Controversies	2. 0.
Item, Calvin uppon the Epistles	1. 0.
Item, Gualther uppon the small prophettes	6. 8.
Item, The golden Chayne	6.
Item, Halls Epistles	4.
Item, an exposition of two chapters of the proverbes	4.
Item, Hemmeng uppon James	6.
Item, a part of Titus Livius	1. 0.
Item, Salust	4.
Item, The pedegree of popish heretiques	4.
Item, Doctor Playfayres sermons	4.
Item, The Anatomie of Abuses	4.
Item, Gritches sermones quadragessimales	2.
Item, Talens Retorique	2.
Item, A greeke Testament & a Clenardes grammar	1. 8.
Item, one volume of Tullies orations	4.
Item, Piscator uppon the Epistles	8.
Item, Gibsons meditations	4.
Item, Ramus log:	3.
Item, Valerius Flaccus Argo:	6.
Item, Catullus, Tibullus & Propertius	1. 0.
Item, Five bookes of moses in laten with a commentarie	8.
Item, A statute booke	1. 0.
Item, a treatise of Christian equititie	2.
Item, The treasure of Evonimus	4.
Item, Michaell de Hungaria	1. 0.
Item, Litosthenes Apothegmes	1. 0.
Item, Tullies Tusculan quest	1. 0.
Item, Salust	6.
Item, An English Bible	3. 4.
Item, Brocard uppon the Revellations	1. 0.
Item, Clenardes greeke grammar & Clarke de Aulico	6.
Item, The English secretarie with three old bookes	6.

Somme £5 16s 0d

The somme of his apparrell, bookes & impleementes £10 8s 4d

Dettes owing by the said Mr Lowdin

Imprimis, for funerall expenses	1.12. 4.
Item, to Mr Allondson	1.10. 0.
Item, to Widdowe Dent	12. 0.
Item, to Richard Boyes	10. 0.
Item, to Anthonie Raynold	14. 4.
Item, to Cutbert Hodgshons wiffe	13. 4.
Item, to Mr William Bore	1.17. 0.
Item, to John Bradeley	2.16. 0.
Item, to Richard Bradocke	1. 4. 3.
Item, to Robert Ward	1. 6. 9.
Item, to Widdow Johnson in Northgate	10. 6.
Item, to Mrs Dennise	9. 6.
Item, to Mrs Jackson	18. 6.
Item, to Thomas Robinson	2. 0. 0.
Item, to Simon Browne	10. 0.
Item, to John Scottes wiffe	
Item, to Nichlas Goodabyre	2. 0.
Item, to Grace Rowell in lent money in tyme of his sicknes	4. 9.
Item, to two women for keeping him five weekes in tyme of his sicknes what the caurt will allowe	
Item, to Anthonie Raynold for 4 weekes table, for chamber & bed, fire, & washinge	1. 4. 0.
Item, laid forth to a proctor for sendinge of me a monicion & for obteininge of letteres of administracion	4. 9.
Item, for lettres of administracion under seall & for ingrossinge of the inventories	9. 6.
Item, to the apparritor	8.
Item, for my charges and my sureties in goinge twice to Durham	5. 4.

Dettes owing to Mr Lowden

Imprimis of Anthonie Branson & Mr Lowden ought him for two falling bandes	10. 6.
Item, Mr Pegeat of Middleham	5. 0.
Mr John Blakeston	5. 0.
Item, owinge unto him by Henrie Oswould for his waiges by the appointement and direction of my Lord Bishopp of Durham	10. 0. 0.

Somme of debtes dewe to the deceased £11 0s 6d

Somma totalis Bonorum et debitorum £21 8s 10d

[*Paper, 4 ff., sewn.*]

In dei nomine, Amen, I, Michaell Jeffreyson, of Darlington in the county of Durham, tanner, sick in body but of good & perfect remembrance, thanks be to Almighty God, do make this my last will & testament, in manner folowing. First, I bequyth my soule to the Almighty God of Heaven, my Saviour & Redeemer, and my body to be buryed in the church yeard of Darlington aforesaid, nere where my father did ly. Item, I gyve towards the amending of the carsay leading to the Armytage, iijˢ iiijᵈ, within one yeare next after my decease. Item, I will that Elizabeth, my doughter, shall yearly, after my decease, pay out of my lands & tenements to her discending from me, unto Janett Jeffreyson, my sister, the some of sex shillings & eight pence, during her lyf naturall. Item, I will & bequyth to Catherine, my wyff, all my Highe Close above High Park, during her lyf. Item, all the rest of my goods, as well reall as personall, my debts paid, my funerall expense deduct & dischardged, I will & bequyth to Mathewe Bellamy of Richmond, mercer, my trewe & trusty frynd, to the intent he shall trewly as well dischardg my said debts as also pay, out of my cleare estait, my loving wife her thirdes thereof, my said doughter her child part, & my legaces dischardged, and him, the said Mathew, I do make my sole executore of this my last will & I do desier Robert Ward of Darnton to be supervisor hereof, to see the same performed according to my intent. Dayted this 7t day of February, Anno Domini, per computatione Angliae, 1611 [1612].

Item, I, the said Michaell Jeffreyson, do also, by thes presents, will & bequyth, after the decease of Elizabeth, my said doughter & heirs, yf she shall happen to dy without yssue of her body, lawfullie to be begotten, all sutch lands and tenements as she shall have by my decease, to go com & be to the said Mathew Bellonby, his heires & assigns for ever, according to my sole intent.

The cubbord & hall seat, morter & pestle, to his daughter in her childs part.

Robert Challenor

Debts by him owen to the schoole iiijˡⁱ or thereabowts
to Robert Ward   1.11. 7.
to Robert White   20. 0. 0.
to Thomas gryndy   iiijˡⁱ or thereabowts
to William bower   3.14. 0.
Wytnesses hereof Robert Challenor Mathewe Bellamy Robert Warde
[*Paper, 1 f., seal.*]

The inventorye of all the goods
moveable & unmoveable, quick & dead,
of Michaell Jeffereyson, lait of Darnton,
tanner, deceased, praysed by Lawrance
Cathericke, John Fawcett, John Watson
& Robart Ward, the xth day Fabruarye,
Anno Domini, 1611

Inprimis, in the hall

Item, a cubbord, with a cover or valt	2.10. 0.
Item, a morter and pestle	1. 0. 0.
Item, a longe table & frame	10. 0.
Item, tow longe settles	10. 0.
Item, a counter	5. 0.
Item, a forme, a chaier and a seat	2. 0.
Item, tow thre footed stoles	1. 0.
Item, a shelf, a paier of tables, 3 pictures, a glasse case & 6 glasses, a stole and a water seat	3. 4.
Item, sex quishings	2. 0.
Item, 17 peces of pewther	1. 5. 6.
Item, two beare pots and an ewer	6. 8.
Item, a chamber pott, three pewther candlesticks, 6 salts, tow litle cups, v sawcers	9. 0.
Item, a brasen morter and pestle, viij brasse candlesticks and a chaffin dish	12. 0.
Item, tow spets, a reckincrooke, ij pare of tongs, a fier shovell, a chopping knif, a shering knife, a rosting iron, a broyling iron, a scommer, ij baisters and a fleshcroke	10. 0.

In the butterye

Item, iiij brasse potts	16. 0.
Item, ij kettles & iij panes	6. 0.
Item, xviij peces of pewther	9. 0.
Item, xviij sponnes, iij sawcers, j pottinger, a quart pott, and a pint pott	2. 0.
Item, shelves, with stoupes & a boord	3. 4.
Item, ij boules, v kanes, v jackes, iiij potts, dishes, trenchers & a lantherne & other litle implements & grater	5. 6.
Item, a paire of racks of iron, an ould fryinpan	2. 0.

In the kitchin

Item, a paire of great rackes, a drippin pane, a reckincroke	11. 0.
Item, a cauldron & a kettle	1. 5. 0.
Item, a maskefatt, a cooling tub, a draftub, a sae, two skeles & a litle bordd	10. 0.
Item, iij seckes and tow pooks	2. 0.

In the vault

Item, ij hogs heads, ij stands, a kit, a barrell, ij ould tubs, ij chernes, formes, shelves and a iij foted stole	12. 0.

In the parler

Item, a stand bed with a feather bed boulster, ij blanketts, a coverlet & an oversea covering with courtings	3. 0. 0.
Item, a table with a frame	10. 0.
Item, v buffet stoles, ij formes and a seat with a chaier	11. 0.
Item, a window leass, a gallowbawke, stoupes & a chist	5. 6.

In the inmost chamber

Item, a longe table, with a frame	8. 0.
Item, an ould presser & a trindle bed	6. 8.
Item, a spinning whele, an ould saddle, spads, shoule & a spattle staff	12. 0.
Item, ij flicks of bacon	6. 8.

In the middlemost chamber

Item, iij stand bedd steads & a trindle bed	1. 6. 8.
Item, iiij feather bedds	4. 0. 0.
Item, other beddinge clothes belonging to them	1.10. 0.
Item, a square table & a frame	6. 8.
Item, a shelf	6.

In the chamber over the entre

Item, a stand bedd, a waineskott chist & a seat	1. 3. 4.
Item, cart geare, raicks, staves & other odd woodd at	8. 0.
Item, bedd clothes with a feather bed	6. 8.
Item, a side saddle	3. 4.
Item, ij lodde saddles & a ridinge saddle	10. 0.

In the chamber over the parler

Item, iiij stand bedd steads	8. 0.
Item, bedding, v matterisses & other clothes	2. 0. 0.
Item, ij litle chists, a temps, a swill	3. 0.

naperye

Item, vij paire of linne shets, iij pare of harne shets, v pillovers & iij bordcloths	3. 0. 0.
Item, x table napkins	3. 4.
Item, his apparell	1. 0. 0.

In the stable

Item, a paire of cart wheles & a paire of cart bound wheles	16. 0.
Item, a stone trough	2. 6.
Item, x trisses	3. 4.
Item, ij stees	2. 0.
Item, iiij paire of siles, ribb & a stres	2. 0. 0.

Item, a cowe 2.13. 4.
Item, a stirck   13. 4.
Item, a haystack   2. 6. 8.
Item, v sheeppe   1. 5. 0.
Item, ij swine   10. 0.
Item, racks and maingers in the stable   6. 8.
            Somma huius Inventorii £46 8s 4d

[*Parchment, 2 mm., sewn. Will and inventory in hand similar to 1, 2, 15, 16,
22, 24 will, 30, 41, 42 and 45 wills.*]

33 John Sober of Darlington, 1613

The xijth of may, Anno Domini, 1612, in the name of God, Amen, I,
John Sober of Darlington, being sicke of bodie but whole of mynde
and in sound and perfect remembrance, do make this my last will
and testament, in manner and forme followinge. First, I bequeath my
soule unto thalmightie God, my Maker and Redeemer, and my bodie
to be buried within the parish church yard of Darlington. Item, I give
and bequaeth unto Jane, my now beinge wife, all that my now
dwellinge house, scituate and beinge within the burrogh of
Darlington, with one brewhouse on the backside and all other
thappurtencances thereunto belongeinge or in anie wise apperteineinge, for and dureing the life naturall of the said Jane, my wife.
Item, I give and bequeath unto Richard, my son, all that myne
aforenamed dwellinge house, with all and singullar thappurtenances
thereunto belongeinge or in anie wise apperteineinge, after the
decease of the aforenamed Jane, my now being wife, with all other
comodities whatsoever unto the same belongeinge and to his heirs
for ever; provided that the said Richard shall pay or cause to be paid
unto Margarett, my daughter, the whole and iust some of five
poundes of current monie of England, within the terme or space of
one whole year next followinge after the said Richard shall enter
unto thaforesaid house; and in deffault of such payment, the
aforenamed Margarett to enter upon the premisses and the same, to
enioy and posses as her owne enheritance, untill the said some of
five poundes be fullie satisfied, and paid. The rest of all my goodes,
moveable and unmoveable, I give and bequeath equallie to be
devided amongst my afforenamed wife, son and daughter, my debtes
and funeralls expences beinge clearlie discharged. Witnesses hereof
ar Willaym Sober, Thomas Sober with others.

[*Paper, 1f.*]

34 Agnes Claxton of Darlington, 1613

Agnes Claxton goodes by will bequeathed
to An, her Child

Imprimis, her best coate

Item, her best petticoate

Her best hat

Her best bande and partt cloth

Her best smocke and apron a payer of blancketts

Two payer of sheetes

One payer of lyn

Another of harden both newe

One new kettle

A coverlett, a codd and a codware, one payer of silke sleeves, vj peeces of
pewder, two candlestickes, two panns, one brasse pott

All these parcells were praysed to v^{li} by Franncis Castle, Vincent Hodgson,
Roger Coniers and Henrye Thompson

And all these parcells were delivered in the presence of the prazers to
Anthoney Claxton, brother unto the said deceased, Agnes, to and for the use
of An her daughter

[*Paper, 1 f. In hand similar to inventories 42 and 45.*]

35 William Robinson of Blackwell, 1613

In the name of God, Amen, the xxvth daie of Aprill, 1612, I, William
Robinson of Blackwell, in the countie of Durham, weaver, sicke in
bodie but of good and perfect remembrance I give God most hartie
thanckes, do make and ordaine this my last will and testament in
maner and forme followinge. First, I bequeath my soull into the
handes of Almightie God, my Creator and Redemer, through whose
death and passion I faithfullie beleve to be saved, committing my
body to the earth frome whence it came and to be buried in the
parish churchyarde of Darlington, at the discrecion of my supervisor
hereafter nominated. Item, I will that, whereas all my children are in
their minoritie and infancy, not able nor fit any way to sustaine
themselves without some meanes left them and aide of charitable
and well disposed freindes, my will is that a leasse (if conveniently it
may be so effected, if not by the charitable permission and license of
the lord, shalbe granted to certaine feoffes in trust frome the day of

my death for twelve yeares, for the educacion and advancement of my five children, vicz., Thomasine, John, Lawrence, William and Faithe, to be yearely imployed for their said educacion and advancement, of some porcion so farre forth as the yearely profitts of my tenement will extend. And for that I thinke it most necessarie, I will that the yongest, vicz., my daughter, Faith, shall begynne and receive the first yeare's rent. And so ascending to William, and then Lawrence and John the fourth yeare and Thomasine the fifte, and so likewise accordinglie for other five yeares, and the last two yeares of this my said grant to be likewise equally divided a mongst these said five children, to everie of them a like porcion thereof. Item, I give to my eldest sonne, Cuthbert (if this my will shalbe performed and goe forward for these twelve yeares) a lynnen loame lait bought of Thomas Potter. The rest of all my goodes and chattells, not given nor bequeathed, I give to my said five children, Thomasine, John, Lawrence, William and Faith, and do make my brother-in-lawe, Robert Horner, my whole exequator, entreating my cosine, John Wheatley of Norton, and my brother, Simon Robinson, to be supervisores of this my said testament and to se the due execucion thereof, according to thintent abovesaid. Witnesses hereof as followeth, Robert Garnet, Anthony Garnet, John Wheatley, Simon Robinson, William Robinson and Richard Pickeringe.

[*Parchment, 1 m.*]

A true inventorie of all and singular the goodes and chattelles, moveable and unmoveable, of William Robinson of Blackwell, lait deceassed, praised the xxviij^th daie of Aprill, 1612, by John Midleton thelder, John Dobson, John Wheatley and Roger Rawline, as followeth

First, his apparrell and the mony in his purse	1. 6. 8
Item, one litle cupbord and an old ambrie in the forehouse	12. 0
Item, eleaven milke bowlles with a great washing bowll, a kneading bowll with dishes, three wood dublers, 3 cannes and other litle implementes	5. 0.
Item, 2 standes, 2 skeeles, one chirne, one gallon pott with one earthen pott	3. 4.
Item, one brasse pott, a ketle, 3 pannes, 2 pewther doublers, 2 brasse candlestickes and a salt	17. 0.
Item, two reckingcrookes, a paire of tonges and a paire of pottkilpes	2. 0.
Item, a fryinge panne, a speet and one iron shoehorne	1. 6.
Item, three skelfes with the hangers	1. 8.
Item, one table, a chaire, five stooles with three batledoores	2. 8.
Item, one paire of sheares, a hammer, a paire of pinsers and other implementes of iron	1. 4.

Item, one great tubb, a stone trough and the mell	1. 8.

In the chamber

Item, two beddsteades and two chistes	7. 0.
Item, a tempze and a peece of leather	2. 8.
Item, seaven happines, three paire of harden sheets and fower codds	1. 2. 0.
Item, an old arke, a bord, a forme and other implementes	2. 6.

In the lofte above the chamber

Item, xv^{ene} yardes of harden and two yardes of lynnen cloath	11. 2.
Item, 3 beehives, two pound of wooll, 2 mold rakes, three sickles and a litle mawnd	2. 8.
Item, a swingle and swinglestocke a paire of woollen cardes and a cradle with other implementes	2. 0.
Item, five peckes of beanes and a newe sacke	8. 0.
Item, weighscales with the weightes and an old ladder	8.

In the wolkehouse

Item, a lynnen loome	11. 0.
Item, the lynnen geares, the barretrees, the workefatt, the frame and spooles with wheeles and yarnewindle blaydes & stocks and ratles	1.14. 4.
Item, an old doore, an old sadle, an old ladder, a grope, a barrey, & a spade	6. 8.
Item, 2 forkes, a paire of weighscales with burthen ropes	1.10.
Item, a woollen loome and three geares	11. 0.
Item, one old painted cloath and an axe or hatchet	10.
Item, in lynnen yarne wrought into cloath	1. 6. 0.
Item, a spade shell with a litle panne	3.
Item, 2 kyne	4. 0. 0.
Item, iiij^{er} ewes with iiij^{er} lambes	1.10. 0.
Item, in timber wood lying on the backside as syles, sparres & other thinges	1. 4. 0.
Item, twentie loades of dunge	6. 8.

Summa £18 12s 1d

Debtes owinge by the Testator at his death

First, to John Dunsforth	4. 0. 0.
Item, to George Taylor	7. 6.
Item, to Elizabeth Turner for a pecke of rye	1. 9.
Item, to Agnes Simpson, a pecke and a halfe of rye	2. 7.
Item, to Cicily longe	6.
Item, to Barnarde Longstaffe for coales	10.
Item, to John Harrison for yarne and coales	1. 6.
Item, to Widowe Sisson of Haughton	3. 0.

Item, bestowed in funerell expences and for writing the will and
  inventarie with other accomptes   1. 0. 6.
Item, to Robert Horner in borrowed mony in the time of the
  testators sicknes   3. 4.
Item, to Mr Giffard for a mortuarie   3. 4.

Summa debitorum £6 4s 10d

Debtes owinge to the testator at the hower of his death

First, John Dobson   1. 0.
Item, John Harrison   2. 5.
Item, Isabell Harrison   8.
Item, Nynian Smelt   10.
Item, Jane Tailor, desperate   8. 4.
Item, Robert Glover, desperate   3. 4.

Summa 16s. 7d.

Summa totalis debitis deductis £13 3s 10d

[*Parchment, 1 m., indented. Will and inventory in hand similar to 6, 10, 11,
12, 14 inventory, 23, 27 will, 28, 36 will, 43, 44, 46, 48 will, 49, 50, 51 and 56.*]

36   Ann Dent of Darlington, 1615

xvij die Aprilis 1615

In the name of God, Amen, 1615, I, Ann Dent of Darlington,
widow, sicke in body but in good and perfect remembrance, I
yeald God most harty thancks, do make this my last will and
testament in manner and forme following. First, I bequeath my
soull into the hands of Almighty God, my Creator and Redemer,
through whose death and passion I faithfully hope to be saved,
and my body to be buried in the parish churchyard of Darlington,
as nearr unto my lait deceassed children as possibly cann be
devised, at the discrecion of my brothers-in-law, William Laxe and
Ralf Taton. Item, I give unto Jennet Jackson, my sister daughter,
one ffether bed in the over parlour, with sheets and blanketts and
other thappurtenances, the beddstocks excepted. Item, I give to
Elen Cawthorne, my servant, one smock, my hose and shoes with
two harden aprons. Item, I give to my sisters, Elizabeth Laxe and
Dorithy Taton, to either of them, a band, a raill and a lynnen
apron. Item, I give to Mr Brian Grant, the Viccar, for his paines in
visiting me, iij^s iiij^d. Item, to Richard Pickering, the parish clarke,

other iij⁵ iiij^d. The rest of all and singular my goods and chattells, not given nor bequeathed., I give and bequeath to my two brothers-in-law, William Laxe and Ralfe Taton, whome I make my whole executors of this my said last will and testament, as ffeoffees in trust for thonely benefit, use and behofe of Isaac Dent, my onely naturall sonne, the educacion of which my said sonn I wholly comitt to the two, desiring them as soone as time will permit, to put him to the occupacion of a glover. Provided alwaies that if my said sonne shall dye before his accomplishment of full age of twenty one yeares, then my will is and I do hereby clearely give all my said goods and chattells whatsoever, moveable and unmoveable, formerly to them bequeathed for thuse and behofe of the said Isaac, to the sole and proper use and behofe of them, the aforesaid William Laxe and Ralfe Taton, their executors and assignes for ever. In witnes whereof I have hereunto subscribed with myne owne hand, the day and yeare first above said, in the presence of us. Ann dent [*mark*]

Witnesses hereof, Brian Grant, Henry Colling[*mark*], Richard Pickeringe.

[*Paper, 1 f. In similar hand to 6, 10, 11, 12, 14 inventory, 23, 27 will, 28, 35, 43, 44, 46, 48 will, 49, 50, 51 and 56.*]

An inventorie of all the goods and chattalls,
moveable and unmoveable, as Ann Dent,
late of Darneton, widow, deceased, dyed
possessed of, apprased the xxvj^th of Aprill,
1615, by John Fawcett, William Hodshon,
Richard Boyes and Anthonie Somer,
as followeth

Imprimis, one violett coate of howswife cloth	13. 4.
Item, one hatt lyned with velvett and one violett colored petticoate	12. 0.
Item, an other howswife coate & a petticoate	10. 0.
Item, all her lininge and naperie	5. 0.

In the hall howse

Item, one cubbord, 2 tables, 2 buffett firmes, 2 seats belonginge to the bords & 2 chayers	2. 6. 8.
Item, all the puther vessell, vidz. doublers, candlesticks, tin potts & salt sellers	2. 8. 0.
Item, all the brasse potts & pannes, a greatt kettle & two brason morters	1.16. 0.

Item, one payer of great rackes, 3 spitts, 2 dripping pannes, 2
choppin knifes, with all other iron geare in the howse   16. 0.

In the upper parlore
Item, one table, one chayer, a buffett firme, a longe settle & a
payer of bed stocks   1. 6. 0.
Item, fower chists   13. 0.

In the lower parlore
Item, 2 bedsteeds, 2 chayers, one table, 2 seats and a little iron
chimney   2. 0. 0.

In the buttrie
Item, all the barrells, stands & tubbs with kans and cupps with
all other implements ther   10. 0.

In the brewhowse
Item, one stone trough a mask fatt one old arke a firme with
all other implements ther   10. 0.

In the stable
Item, all the wood geare   3. 4.
Item, a horse heck & a manger   1. 0.
Item, a stone trough   8.
Item, a cowe   2. 0. 0.
Item, broken wood vessell   1. 0.

In the chamber over the howse
Item, 3 bed stockes   1. 0. 0.
Item, 3 fetherbedds, 3 codds & 3 bolsters   2.10. 0.
Item, 3 coverletts & five blancketts   13. 4.

In the chamber over the upper parlore
Item, 4 bedstockes   10. 0.
Item, 2 mattresses, 7 codds & 4 old coverletts   1. 0. 0.

In the chamber over the doers
Item, a long chist, a loade saddle, a payer of woolle cards, an old
tubb with other implements in the said chamber   3. 0.

In the lower & upper parlore
In both the parlors, 3 fetherbedds with codds & bolsters
belonging to them   3. 0. 0.
Item, 4 blanketts, 3 coverletts & a grene rugg   1. 0. 0.
Item, one payer of bed coverlays   3. 4.
Item, 2 coverletts & a payer of blancketts   6. 0.
Item, 2 swords   5. 0.

Item, one fetherbed, one bedsted, a grene rugg, a bolster, a cod with a payer of shetes & blancketts	2. 6. 8.
Item, 8 payer of harden shetes, 2 payer of lin shetes, eight codwares, 2 towells, two bord clothes, 9 napkins, two hand towells & one square bord cloth	2. 0. 0.
Item, 8 quishions	4. 0.
Item, a brewe grater	4.
Item, the revercion of the lease of the howse for 3 yeares yet enduring	6. 0. 0.
Item, a stone morter	8.
Item, a payer of tables & a table cloth	2. 6.

Summa totalis £37 16s 10d

debts owen to the said testatore

Item, Mrs Ursalie	6. 0.
Item, Mr Samuell Hilton	4. 0.
	10.0.

Summa bonorum et debitorum £38 6s 10d

[*Paper, 1 f. In different hand to will.*]

37 Edmund Fawell of Cockerton, 1615

In the name of God, Amen, the fifte day of Januarye in the yeare of our Lord God, 1614, I, Edmund Fawell of Cockerton in the parishe of Darlington, yoman, beinge of wholl mynd & in good & perfite remembrance, laud & prayse be to Almighter God, make & ordeyne this my presente testament concerninge heare in my last will in maner & forme followinge, that is to say, firste, I comend my soule unto Allmightie God, my Maker & Redemmer, & my body to be buried in the churche yard of Darlington. Item, I geve & bequeath to my daughter, Merriall Fawell, on counter & on blacke cow that was given to her by hir grandmother of a whye calfe. Item, I give & bequeath to my daughter, Margreat Fawell, on cobborde & my better whie stirck by legacie. All the residue of my goodes & chattles, moveable & unmoveable, unbequeathe, to be equallye devided to Jenne Fawell, my wife, Merriall Fawell & Margreat Fawell, my ij daughters, whom I maker joyntley executors of this my last will &

testament. Item, my will is that Raphe Blackwell & Peter Bowebancke have the keppinge, government & bringinge up of my ijᵒ children duringe ther nonage. In witnes wherof I have caused these presentes to be written befor Thomas Mason, Thomas Bowebancke, Henry Robinson and Raphe Blackwell.

[*Paper, 1 f.*]

A trew inventorye of all the goodes &
chattles of Edmund Fawell of Cockerton,
in the parishe of Darlington, lait deceased,
praysed the 22 day of Januarye, 1614,
by Thomas Emerson, George Goundrye,
William marshall & Edward Marshall

First, all his apparrell	1. 6. 8.
Item, hay in the field	3.10. 0.
Item, v kyne, j why stirke & calfe	13. 0. 0.
Item, on why stircke geven by legacie margreat ffawell	18. 0.
Item, iiij mears, praysed to	9. 0. 0.
Item, in the little howse, 4 sadles with divers other implementes	1. 0. 0.
Item, hay in the garth praysed to	1.10. 0.
Item, 24 bowles with other imeplements	9. 0.
Item, ij irons, forkes & other imeplementes	3. 0.
Item, j chese prese, j stey, other imeplementes	2. 0.
Item, 3 kettles, ij panes	1. 4. 0.
Item, 9 peece of puther, 3 candlestickes, iiij salts, 6 spones, j tin potte	12. 0.
Item, on corbord given by legacie to my daughter margreat	1. 4. 0.
Item, j spence, j amerye	9. 0.
Item, iiij hingers, ij bordes	1. 0.
Item, j reckinge crocke, on speat, on pare of tonges, j pare of potcilps, on iron potte	7. 0.
Item, iij skelles, with other imeplementes	4. 0.
Item, salt fleshe	10. 0.
Item, in hemp, lint & yarne	8. 0.
Item, j pented cloth, j grat, j seafe	1. 0.
Item, 4 coodes, 3 happens, 4 pare of harden sheetes	1. 0. 0.
Item, j bed & the cloth over it	7. 0.
Item, 3 linen sheetes, ij codworths, j towell	13. 0.
Item, ij standes, ij chirnes, ij kirne stafes	6. 0.
Item, iiij eathen muges, j spad	2. 0.
Item, iij chistes	4. 0.

Item, j table, j bord	3. 0.
Item, iiij chese fates, ij sinckers, j mand, j tempes	4. 0.
Item, j tub, j cawell, j pare of scaylles	4. 0.
Item, j counter, with other imeplementes	4. 0.
Item, j trayll steed, j hecke	3. 0.
Item, v hens, j cocke	4. 0.

Debtes owne to the testator

First, Wedo Ward	4. 0.
Item, Edward Elgie	3. 0. 0.
Item, Edward Marshall	13. 0.
Item, Geo Stanine	4. 8. 0.
Item, Thomas Sadler	3. 0.
Item, William Atkenson	2. 0.
Item, John Bell	11.
Item, Arthur Stockdle	2. 5.

Sume £49 5s 0d

debtes that the testator
did owe at his death

Imprimes, to Wedo Surties	6. 0. 0.
Item, to Anas Surties	2. 0. 0.
Item, to John Hodgshon	3.13. 4.
Item, to Thomas Bowebank & Rappe Blackwell	19. 6.
Item, for his mortuall	10. 0.
Item, to sum wife for fedeinge of his beastes	2. 0.
Item, to Roger Woodmes for a chese	2. 6.
Item, our charges to Durham the first day	3. 6.

Sume £13 10s 10d

[*Paper, 3 ff., sewn*.]

A trew inventory of all the goodes of Edmund
Fawell of Cockerton, lait deceased, as they
weare all sould

Imprimes, iiij kyne were sould for	13. 0. 0.
Item, ij meares sould for	6.13. 4.
Item, one cowe given to Meriall Fawell, sold for	4. 0. 0.
Item, on why sturcke	16. 0.
Item, ij mears, sould for	4. 0. 0.
Item, j why given to Margaret Fawell, sold for	1. 7. 0.
Item, his apparrell, sould for	1. 8. 0.
Item, all the implementes in the little howse	1. 0. 0.
Item, the hay in the garth, sould for	1. 8. 0.

Item, the hay in the field & the eatishe of the field	4. 0. 0.
Item, 24 bowles, with other implementes	9. 0.
Item, ij iron forckes, with other implementes	3. 0.
Item, j chese presse, j stie & other implementes	2. 0.
Item, 3 kettles, 2 panes	1. 4. 0.
Item, ix peece of puther, 3 candlestickes & other implementes	12. 0.
Item, j spence, j ammery	9. 0.
Item, iiij hinges, ij bordes	1. 0.
Item, j reckin crock, j speat & other implement	7. 0.
Item, iij skelles, with other implements	4. 0.
Item, salt fleshe	10. 0.
Item, in hemp lint & yarne	8. 0.
Item, j paynted cloth, j grat, j seafe ...[illegible]...	1. 0.
Item, iiij coodes, with other implements	1. 0. 0.
Item, j bed, j paynted cloth	7. 0.
Item, iiij lynen sheetes, ij coodwortes, j towell	13. 0.
Item, ij standes & other implementes	6. 0.
Item, iiij earthen muges, j spad	2. 0.
Item, iiij chistes	4. 0.
Item, j table, on bord	3. 0.
Item, iiij chese fates, with other implementes	4. 0.
Item, j tub, with other imeplementes	4. 0.
Item, j counter, with other implements	4. 0.
Item, j trayll stead, j hecke	3. 0.
Item, v henes, j cocke	4. 0.
Item, the lease of his ground, which he took of John Hodgson, &, after his decease, turned over to the said John	1. 6. 8.
Item, one cow, sould for the sume of	2.13. 4.
Item, a cupbord given to Margaret Fawell, sold for	1.13. 4.

Summa bonorum £51 5s 8d

Debts owen to the testator

Item, Wedo Ward	4. 0.
Item, Edward Elgie	3. 0. 0.
Item, Edward Marshall	13. 0.
Item, George Stanyne	4. 8. 0.
Item, Thomas Sadler	3. 0.
Item, John Bell	11.
Item, William Atkenson	2. 0.
Item, Arthure Stockdle	2. 6.

Summa £8 13s 4d

Summa totalis £59 19s 0d

Debts that the testor did owe
at his death

Imprimis, to John Surties	6. 0. 0.
Item, to Anas Surties	2. 0. 0.
Item, to John Hodgshon, for rent	3.13. 4.
Item, to Thomas Bowebancke & Rapp Blackwell for funerall expences	19. 6.
Item, his mortuall	10. 0.
Item, payd to a wife for the time that she did serve the beasts	2. 0.
Item, to Roger Woodmes for a chese	2. 6.
Item, for hempe which he bought at Thrisk	8. 0.
Item, for charges att Durham aboute the provinge of the will, going thrice there, for a proctor fee & for the probate of the will & tuicion of the children.	2. 0. 0.

Summa £15 15s 4d

[Paper, 2 ff., sewn. Will and inventory in similar hand to 5, 20 will, 26, 38 and 39 inventories, 40, 54 and 57.]

38   Jane Surties of Cockerton, 1615

Memerandum that Jannett Surtice, layt of Cockerton in the county of Durham, wedoe, did make hir last will and testament, the second day of January, 1614 [1615], in maner and forme following. First, she bequethed hir soule to Almighty God and hir body to be buryed in the church yeard att Darnton. Item, she did give and bequeth to Margert Fawall, daughter, to hir sone, Edmond Fawell, five shilling and to Mirioll Fawall, his eldest daughter, five shillinges and to Robert Fawell, son of Christofer Fawell, five shillinges and to Elezebeth Maison, her daughters daughter, five shillinges, and to every one of hir cossin Thomas Bowbancke, his six children, xijd, a peece. All the rest of hir goodes, movable and unmoveable, she give to hir daughter, Angnes Surtice, and she did appoynt hir cossin, Thomas Bowbancke, and Rawffe Blackwell to se that all those hir bequestes be executed. All these wordes or the effecet therof she repetted in the presentes of Thomas Bowbancke and Rawffe Blackwell, the day & year first above written.

[Paper, 1 f. In hand similar to will 39.]

A trew inventory of all the goodes, chattles & creditts
of Jene Surties of Cockerton, in the parrishe of
Darlington, wedo, lait deceassed, praysed the
xxj day of May, Anno Domini, 1615, by these iiij men,
Thomas Bowebancke, William Marshell, Rappe
Blackwell & William Staynsbey, as followeth

Imprimes, vj peece of puther, ij candlestickes, with other implementes 17. 0.
Item, j coverled, j wood trow 5. 0.
Item, ij potes, ij chistes, five sheetes, with other implementes 1.14. 4.
Item, j bed, j ammerye, with other implementes 1. 6. 8.

Debtes owen to the deceased

Item, thexecutors of Edmund Fawell 6. 0. 0.
Item, Gregory Mason 2. 5. 0.

Some £12 8s 0d

[*Paper, 1 f.. Inventory in hand similar to 5, 20 will , 26, 37, 39 inventory, 40, 54 and 57.*]

39   Ann Surtis of Cockerton, 1616

In the name of God, Amen, I, Ann Surtis, laite of Cockkerton within the county of Durham, spinster, but remayninge now within the Citie of Durham, beinge sicke in bodie but in good and perfect remembrance, thankes be to Almighty God, do make this my last will and testament, in mannor and forme followinge. First, I bequeethe my soule in to the handes of Almightie God, my only Maker and Redemer, by whome I trust and ame full assured to be saved, and my bodie to be buryed in the parishe church yard of St. Oswoolds in Durham if my friendes will not do so much as for to carrie me to Darlington to be buryed amonge my frindes their. Item, l give unto Elizabeth Mayson of Cockkerton, my sister doughter, xxˢ for a tokin. Item, l do give unto Robert Fawell of Cockkerton xxˢ for a tokine. Item, I do give unto Sebell Fawell of Cockkerton xxˢ for a tokine. Item, I do give unto the powre of Cockkerton vˢ, to praie for me. All the rest of my goodes, moveable and unmoveable, my debtes, legaces and funerall expences to be first paide and discharged, I do make John Walker of Elvitt within the suburbes of the Citie of Durham my full executor of this my last will and testament. In wytnesse whereof, I, the saide Ann Surtis, to this, my last will and testament, have sette my hand, the xth daie of September, 1616.

Ann: Surtis [*mark*]

Signed and delivered in the presentes of Symond [*mark*] Grenn, Thomas Wright [*mark*], Thomas Atkinsonn.

24 September 1616

[*Paper, 1 f., sewn to inventory, in hand similar to 38.*]

Ann inventore of all the goodes and chattles of Angnes
Surtise, lait of Cockerton, deceased, prayssed by these
fower men, Roger Heighington, Rawff Blackwell, John
Sympson and William Staynforth, as followeth

Imprimis, all hir wearing apperall	1. 0. 0.
Item, one cabbert and v chistes and a wood trowe	1. 0. 0.
Item, six peece of puther, two candlestickes, with other implementes	5. 0.
Item, one mattrice, one blankett, two coverledes, two happinges, one bolster, one cod and there quesshones	1.10. 0.
Item, one pare of bedstockes	1. 0.
Item, two pottes and a pane	10. 0.
Item, there pair of harden sheates and one pair of lyne fower pillowes, two towelles, one bord cloth	1.13. 4.

debtes owing to the deceased

Item, remaining in the cusstody of the Consistory Cowert att Durham.	6. 0. 0.
Item, Gregory Mayson, as by theis bills appeareth, whereof he saith he hath paid xlvˢ	3.15. 0.

The som in totall £15 14s 4d

John Simpson, Rawffe Blackwell [*mark*], Roger Heighington [*mark*], William
Staynforth [*mark*]

[*Paper, 1 f., sewn to will, in different hand similar to 5, 20 will , 26,
37, 38 inventory, 40, 54 and 57.*]

Memorandum, Mr Channcelor, within named, did order that John
Walker, executor of the testament of Agnes Suretisse, should paie vs
a peece unto Robert Fawell and Isobell Fawell, children of Margarett,
lait wiffe of Christofer Fawell of Cockerton and now the wyffe of
William Stainforth of Cockerton, which tenne shillinges was paid
accordinglie unto the said William for there use, the xxjst of March,
Anno Domini, &c., 1616. And, besides that xs, there was paid also by
the order of Mr. Channcelor to the handes of the said William
Stainforth for the use of the said children, fortie shillinges.

in the presence of us, hear undernamed, the said
some of fiftie shillinges was paid to the handes
of the said William, to the use of the said Robert
Fawell and Isabell Fawell, this xxvjᵗʰ of March,
Anno Domini, &c., 1616

Signed [*mark*] dictus William Stainforth

In the presentes of us, Thomas Chaytor
[*Paper, 1 f.*]

40 John Glover of Darlington, 1616

In the name of God, Amen, I, John Glover of Darlington within the county of Durham, weaver, being sicke in body but of sound and perfect remembrance, thankes be unto Almightie God, do make this my last will and testament in manner and fourme following. First, I bequeath my soule into the handes of my Redeemer, Jesus Christ, who with his pretious bloud bought me, and my body to be buryed in the churchyard of Darlington, neere unto the place wher my father was buryed. Item, I do give unto John Glover, the sone of Thomas Glover, my sonne & his heires, the house wherin Thomas Glover now dwellith (except the kitchin and stable belonging to the said house). Item, I do give to my sonne, Thomas Glover, all my loames and warkgere. Item, I do give to my sonne Thomas, my apprentice, Richard Collin, with his Indentures. Item, I do give unto my wife, Katheron Glover, the house I now dwell in for hir lyfe, with the stable and kitchin befour excepted. I do give unto my said wife all the household stuffe in my said house and kitchin. Also I do make my wife Katheron my sole executrix of this my last will & testament. In wittnes whereof, I have hereunto sett my hand, the 3 of October in the l3th year of his highnes reigne that now ys.

wittnesses herof Henry Oswalde, Lawrence Cateryck, John Glover [*mark*], Raphe Blackwell [*mark*].

[*Paper, 1 f.*]

An inventory of the goodes and chattels,
moveable and unmoveable, of John Glover
of Darneton, deceased, praised the second
of November / 1615 / by Lawrence Katericke,
Raphe Blackwell, Anthony Glover & Henry Elstoobe

In the haule

Imprimis, j long table with a frame, ij forrmes, one longsettle, j chaire, ij buffett stooles, j round table	13. 4.
Item, j shelfe, v queschions, j brasin morter, j paire of tables	6. 8.
Item, ij reckincrukes, j paire of tounges	2. 0.

In the buttery

Item, stanndes, blacke pottes & kannes	4. 0.
Item, xv peece of pewder, iij candlestickes, iij saltes	1. 0. 0.

In the chamber

Item, j cubbord, ij chestes	10. 0.
Item, his apparrell and purse	2. 0. 0.

In the lofte over the haulle

Item, iij stand bedes and iiij fetherbeddes, iij bolsters, iij coodes, vj coverlettes, iiij blankettes	8. 0. 0.
Item, ij tricklebeddes, ij matterresses, ij coverlettes, j blanckett, j bolster and one code	1. 0. 0.
Item, viij paire of linnen sheetes, ij paire of harden sheetes, v pillowbers	1. 0. 0.
Item, ij counters, j long chest, ij foormes, j table clothe	13. 4.

In the kitchin

Item, ij kettles, ij brasse pottes, j panne	1. 6. 8.
Item, j paire of rackes, ij speetes, j paire of tonges, j fire shovell, j reckin crooke, j broyling iron, j dreping pann, j chopping knyfe, j fleshe crooke	13. 4.
Item, j maskfatt, j guylfatt, j cooling tubb, ij standes, j beefe kitt, j brake, j chopping bord, with other wood vessell	10. 0.

In the worke house

Item, j coverlett, loome and a linne loome	2.11. 0.

In the stable

Item, j loode of hay	1. 0. 0.
Item, wood fleekes, with other wood	1. 0. 0.

Sum £22 9s 4d

Debtes owing by John Glover

To Lawrence Caterick	3. 0. 0.
For rent	1. 0. 0.

Lawrence Catryck, Raphe Blackwell, Anthony Glover, Henry Elstobb

[Paper, 1 f. Will and inventory in hand similar to 5, 20 will , 26, 37, 38 and 39 inventories, 54 and 57.]

41 Cuthbert Corneforth of Blackwell, 1616

In the name of God, Amen, the xxiiijth day of March, 1615, I, Cuthbert Corneforth of Blackwell in the county of Durham, yeoman, syck in body but of good & perfycte remembrance, thanks be to Allmyghtye God for the same, maketh this my last wyll & testament in maner & forme followinge. Fyrst & pryncypally, I do gyve & bequeth my soule into the handes of Allmyghtie God, my Maker and Creator, trustinge to fynde mercye & forgyveness at his handes (onely) for the merytes of Jesus Chrysts his sake, my onelye Savyor & Redemer and by no other meanes; and my body to the earth from whence yt came & to be buryed in the church of Darneton if God so provyde & in my father's grave. Item, I gyve and bequeth unto Agnes, my dowghter, lxx^{li} when she shalbe advanced in mariag or com & be xxj years of aige. Item, I do gyve & bequeth unto my dowghter, Margaret, lxx^{li} when she shalbe advanced in mariag or come & be of xxj yeres of aige. Item, I do gyve & bequeth unto my dowgter, Jane, lxx^{li} and that out of [mark]nfeild lands shalbe paid 6li yearlie for fowertene yeres to her also. Item, I do gyve & bequeth to my sone, Wylliam, xx^{li} and three cottages at Blackwell Towne ende, and xij acres of land belonginge unto them lyinge on the more, and xv acres of lande on the more and viij acres of land lyinge in the snype adioyninge to the more, Item, I gyve & bequeth unto my sonne, John, xx^{li}.* Item, I do gyve & bequeth to every of my servantes iij^s iiij^d. Item, I doe gyve & bequeth unto Thomas Cay one bay mayre which I did lett hym have. Item, I do gyve & bequeth to everye of his chyldren one gymer lambe, Item, I do gyve unto my sister, Margery Jackson, one angell in gold. Item, whereas my brother, John Jackson, ys indebted unto me at whytsonday next the some of xj^{li}, my wyll ys that the said xj^{li} shalbe distrybuted in this maner, videlicet, to George Jackson, sonn of the said John, xx^s, to Ralfe Jackson, sonn of the said John, iiij^{li}, to John & Lowrance Jackson, sonnes of the said John, eyther of them, fyftye shillings. And to Margeret, dowghter of the said John, xx^s. Item, I do gyve & bequethe unto my brother, Anthony Bramson, for a remembrance, x^s. Item, I do gyve Robert Ward x^s. Item, I do gyve to Edmond Elgye vj^s viij^d. Item, I do gyve and bequeth unto the use of the poore of Blackwell xl^s, besydes xl^s which my ffather did wyll, which iiij^{li} my wyll ys that the same shalbe lett forth to some honest man by the church wardens of this parishe and the interest thereof to be distrybuted yerely unto the poore of Blackwell for ever. Item, my wyll ys that my executor shall lende unto my nephew, Ralfe Jackeson, for ij^o yeares, xx^{li} without any consyderation payinge for the same, he lyinge in good and suffycient securytye to them for the payment of the said xx^{li} agayne at the ende of ij^o yeares. The resydew of all my goodes, both moveable & unmoveable, my debtes, legacyes & funerall discharged, I do gyve & bequeth unto Richard, Wylliam & John, my said sons, whome I do make joynt & sole executores of this my last wyll and testament. And I do request & appoynt my brother, Henry Bayles, and his sonne Ralfe, Franncis Foster and George Jackson, my nephew, to be supervysors of this my last wyll & testament and to se the same truly performed. And to be aydinge & assystinge unto my wyfe & chyldren and, as my trust ys in them, not to suffer them to take any wronge wherein they may ryght them and

I do gyve to everye of them, xx⁵. In wytnes hereof, I have sett my hande & seale in the presents of   Cuthbarte Corneforthe
Sealled & signed in the presence of Henry Bayles Francys Foster Robert Warde

*At this point is crossed out "Item, I gyve & bequeth unto my sonne Thomas xlˡⁱ"

[*Paper, 1 f., seal ; another copy on parchment, 1 m.*]

A codicill to be annexed unto my will, this day, alltered by myne owne deliberate mynd, upon my more deliberate & further consideracion of the advanncment of my yonger children, & for all their weales as I hope, made, sealled & subscribed unto this xvjth day of Aprill, Anno Domini, 1616

First, whereas heretofore I have surrendred certen of my copyhold landes to three, viz., to Henry Bailes Frannces Foster & John Jackson, my loving frendes, in trust as by the same doth appeare, to thusses in a wryting therof made & specified, the consideracion partly therin declared, as also hereby to be declared, viz., that they, the said feoffees, shall, immediatly after my decease, yearly reserve out of those copyhold landes to my son, Richard, intended during his non aige, being 7 years, the some of ten poundes and the same gyve, according to my reformed will, unto John, my yongest son, and for the yearlie revennewe thereof, over the same, I will shall go to my said feoffees & by them to be disposed of according to my secret will & trust to them wholie commytted. And whereas I have bargayned for certen copyhold land with one John Marknfeild, the which I intend, by godes grace, to be passed to the said feoffes, in like trust & upon like consideracion, to thuse of Thomas, my son, my will is also that they the said feoffees shall yearly, during the terme of xiiijtene yeres & within the nonaig of the said Thomas, my son, immediatly after my decease, reserve yearly sex poundes for & to thuse of Jane Cornforth, my yongest doughter, as in my said will is expressed. And whereas also my children in my said will mentyoned, being yong & tender, may som of them, by the good pleasour of god, dy & depart this present lyff before they or som of them accomplish their full aige, by reason whereof the portions to sutch of them dewe may make discention amongst the rest for clearing whereof my will is that the goodes of sutch to be departed shall only go & come to my other children survyving & to none other. Also I gyve & bequith to the son of Christofer Foster, whom I christened, vs.

Cuthbarte Corneforthe

Sealled & subscribed before us John Marknfeild [*mark*], Francys Foster, Raphe Bayles, Robert Warde.

[*Paper, 1 f., seal ; another copy on parchment, 1 m.*]

An inventory of all the goods, chattells and creditts
of Cuthbert Corneforth of Blackwell,
in the county of Durham,
dasceased, praysed the vij day
of Maij, 1616, by Thomas Ritcheson,
Christofor Rytcheson, John Warde &
John Markinfeild, as followeth

Imprimis, vj oxen	25. 0. 0.
Item, ij° stottes	6.13. 4.
Item, xj kye & a bull	30. 0. 0.
Item, ij° mayres & a horse	8. 0. 0.
Item, iiij°ʳ yonge horses	6.13. 4.
Item, ij° steeres & ij° whyes	8. 0. 0.
Item, vij styrkes	10.10. 0.
Item, xxviij ewes & lambes	10.10. 0.
Item, xxᵗⁱᵉ ewes & lambes	12. 0. 0.
Item, xxviij hogges & tuppes	9.16. 0.
Item, corne in the barne	16. 0. 0.
Item, corne on the grownde	70. 0. 0.
Item, hay in the barne	30. 0. 0.
Item, iiij°ʳ swyne	2. 0. 0.
Item, tymber wodd & other wodd, viij stees & a rayle staggarth	3. 6. 8.
Item, in the ox howse, two cubbordes & 4 chystes	16. 0.
Item, a servantes bed & clothes	8. 0.
Item, 4 loode saddelles and ij° rydinge saddles	13. 4.
Item, waynes & wayne geare, plowes & plow geare, silmes & all other things belonginge to husbrandry	11. 0. 0.

In the hall howse

Item, ij° cubbordes	4. 0. 0.
Item, one table & a counter, 4 chayres, 6 quissions and two formes	1. 0. 0.
Item, xxj puther dublers and a bason, with other candlestyckes, saltes and pynte pottes	3. 6. 8.
Item, 3 payre of tonges, v speetes, racking crookes and certain kytchyn stuffe	1. 3. 4.

In the chamber
Item, one cubborte one lyvery table, one chist, 4 peaces of puther,
  4 sawcers, 2 candlestyckes, 2 saltes, 2 quissinges, a buffett stole & a
  chamber pott   1.10. 0.

In the parler
Item, one table & frame, 3 chayres, 8 buffet stolles, a table cloth &
  one buffet forme   1.13. 0.
Item, x quissinges   10. 0.
Item, one cubbord & bason & ure   1. 0. 0.
Item, one ffether bed, beds and bedclothes   2.13. 4.
Item, 5 coffers   16. 0.
Item, xj payer of lynn sheetes, vij pyllowbers   5. 0. 0.
Item, vj table clothes, 4 dussen of table napkins   2. 1. 0.
Item, 8 payre of harden sheetes, 3 table clothes   2.10. 0.

In the buttery
Item, 23 peaces of puther, 10 sawcers, 3 saltes   1. 3. 0.
Item, one great chyst, 4 barrelles and other hushowd stuffe   1. 0. 0.
Item, 5 sylver spones   1. 5. 0.
Item, 3 dussen of tynn spones   3. 0.

In the kytchyn
Item, one table, one cawell, one stone trow, & one wodd trow, one
  forme, & other wodd geare   1.10. 0.
Item, 3 caldrons, 2 kettlles   2.13. 4.
Item, 7 brasse pottes, 5 pannes and ij° posnettes   2.13. 4.

In the mylke howse
Item, certayne tables, bordes, barrelles, bowles & other stuff   1. 6. 8.

In the lofte over the howse
Item, wheat & rye   6. 0. 0.
Item, ottes   15. 0.
Item, malt   4.10. 0.
Item, one stand bed, fether bed and furnyture thereto belonginge   1. 6. 8.
Item, one tredle bed, fetherbed and furnyture thereto   1. 4. 0.
Item, one arke, 3 chystes and other implementes   1. 0. 0.
Item, one green rugge   1. 4. 0.
Item, one coverlet, a payre of blankettes, & 4 happins   2. 0. 0.
Item, one fetherbedd teek & coddes   18. 0.
Item, 3 fether coddes   13. 4.
In the lofte over the kytchyn
Item, grootes & pease   2. 0. 0.
Item, certayne garne, wooll, & other implementes   2.10. 0.
Item, a payre of cobirons   3. 4.
Item, one great arke, and certayne bread salt fleshe ...[faded]... 2.10. 0.

Item, gease & pullen	9. 0.
Item, 12 yeardes of seckwebb, one windowcloth, & 3 seckes and ijᵒ pookes	1. 6. 8.
Item, his purse, and his apparell & furnyture	35. 0. 0.

Some £340 2s 4d

debts awinge to the testator

Imprimis Roberte Browne	10. 6. 0.
Item, John Vaysy	6.12. 0.
Item, Robert Coundell	1. 0. 0.
Item, Thomas Pudsey	9. 0. 0.
Item, John Dennam	4.10.
Item, Thomas Gregory	8. 0.
Item, John Ritcheson	7. 6.
Item, Edward Thursbee	10.10. 0.
Item, John Hixon	5. 0.
Item, Steven Chambers	12. 0.
Item, Umfra hall	5. 0.
Item, John Linskell	1. 5.
Item, John Hodgeson	5. 0.
Item, Ralfe Coorser	5. 0.
Item, John Atkinson	1. 0. 0.
Item, Lawrance Elgie	7.10. 0.
Item, Cuthbert Gibson	1.10. 0.
Item, John Hodgeson & Edwarde Elge	8.16. 0.
Item, John Symson and ..[faded]... Dack	2. 5. 6.
Item, John Dobson and Robert Dobson	6. 0.
Item, Richard Garnet & Robert Garnet	5. 0. 0.
Item, Thomas Bowbank & Peter Bowbank	11. 0. 0.
Item, Christofor Garthorne	8.16. 0.
Item, Gregory Mayson & Thomas Mayson	3. 3. 4.
Item, Wylliam Staynsbee	4. 9. 0.
Item, John Herreson	2. 4. 0.
John Jackson	11. 0. 0.
Item, Edward Marshall & Thomas Marshall	3, 6. 0.
Item, John Garthorne & Christpher Garthorne	22. 0. 0.
Item, Lawrance Hobson	9. 0. 0.
Item, George Stanyne & Peter Stanyne	2.10. 0.
Item, Robert Garnet	3.11. 6.
Item, Henry Bayles	63. 0. 0.
Item, Ralfe Bayles, for a horse	6. 0. 0.
Item, Robert Dobson	2. 2. 0.
Item, Thomas Bowbank and Rappe Blackwell	12. 4. 0.
Item, Lawrance Staynesbie	22. 0. 0.
Item, John Symson	22. 0. 0.
Item, Mathew Dack	11. 0. 0.

Item, Thomas Bowbanke	11. 0. 0.
Item, Wylliam Marshall	3. 0. 0.
Item, Wylliam Tompson	2. 4. 0.
It{em George Staynynge	4. 8. 0.
Item, Ralfe Blackwell	2. 4. 0.
Item, John Garthorne	2. 4. 0.
Item, John Myddleton	21. 0. 0.
Item, John Jackson, more	10. 0. 0.
Item, John Atkenson & Thomas Colson	11. 0. 0.
Item, Robert Horner	4. 8. 0.
Item, James Johnson	1. 0. 0.
Item, Anthony Shorte	5.10. 0.
Item, Thomas Ke	3. 0, 0.
Item, John Hodgeson	2. 4. 0.
Item, James marshall	3. 6. 0.
Item, Ralfe gregorye	2.15. 0.
Item, Wylliam Staynsbee more	5.10. 0.
Item, Robert Dobson	19.16. 0.
Item, John Chambers	4. 0. 0.
Item, George Tayler	1. 2. 0.
Item, John Wethereld	4. 0. 0.
Item, John Markinfeild	6. 0. 0.
Item, John ..*[faded]*...	..*[illegible]*...
Item, Ralfe Coser	1. 2. 0.
Item, Ralfe Coser & Henry Staute	2. 4. 0.
Item, John Rutter	2. 2. 0.
Item, Edwarde Elgie	22. 0. 0.

Summa debitorum £478 15s 1d
Summa totalis £816 19s 5d

debtes owinge by the testator

Item, Ralfe Wyld	3. 0. 0.
Item, hys cosyn Ward	2. 0. 0.
Item, to his cosyn Ward syster	4. 0. 0.
Item, to Margery Jackson	10. 0. 0.
Item, to George Jackson	1. 0. 0.
Item, to Lawrance, Ralfe & John Jackson	9. 0. 0.
Item, to Thomas Bowbank	11. 0. 0.
Item, to the poore of Darneton	2. 0. 0.
Item, to Isabell Bayles	1. 0. 0.
Item, to Mary Askew	2. 0. 0.
Item, rentes	2. 1. 6.
Item, funerall expenses	9. 6. 8.
mortuary & layrestall	13. 4.

Somma £46 13s 6d *[deleted]*

[Parchment, 3 mm., sewn . Will and inventory in hand similar to 1, 2, 15, 16, 22, 24 will, 30, 32, 42 and 45 wills.]

42 Margery Lassells of Darlington, 1616

The 5th Junij 1616

In Dei nomine, Amen, I, Margery Lasselles, of Darlington in the county of Durham, wydow, sick in body but of good & perfect memory (praised be God), do make this my last will & testament in manner & forme folowing. First, I commyt my soule into the handes of Almighty God, my Creator & Redeemer, and my body to be buried in the parish church of Darlington afore said, and of my temporall goodes I thus dispose. First, to the poore people of Darnton parish xxx^s and to the poore people of Auckland parish, wher I was borne, xxx^s. Item, I gyve & bequyth to Rauph Bailes, the son of William Bayles deceased & my sister son, the howse, burgaig, tenement or messuage wherein John Bygot & my self nowe dwell in Darnton abovesaid, to have & to hold to him his heires & assigns for ever. Item, I gyve & bequyth to Elizabeth Bayles, my sister daughter, my close over the Skearne belonging to my said burgaig wherein I dwell, to have & to hold to her, her heires & assignes for ever. Item, I gyve & bequyth to Margret Bailes, the daughter of my said sister, the Armytage howse, garth & orchard therto belonging, to have & to hold to her, her heires and assigns for ever. Item, I gyve & bequyth to Elizabeth Jeffreyson, Michaell Jeffreyson doughter, xxx^{li}. Item, I will that to satisfie a bond, wherein I stand bound to gyve xx^{li} to the children of Rauf Mayson at my dying day, that Thomas Mayson, the son of the said Raufe Mayson, shall have v^{li} and that Anne, an other of the said Mayson children, shall have xv^{li}, in full dyscharge of the said xx^{li}. Item, I will & bequyth forever to remayne as heirlomes unto this howse, to the said Rauf Bayles, my round cubbard nowe standing in the hawle, a brasen morter & pestle. Item, I gyve to every child I cristened 12d a pece now lyving.

Item, I gyve to Mary Barnes, doughter of Tymothy Barnes, x^{li}.

Witnesses, Brian Grant, John Atkinson, Robert Warde .

Item, the said Margerie did give & bequeath the yearelie rent of the house, wherein John Bigott doth dwell, to Margaret Bales duringe the minoritie of Raph Bales, her brother.

Witnesses hereof, Brian Grant, John Atkinson, Elizabeth [mark] Barnes

debtes which she owes

to her syster Barnes	4. 5. 8.
to Robert Ward	1. 0. 0.

[Paper, 1 f. In hand similar to 1, 2, 15, 16, 22, 24 will, 30, 32, 41 and 45 wills.]

The inventorye of all the goodes, moveable and
unmoveable, quick and dead, of Margery Lasselles, lait of Darnton
wydow, deceased, praised by John Atkinson, Richard Boyes, William Lawson,
Robert Ward and Robert Printiz, the 12th day of June,
1616,

Imprimis, 25 napkins for table at	12. 6.
Item, 4 pece of nappery at	6. 0.
Item, a silver salt at	13. 4.
Item, 14 silver spoones	3. 0. 0.
Item, two silver cuppes	3. 6. 8.
Item, 12 paier of lynning sheetes	4. 0. 0.
Item, 10 paier of harden sheetes and a sheete	2.10.0.
Item, 12 pyllovers	10. 0.
Item, 3 bord cloothes of lynnen	6. 8.
Item, 2 lynne towells and v others	3. 4.
Item, a trunke, with lock and keas	6. 0.
Item, a morter and pestle	1.10. 0.
Item, a little morter and pestle	2. 0.
Item, a looking glasse	1. 6.
Item, a cubbard	1. 0. 0.
Item, a polke or cubbord, with little trifles in it	16. 8.
Item, 10 pece of pewther on the cubbord head	1.13. 4.
Item, 3 flaggyngs	12. 0.
Item, 3 pint pottes and a flaggyng of pewther	8. 0.
Item, a posset bowle of pewther	4. 0.
Item, an aquavite bottle, a shank panne and a skein of lace	2. 6.
Item, a brasse chafyndish and v brasse candlestickes	7. 0.
Item, 3 pewther candlestickes, a bason and ewer, 5 dishes, a plait,	
6 potting dishes	13. 0.
Item, a salt of pewther and 2 store potts and a head	1. 0.
Item, a paier of tables	2. 6.
Item, a brod chist and with kea	8. 0.
Item, a long settle and holdfast	10. 0.
Item, a standbed stead and all furniture to it	3. 6. 8.
Item, a tryndle bedd with all furniture	1.13. 4.
Item, one chamber pott	1. 0.
Item, a table cloth	5. 0.
Item, 2 three footed stooles and 3 quisshings, a chaier, with	
divers other little trifling thinges	5. 6.
Item, a lynnen wheele, one speate, a paier of racks, one paier	
of tonges, a paier of pottkilpes, a fyer shovell, a frying panne	11. 0.
Item, a pillion seat, a brandred	2. 0.
Item, divers little peces of wudd, with other little thinges	
of howshold	4. 0.

in the high chamber

Item, a bedd and bedstead, with furniture	2. 0. 0.
Item, an other beddstead, with clothes	2. 6.
Item, a livery cubbord, x quysshings and a limbeck	1. 2. 6.
Item, a counter, with covering	6. 8.
Item, 2 iron chymbneyes	3. 0.
Item, 9 pece of larg pewther and 9 pece of lesse	1. 4. 0.
Item, 15 sawcers	5. 0.
Item, 4 potting dishes and 2 chamber potts	2. 0.
Item, a chist	3. 4.
Item, 7 brasse potts and a chafer	2. 6. 8.
Item, 6 kettles	2.10. 0.
Item, divers other little tryflinges of howsehold	1. 0.

In the hall

Item, 20 pece of pewther, 2s pece	2. 0. 0.
Item, 20 pece of pewther, 16d pece	1. 6. 8.
Item, 20 plates and sawcers, 4d pece	6. 8.
Item, 2 basons and ewers	10. 0.
Item, 2 saltes of pewther	1. 0.
Item, 5 brasse candlestickes	6. 0.
Item, 2 pewther candlestickes	3. 0.
Item, 4 chamber pottes	3. 4.
Item, a cubbord	..[no entry]...
Item, 2 hand basons	3. 0.
Item, 2 pottle pottes, 3 livery pottes and 7 quart pottes	1. 0. 0.
Item, a laver of brasse	6. 8.
Item, a long table	1. 6. 8.
Item, a square table	10. 0.
Item, 3 buffet firmes	3. 0.
Item, a flanders chist	5. 0.
Item, all the iron with a chimbney	1. 0. 0.

in buttery

Item, a bey and other wudd	5. 0.

in the kittchin and brewhowse

Item, 2 dripping pannes	6. 0.
Item, 2 braying stones and a cawell	4. 0.
Item, a wurt stone and 3 drissing tables	10. 0.

the dark buttery

Item, 2 shelves, a cubbord, a bedstead, 2 chistes, a bread brake and a candlecase	1. 8. 8.

in the parlor

Item, a bedstead, with other furniture thereto belonging	4. 0. 0.
Item, a long table, 3 firmes and a buffet stoole	13. 4.
Item, a bedstead	13. 4.

in the chamber over hall, all thinges there

Item, a buffet firme, a livery table, 3 square stooles, with beddes & bedsteades	8. 0. 0.

in chamber over entry

Item, a bedd and bedstead	3. 0. 0.

in the kitchin chamber

Item, a table & frame with firmes, a bedd and bedstead with cloth	2.10. 0.
Item, 3 beddes and furniture	6. 0. 0.

in stable

Item, a ladder	10. 0.
Item, divers other thinges, in divers places, now remembred	5. 0.

Suma totalis 78 18s 10d

debtes owen to the deceased

Cuthbert Parkinson of Darlington	10. 0. 0.
Lancelott Hutton, a desperat debt	5. 0. 0.
Mr Hearon of Bowenfeild	5. 0. 0.
Thomas Norton	40. 0. 0.

[*Parchment, 2 mm., sewn, indented. In hand similar to 34 and inventory 45.*]

43 John Fawcet of Darlington, 1617

In the name of God, Amen, the 22º of Aprill, 1617, I, John Fawcet, of Darlington in the countie of Durham, cordiner, sicke in bodie but of good and perfect remembrance I give God most hartie thanckes, do mak this my last will and testament in maner and forme following. First, I commend my soule into the handes of Almighty God, my Creator and Redemer, and my body (if it please God to take me to his mercy) to be buried within the parish church or churchyard of Darlington, at the discrecon of myne executor. Item, I give and bequeath unto Agnes, now my wiefe, my now dwelling house in Darlington, with thappurtenances thereunto belonging, with a litle close which I purchased of Thomas Bland and Christopher Bland, adioyning upon Robert Ward of the south and Frances Foster upon the west and the Kinges street upon theast, for the term of her liefe

naturall. And after her deceasse, I give and bequeath the said house
and close, with their appurtenances whatsoever, to Oswold Fawcet,
my yongest sonne, his heires and assignes for ever. Item, I give and
bequeath unto my said sonne, Oswald, one skware table and a round
table, standing in the hall house, with a table now standing in the
low parlour, and frames to them belonging, with one paire of bed
stockes standing in the loft without the back doore, with condicion
that my will is, neverthelesse, that my said wiefe, Agnes, shall have
and enioy the use of the same during the terme of her liefe naturall.
Also, my will is further that Agnes, my said wiefe, and my said
sonne, Oswold, whome I purpose to make myne executor, shall (if
anie benefite of one annuall rent of xij^{li} per annum for certaine
yeares, yeat enduring joyntly to me and my cozan, James Eden,
belonging, befall dew to myne executor after the deceasse of the said
James) that then my said executors shall pay or cause to be paid
unto my sonnes, Christofer Fawcet, John Fawcet and Agnes
Hodgshon, my daughter, to every of them, sixe poundes a peece.
And if the benefite of the said annuitie shall not happen to fall before
the death and deceasse of my said wiefe, then my will is that my said
sonne, Oswold, shall pay or cause to be paid unto the said Christofer
and John, in liewe and consideracion of their ffiliall and childes
porcions, to either of them, fowre poundes a peece, and to the said
Agnes, my daughter, sixe poundes. The rest of all my goodes and
chattelles, moveable & unmoveable, not given and bequeathed, my
funerall expences, debts and legacies deducted, I give and bequeath
unto my said wiefe, Agnes, and Oswold Fawcet, my sonne, whome I
make my joynt executors of this my said last will and testament. In
witnes of these, whose names are hereunto subscribed, John Fawcet,
his marke. Witnesses hereof, Simon Giffard, Ralph Jackson, Lawrence
Catrayck, Thomas Nicholson, Richard [*mark*] Bullock, Richard
Pickeringe.

[*Paper, 1 f.*]

The inventarie of all and singular, the
goodes and chattelles, movable and unmovable, of John Fawcet
of Darlington, deceassed, praised the xiiijth day of May, Anno Domini,
1617, by Symon Giffard, gentleman, Richard Boyes, Henrie
Ellstobb and Cuthbert Hodgshon, cordiners, as followeth

In the hall house

first his apparrell and monie in his purse	6.13. 4.
Item, a longe table and a square table with frames	16. 0.

Item, twoe chayres, five buffett stooles and twoo other throwe
   stooles with other three litle stooles, a longe forme and a
   backe stoole   9. 0.
Item, an ambrie a long skelfe, with dishes & trenshers   5. 0.
Item, xxj^{to} peece of pewther, twoe brasse candlestickes, one pewther
   candlesticke, a pewther bowle, a chafinge dishe, two saltes and a
   potting dish   16. 0.
Item, three speetes, a halbart, a paire of iron rackes, two reckines,
   three paire of tonges, a fire shovell, a drepinge panne, a frying
   panne, a scummer, a baister, a fleshe crooke, with a paire of
   pott kilpes, and all other small trifles in the said hall house   1. 4. 0.

In the buttrie

Item, a cupbord, a presse, a table with a frame, with xvj^{tene}
   peece of pewther, a chamber pott, five candlestickes, with three
   saltes and halfe a dozen tynne spoones   2.15. 0.
Item, fower silver spones   1. 0. 0.
Item, a tubb with standes, barrelles, mylke bowles, a chirne, skelves
   and all other implementes in the said buttrie   15. 0.
Item, three cloths ..[*illegible*]... two towells and other napkines   5.10.

In the lowe parlour

Item, a table, with a frame   10. 0.
Item, a trickle bedd, a long setle, a chaire, a forme, a recking crooke
   and all other implementes in the said parlour   16. 0.

In the chamber over the hall house

Item, iiij^{er} paire of bedd stockes, two fether beddes with
   coverlettes, happines, blankettes, coddes & bolsters   3. 6. 8.
Item, three paire of lynnen sheetes, vj paire of samron sheetes
   and two paire of harden, with ten pillowberes   3. 0. 0.
Item, five chistes, with other implementes in the said chamber   10. 0.

In the chamber over the shopp

Item, v bedsteades, iiij^{er} fether beddes, vj coverlettes, vj blancketes,
   v happines, v bolsters and five coddes, with all other implementes
   therein   7. 0. 0.
Item, iiij^{er} carpet cushions   4. 0.

Implementes in the kitchinge

Item, three brasse pottes, three ketles and three pannes   2. 0. 0.
Item, a mask fatt, a cheese trough, thre skeeles, a stone troughe,
   with all the rest of other implementes therein   1. 0. 0.

Implementes in the chamber over the butterie

Item, viijth stones of tallowe, viij gallons of oyle   2. 0. 0.
Item, a liquor panne, three swalls, two tubbes, a paire of tresles,

a window cloth, twoe sackes, two riding sadles, with all other
implementes there   1. 0. 0.
In the chamber over the kitchinge
Item, one bedstead   10. 0.
Item, twoe coverlettes   3. 4.
Item, an arke, a swall, three hundret lattes, a grindstone, with
forkes, spades, teams and other implementes therein   2. 0. 0.

In the stable
Item, a racke and a peece of wood, with jeastes and other
implementes there.   10. 0.

In the further litle stable
Item, xx^{tie} boordes, xxj jeastes, vij scoathes, iiij^{er} railles, a grindstone
with a trough, a horseheck and other implementes there   1. 6. 8.

In the kilne
Item, an old kilne haire with other implementes and a bucket
with rope and a trough stone   6. 8.
Item, compost in the yard   5. 0.

In the shopp
Item, xix^{tene} paire of maid boates, iiij^{er} dozen of maid shoes, five
paire of children shoes, xx^{tie} paire of unmaid boates, with other
broken lether, with all the shopp geare   12.10. 0.
Item, one brewing leade   1. 6. 8.
Item, one cart with wheles and a cowp carte   1. 0. 0.
Item, iiij^{er} hennes and a cocke   2. 6.

Chattells in the feildes
first, haye in the staggarth with Railles about the same   1.13. 4.
Item, sixe kyne and two calves   18. 0. 0.
Item, one horse and a mare   6. 0. 0.

Somma £82 0s 0d

debtes owen to the deceassed
first, John Brewer   10. 0.
Item, William Allon   2. 0.
Item, Ralfe Corser   4. 4.
Item, William Goldsbrough   4. 8.
Item, Myles Atkinson   2. 0.
Item, Alice Stubbes   2. 0.
Item, Grace Gregorie   2. 0.
Item, John Wrightson   1.10.
Item, Mr. Marmaduke Wivill   2. 8.
Item, Richard Thaddie   8. 0.

Item, Vincent Fearre	2. 6.
Item, Phillipp Johnson	2. 2.
Item, Thomas Wellfatt	5. 0.
Item, Christofer Threlkelt	2. 8.
Item, William Robson	2. 4.
Item, Thomas Collson	8. 8.
Item, William Garrie	2. 3.
Item, Henrie Ellstobb	1. 0. 0.

Suma debitorum debentium testatoris £4 5s 1d
Summa totalis £86 5s 1d

Debita debentes per Testatorem

first, to Lawrence Catheryck	15. 2. 6.
Item, to Widowe Edward	10. 0. 0.
Item, to companie of thoccupacion	2. 0. 5.
Item, to Richard Boyes	16. 2.
Item, to Thomas Hodgshon, his grandchild	2. 0. 0.

Sume debitorum debentium per testatorem £29 19s 1d
Summa totalis debitis deductis £56 6s 0d

desperate debtes owen to the testator

In primis, Edmunde Blande	2. 4.
Item, Robert Brasse	7. 4.
Item, Thomas Deaneham	8. 0.
Item, the said Thomas Deaneham, for which Richard	
Bullocke is pledge	5. 0.
Item, James Drybecke	4. 3.
Item, Robert Bell	2. 6.
Item, ...[faded]... Husband	4. 4.
Item, John Killinghall	8. 0.
Item, John Newby	11. 0.
Item, John Raine	6. 0.
Item, Edwarde Holme	1. 4.
Item, Ralfe Hindmers	1. 0.
Item, Edwarde Marshall	3. 0.
Item, Thomas Marshall	2. 8.
Item, Gyles Smith	2. 0.
Item, Peter Simpson	2. 0.
Item, Thomas Messenger	1.10.
Item, Nicholas Brafferton	2. 4.
Item, Hugh Browne	4. 0.
Item, John Willson	8. 2.

Suma £4 7s 1d

[Parchment, 2 mm., sewn, indented. Will and inventory in hand similar to 6, 10, 11, 12, 14 inventory, 23, 27 will, 28, 35, 36 will, 44, 46, 48 will, 49, 50, 51 and 56.]

44 StephenWard of Blackwell, 1617

In the name of God, Amen, the xviijth day of December, 1616, I, Stephen Warde of Blackwell in the countie of Durham, yeoman, sicke in bodye but of good and perfect remembrance I give God most hartie thancks, doe make this my last will and testament, in manner and forme followinge. First, I commend my soule into the handes of Almightie God and his Sonne, Jhesu Christ, my Creator and Redeemer, by and throughe whose precious death and passionn I faithfullie beleeve to be saved, and my bodie, if it please God to take me to his mercy, to be buried at the South portch doore of the parish church of Darlington, as neare unto my lait deceassed parents as cann convenientlie be devised. Item, I give to the poore of the parish of Darlington, to be distributed at the discrecionn of John Midletonn and Thomas Emerson, fiftie shillinges. Item, I give to my godchild, Stephen Potter, sonne of Thomas Potter, sixe and twentie shillinges, eight pence, to be paid him by my executors, or their gardiners or tutors, at his accomplishment of one and twentie yeares, upon his acquittance for the same. The rest of all and singular my goodes and chattelles, not given nor bequeathed, my debtes, legacies and funerall expences deducted and dischardged, I give and bequeath unto my five yongest childrenn, that is to say, Ralfe Ward, Christofer Ward, John Ward, Stephen Warde and the yonge infant nowe newlie borne, as yeat not baptised, whome I make joynt executors of this my said last will and testament, humblie entreatinge Thomas Emerson and John Midleton the yonger, of Gillinge, to be supervisores of this my said will and to se the execucionn performed, accordinge to the true intent and meaninge of the same. In witnes whereof, I, the said Stephen Ward, to this my said last will and testament, have set my hand and seall, the day and yeare first abovesaid. Witnesses hereof, John Midleton, senior, Thomas Emerson, John Midleton, junior, Richarde Pickeringe and Leonard Emerson.

[*Paper*, 1 *f.*]

A trewe inventarie of all and singular, the goodes and
chattelles, moveable and unmoveable, of Stephen Ward
of Blackwell, lait deceassed, praised the xxij[th] day of
Februarie, 1616[1617], by Thomas Emerson, John Midleton, thelder,
and John Midleton, the yonger, and George Patteson, as followeth

First, his purse and apparell	10. 4. 6.
Item one leverey cuppbord, with bason and ewer and cushions and two table cloathes	1. 8. 0.

Item, one table, a chaire, three chistes and twoe coffers	1. 0. 0.
Item, nyne cushions	10. 0.
Item, in woollen cloth	1. 5. 4.
Item, one truckle bedd, furnished	3.10. 0.
Item, sixe buffet stooles & one brush	9. 0.
Item, lynnen in one chist	3. 0. 0.
Item, in beefe	1. 3. 8.
Item, xxviij^th peece of pewther, xj sawcers, vj candlestickes, two quart pottes, one chamber pott, two saltes, two pewther pottes and two dozen of spoones	3. 4. 0.
Item, two cuppbordes, one chist, a table, twoe formes and one chayre & a cradle	2.10. 0.
Item, two paire of rackes, two speetes and two reckincrokes and two paire of tonges	8. 4.
Item, iiij^er salt fishes	4. 0.
Item, one corslet with a pyke	1.10. 0.
Item, necessarie implementes in the buttery	1. 0. 0.
Item, the brasse vessell	4.13. 8.
Item, one bedd, with clothes and boards, and tubbs in the lowe house	1. 0. 0.
Item, another bedd in the loft, with bolsters and cloathes	3. 0. 0.
Item, one chist, with aples	13. 4.
Item, in iron geare and grotes & one baskett	1. 4. 4.
Item, sackes, poakes and tubbes, with other Implementes	1. 5. 0.
Item, more in tubbes, with one troughstone	13. 4.
Item, in coales	1. 0. 0.
Item, the servantes bedds, one paire of wheles with sadles and boardes and roopes and other thinges in the oxehouse	1.13. 4.
Item, one paire of oxe harrowes, one cowpe, sixe plough teames & two calves	1.15. 4.
Item, one payre of bound wheles, one waine, with old wood and harrowes	2. 5. 0.
Item, fower oxen	20. 0. 0.
Item, five swine	1.10. 0.
Item, fower kyne	13. 0. 0.
Item, sixe yonge beastes	11. 0. 0.
Item, one horse and twoe mares	8. 6. 8.
Item, one bee hive	10. 0.
Item, one paire of wheles, bound	3.10. 0.
Item, twoe geese, one gander, eight hennes and a cocke	9. 0.
Item, thirteene sheepe	5. 7. 0.
Item, in wheat and rye in the barne	13. 0. 0.
Item, thirtie threaves of bigge	14. 0. 0.
Item, in beanes and pease	2. 0. 0.
Item, the hardcorne on the grounde	20. 0. 0.
Item, tenn ewes	3. 0. 0.
Item, in hay	5. 0. 0.
Item, one plough and plough geare	14. 0.

Item, in threshed corne   4. 0.

Suma Bonorum £166 0s 6d

debtes owen to the testator at the time of his death
as followeth

first, Mr Anthonie Catherick, thelder	22. 0. 0.
Item, Richard Smith of Thorneton	66. 0. 0.
Item, Cuthbert Robinson of Cockerton	11. 0. 0.
Item, William Marshall of the same	15. 0. 0.
Item, the said William Marshall, more	10. 0. 0.
Item, John Manfeild of Aldbrough	15. 0. 0.
Item, Lawrence Stainsbie	11. 0. 0.
Item, Edward Elgee	11. 0. 0.
Item, John Midleton, the yonger	22. 0. 0.
Item, Thomas Gregorie	4. 8. 0.
Item, John Atkinson of litle Stainton	24. 3. 3.
Item, Richard Willson of Girsbie	6.12. 0.
Item, John Jackson of Cowpen	2. 0. 0.
Item, Widow Patteson of Redworth	8. 0. 0.
Item, her sonne George Patteson	4. 3. 8.
Item, John Dunne of Midridge	4. 0. 0.
Item, Thomas Garthwait	1. 0. 0.
Item, George Goundrie	1. 0. 0.
Item, Henrie Dobson	1. 0. 0.
Item, Christofer Piburne	1. 0. 0.
Item, Peter Wawbancke of Pearcebridge	5. 0. 0.
Item, William Simpson	6.10. 0.
Item, Robert Dobson for six peckes of bigge	6. 8.
Item, the said Robert Dobson for a bushell of beanes	5. 0.
Item, Anthonie Sotheron	7. 0.
Item, William Stainsbie	5.14. 8.
Item, Mr Garnet	2. 0. 0.
Item, the said Mr Garnet, a bowll of rye and a bushell of wheat	18. 0.
Item, more, for plowing tenn dayes and a halfe	1.11. 6.
Item, Richard Robinson of Cunscliffe	5. 0. 0.
Item, Henrie Simpson	3.13. 4.
Item, William Robinson	5. 0.
Item, the said William, more for a firrdaill	1. 8.

Suma debitorum debentium Testator £271 19s 10d

Suma Totalis £438 0s 4d

John Middltonn, Thomas Emerson, George Pattesonne, John Middletonn

[*Paper, 2 ff., sewn, indented. Will and inventory in hand similar to 6, 10, 11,
12, 14 inventory, 23, 27 will, 28, 35, 36, 43, 46, 48 will, 49, 50, 51 and 56.*]

45 Christopher Foster of Darlington, 1618

In the name of God, Amen, I, Christofer Foster of Darlington in the county of Durham, butcher, sick in body but of good & perfect remembrance, praised be God, do make this my last will & testament in manner folowing. First & principally, I bequyth my soule into the handes of Almighty God, my Saviour & Redemour, & my body to be buryed within the church yeard of Darlington & of my temporall goodes I thus dispose. I do gyve & bequyth to fower of my yongest children, to ich of them, v^{li} vj^s viij^d apece, viz., Margaret, Marke, John & Peter. Item, I gyve unto Frannces, my eldest son, xls. The rest of my goods unbequythed, my debts paid, my funerall expences deducted & dischardged, I gyve unto Jennet, nowe my wyf, whome I make sole executor of this my will dayted this xvijth day of March, Anno Domini, 1617, per computationem Angliae.

Christofer foster [*mark*]

Wytnesses: Robert Warde, Francys Foster, William Sober [*mark*].

[*Paper, 1 f. In hand similar to 1, 2, 15, 16, 22, 24 will, 30, 32, 41 and 42 will.*]

The inventorye of all the goods, moveable and unmoveable,
quyck and dead, of Christofor Foster, lait of Darlington, butcher,
deceased, praysed by Frannces Foster, Robert Shutt, Robert
Ward and John Burne, the vijth day of July, 1618, in manner
as followeth, viz.,

In primis, in the hawle, a cubbord	1. 0. 0.
Item, ij square tables and a counter	13. 4.
Item, a long settle	5. 0.
Item, x pece of pewther	1. 0. 0.
Item, ij pewther candlestickes, 5 pewther saltes & 2 drinking cuppes	4. 8.
Item, one brasse candlestick, a drinking cupp & a bottle	1. 4.
Item, 5 sacers, a chaier, a firme, 3 buffettes stooles and a little child chaire	6.11.
Item, a frying panne, a paier of rackes, a speete, 2 paier of potkilps, a broyle yron, 2 reckon crookes, a paier of tongs and a braying trowgh	7. 8.
Item, 4^r quysshinges and a brush	2. 6.

In the buttery
Item, 20 bowles of wudd, a skeele, a syle, a chirne, 2 kittes, 2 gallon
  pottes, 2 doozen trenchers, 2 dublers, 3 sawcers, a chopping knyfe   12. 9.

in the kitchin
Item, 2 kettles, 2 pannes & 2 pottes   1. 5. 0.
Item, a spynnyng wheele, a stand, a bedstead, with 2 happinges, a
  sheete and a blankett   11. 6.
Item, a swale of wudd   1. 0.
Item, 5 bordes and a firme   2. 0.

in the chamber
Item, his apparell   3. 0. 0.
Item, a bedstead & the bedding belonging it   2. 6. 8.
Item, a square table & a cheist   10. 0.
Item, a troklebed, 3 little chists & 2 buffettes   8. 0.
Item, 12 fleeces of wull   18. 0.
Item, 2 happyns, a coverlett, 3 koddes & a quishing   18. 0.
Item, a kytt & ten score of garne, a temps, 3 pookes, 2 sackes
  & a reale   1. 2. 4.
Item, a paier of garne wyndowes as windlestock   4.
Item, 6 lynne sheetes, 13 harden sheetes, 6 codwares, 3 towells, 2
  bordclothes, a doozen of napkins, fryng for a bedd, 2 drinking
  napkins   4. 0. 0.
Item, a table cloth, a sword, 3 cheeces, a skep & 2 looves   3. 0.
Item, fower kyne, a stirk & xj ewes at   15.13. 4.
Item, a swyne at   6. 0.
Item, in other little implementes not remembred with his shopp geare   5. 0.
Item, in ready money   20. 0. 0
Item, in haye   2. 0. 0.
£58 4s 4d

debts owen to him
Roberte Shutt   14. 0. 0.
John Burnet, yonger   3. 8. 0.
John Bradley   3. 0. 0.
Peter Glover   1. 1. 4.
Richard Bullock   17. 0.
Elizabeth Wudd   1. 6. 8.
William Burnet   14. 3.
Mr Salkeld   8. 0.
£24 15s 3d

Summa totalis £82 19s 7d

[*Parchment, 1 m., indented. In hand similar to 34 and inventory 42.*]

46 John Corker alias Headlam of Darlington, 1619/20 *[filed under 1619]*

In the name of God, Amen, the xxiiij^th daie of January, 1619 [1620], I, John Corker, alias Headlam, of Darlington in the countie of Durham, weaver, sicke in bodie but of good and perfect remembrance, I give God most hartie thanckes, doe make this my last will and testament in maner and forme following, that is to say, first, I give and bequeath my soule into the handes of Almighty God and his Sonne Jhesus Christ, through whose death and passion I hope to be saved, and my bodie to be buried within the parish church yeard of Darlington, at the discrecion of my freindes. Item, I give & bequeath unto Jennet Headlam, my mother, for and towardes her maintennance during her liefe, three poundes with condicion that the said Jennet shall give and bequeath whatsoever thereof shall remaine in her handes unspent, to Michaell Corker, my sonne. Item, my will is that Elizabeth, now my wiefe, shall have the full thirde parte of all my goodes and chattells in respect of her widow right, according to the comon course of widows right in such cases used. The rest of all and singular my goodes and chattelles whatsoever, moveable and unmoveable, not given nor bequeathed, my debtes and funerall expences deducted and discharged, I give unto my sonne, Michaell Corker, whome I make sole executor of this my said last will and testament, appoynting my brother, Toby Corker, as his tutor and gardiner for and during the said Mychaell his minority & nonage, the law so permitting.

John Corker alias Headlam [*mark*]

witnesses hereof, William Corker [*mark*], Ralf Preston [*mark*], Edwarde Coates [*mark*], Toby Corker [*mark*], Richard Pickeringe.

debtes owen to the testator	
First, Lawrence Stainsby	7. 0. 0.
Item, Christofer Robinson	2. 0. 0.
William Coates and Margaret, his wief	3. 0. 0.
William Taylor of Burtry house	3. 0. 0.
Item, John Pollson and Isabell Shawter	2. 0. 0.
Item, John Raine	12. 0.
Thomas Huchinson of Well Rawe	1. 0. 0.
Item, James Pape	11. 0.
Item, in his purse	8. 0. 0.
Item, Richard Appleby	1. 0. 0.

[Paper, 1 f., and another copy on parchment, 1 m., both in the same hand.]

A true inventarie of all and singular, the goodes and chattelles,
moveable and unmoveable, of John Corker, alias Headlam, of
Darlington, in the countie of Durham, weaver, lait deceassed,
praised the twelfth day of Februarie, Anno Domini, 1619 [1620],
by Conand Lawson, William Corker, Ralfe Preston and
Edwarde Coates, as followeth,

First, his apparrel	11. 0.
Item, monie in his purse	8.14. 0.
Item, a soe, a tubb and two kimlines, with a bowle weight	3. 0.
Item, a spynning whele with thappurtenances	1. 0.
Item, a cupborde, fower dublers, three candlestickes, two saltes and a pewther cuppe	1.10. 0.
Item, an old ambrie, a great ketle with a lesse, two litle pannes with a frying panne and two pewter dublers and three litle sawcers	16. 4.
Item, a cawell, with a brasse pott, a panne and other small implementes, as trenshers and dishes	5. 0.
Item, a table and frame, two formes with a chayre and stooles, with an old chist	5. 0.
Item, five busshelles of wheat and rye	16. 0.
Item, in coales	4. 0.
Item, eight score of harden and lynnen yarne	12. 0.
Item, fourtie yeardes of harden	1. 6. 8.
Item, nyntene yardes of unbleacht lynne	18. 0.
Item, sixtene yardes of course harden	7. 0.
Item, another peece of harden of six yardes and a half	3. 0.
Item, seaven quarters of lynnen	2. 0.
Item, fower yardes of lynnen and samron	3. 0.
Item, nine yardes of samron	6. 8.
Item, three whole webbes of lynnen, contayninge three score yardes or thereaboutes	3. 6. 8.
Item, three peeces more of lynnen, contayning fower and twentie yardes	1. 4. 0.
Item, sixe yardes and a half of hempline	5. 0.
Item, twoe peeces of two yardes	1. 8.
Item, more a yeard and a halfe	1. 0.
Item, fower yeards of linsey woolasey	4. 0.
Item, a yeard and three quarters of woollen cloth	2.11.
Item, a peece of plaine white contayning a yarde and a half	2. 6.
Item, another peece of white kersey	5. 0.
Item, three yardes three quarters of linsey wallasey	5. 0.
Item, two poundes of heckled flaxe	1. 8.
Item, two webbes more of harden at the weavers	1. 0. 0.
Item, in lynnen sheetes, towelles and pillowberes	9. 0.
Item, two samron sheetes	2. 4.
Item, three hennes and a chicken	2. 0.

Sum £25 2s 5d

debtes owen to the testator at the time of his
death as followeth

first Lawrence Stainsby	8. 0. 0.
Item, Christofer Robinson	2. 0. 0.
Item, William Coates and Margaret, his wiefe	3. 0. 0.
Item, William Tayler of Burtriehouse	3. 0. 0.
Item, John Powllson and Isabell shawter	2. 0. 0.
Item, John Raine	12. 0.
Item, Thomas Huchinson of Wellrawe	1. 0. 0.
Item, James Pape	11. 0.
Item, Richard Applebie	1. 0. 0.
Item, Margaret Potter	5. 0.
Item, Robert Thompson, currier	3. 4.
Item, Humfrey Hall	2. 1.
Item, Elinor Dennis, widowe	2. 0.
Item, Myles Collson	1. 4.
Item, Thomas Lumbley	1. 4.
Item, Mathew Corker	5. 0.
Item, Edwarde Coates	2. 2.
Item, Toby Corker	10. 0.
Item, John Stainsbie of Cockerton	3. 4.
Item, Arthure Swainston	2. 6.
Item, Parcy Marshall, alias Tipladie	3. 8.
Item, Agnes Gybsonn	1. 1.
Item, Henrie Appleby	8.
Item, Ralfe Preston	10. 0.
Item, Elizabeth Wood	1. 0. 0.
Item, John Spedlinge	1. 0.
Item, Jane Coltard, alias Snawdon	2. 0.

Summa debitorum £25 1s 6d

Summa totalis £50 3s 11d

[parchment, 1 m. Both wills and inventory in hand similar to 6, 10, 11, 12, 14 inventory, 23, 27 will, 28, 35, 36 will, 43, 44, 48 will, 49, 50, 51 and 56.]

47 William Sober of Darlington, 1620

In the name of God, Amen, I, William Sober, of Darlington within the country of Durham, yeoman, being sicke in body but yet, God be praised, of good and perfect memory, doe make this my last will and testament, the xxvth day of ...[torn]... in the yeare of our Lord God, one thousand, six hundreth and twentyeth, in manner and forme following. First, I committ my soule to Almighty God, our Heavenly

Father, trusting and fully assuring myselfe to possesse the heavenly joyes of His kingdome, through the merits of His Sonne, Jesus Christ, my Saviour and Redeemer, and my body to be buryed within the churcheyeard of Darlington aforesaid. Item, I give and bequeath unto Richard Sober, my fourth sonne, two branded oxen, one stand bedd with a teaster standing in the chamber over the shopp, & one fether bedd, two coverletts, two blancketts, one bolster, & two codds, all the which before recyted premisses doe belong to the same bedd, and also one square or round table with the frame standing in the same chamber, which is over the shopp, in leiwe and consideracion of his bringing upp, and towards the setting & putting him to a trade or occupation. Item, I give unto Agnes Sober, my youngest daughter, ...[torn]... branded cow which I have had of hers long in my hands, given to her by the last will and testament of one Hellen Browne, late of Bongate, deceased. Item, I give and bequeath unto Christopher Sober, my youngest sonne, two black oxen towards his bringing upp and putting him to a traide or occupation. Item, I give and bequeath unto Jayne Sober, my wiffe, one whyte gray meare. Item, I give and bequeath unto Agnes Pearson, my daughter and wyffe unto Thomas Pearson of Darlington aforesaid, the some of vj^s viij^d, in full satisfaction of her filyall & childs parte, by reason she hath had a sufficient & reasonable porcion of me heretofore. Item, I give and bequeath unto Francis Grante of Darlington aforesaid the some of iij^s iiij^d. All the rest of my goods & chattells, moveable and immoveable, not before named, given, nor bequeathed, my debts, leagacyes, and funerall expences payed and discharged, I give unto Jayne Sober, my wife, Ralphe Sober, William Sober, John Sober, Richard Sober, Christopher Sober, my sonnes, Johne Sober and Agnes Sober, my daughters, to be equally distributed and devided amongst them, Jayne Sober my wyffe first having her thirds forth of the same, according to ...[torn]... custom of this countrey. And also I doe make and ordeyne Richard Sober, my fowrth sonne, my full and sole executor ...[two lines torn and missing]... Christofer Wilkenson of Barton to take some paynes to see my ...[torn]... of this same my will & testament. In witnes whereof, that this is my full mynde & trewe will which is before rehearsed in this writeing, I have hereunto sett my hand the ...[torn]... and yeare first above written. In the presence of John Bygott [mark], Thomas Lumley and Franncis Grante.

     William Sober

[Paper, 1 f.]

A true and perfect inventorie of the goods
and chattles of William Sober of Darlington, deceassed,
taken the xxijth day of June, 1620, and praised
by Thomas Emerson, John Bygoot, Henry Elstob
and Anthony Raynton

Imprimis, in his purse and his apparell in the house	...[*damaged*]...
Item, xxiiijth peece of pewther wyne quarte pott, one other quarte pott, ij chamber potts, two pewther candlesticks, iij plats, ij pewther tuns, ij saucers	...[*damaged*]...
Item, two tables with frames, one buffet forme, other little formes, one stoole without ...[*torn*]... one chayre, one payre of tables, one shelve, one shelve, iij quishens	10. 0.
Item, two cubbards	1. 2. 0.
Item, one recken crooke and one payre of tonngs	1. 6.

In the camber over the shoope

Item, one bedstead, one square table with frames, one fether bed, ij blanckets, one bolster, one codd, ij Coverletts	2. 3. 4.
Item, one bedstead with a paynted cloth teaster, one fetherbedd, one codd & one bolster, ij coverlets, one blanckett	1. 0. 0.
Item, one payre of lynnen sheets, ij pyllebears	12. 0.
Item, one chayre, one forme, one little coffer and one ould cheste and one olde wheele	1. 8.

In the camber over the house

Item, one happinge & one old codd	1. 4.
Item, one table, with frame & one forme	4. 0.
Item, one old windowe cloth and iij sacks	3. 4.
Item, one kettle & one bushell, one old chest, with other housements	10. 8.

In the buttre

Item, all the wood vessell there, with other implements	10. 0.

In the kitchinge

Item, one brasse pott, iij kettles, ij pannes, one chaffing dishe, iij candlestickes	2. 0. 0.
Item, two paire iron racks, one spyt and one recken crooke	8. 0.
Item, one old matteryss, with other huslement	2. 0.
Item, certaine old wood vessell, ij old load sadles, one cheese presse, ij hay racks	10. 0.

Item, one stone throughe	1. 0.
Item, lyme and stones	2. 0.
Item, the irone plowe geare with irone teames, one poake, ij harrowes, one hay spade, one woorke dragge & other irone wayne geare	13. 4.

In the stable

Item, one steighe and other wood powles	7. 0.
Item, two old ploughes, one harrowe, other implements	4. 0.
Item, one payre of waynne blaydes, one coope wayne with a payre of irone bound wheles	2.10. 0.
Item, certaine mault & oats in a chamber att Jo Bygotts	7.10. 0.
Item, two branded oxen	8.10. 0.
Item, one branded cowe & caffe	2. 0. 0.
Item, two other cowes and one younge calfe	3.16. 7.
Item, one cowe and ij ...[illegible]... piggs	16. 0.
Item, one graye meare	4. 0. 0.
Item, one bay nagge	2. 1. 8.
Item, xxviij cutts of harden yearne & j^{li} of wollen yearne	2. 2.

In the house in Bongaite

Item, one kylne haire ...[illegible]...	1. 4.
Item, the bigg sowen in the ...[illegible]... of the backsid of the house in Bongayte	1. 0. 0.
Item, vj scoores bushells of otes, in Bongaite house	7. 0. 0.
Item, xj hennes & j cocke	5. 0.
Item, wynter corne & waire corne in Grange Cloose	10. 0. 0.
Item, the corne in the feilde called Bennet	9. 0. 0.
Item, the corne in the kylne garth	1.13. 4.
Item, the corne in the Becke field	9. 6. 8.

Summa [blank]

Debts owing to the said William Sober, deceased

Imprimis, John Potter of Stappleton	10. 0.
Item, Christofer Wilkinson for a yoake of oxen	7.10. 0.

desperate debtes

Imprimis, Christofor Fawcett	6. 0. 0.
Item, of one Ferrar, the hinde, at Oxen Flatte	5. 0.

Summa [blank]

Summa totalis bonorum et Creditorum [blank]

Debts owing by William Sober at the
day of his death

Imprimis, for the rent of Graynge Close	2.15. 0.
Item, for rent of the Beck feilde	2. 0. 0.
Item, for rent to Mr Knype	6. 0. 0.
Item, for rent of the lyttle garth	1. 0. 0.
Item, owing to Thomas Orray	8. 0.
Item, owinge to Ralphe Jackson	2. 8.
Item, owinge to Mr Tymothie Huton	2. 4.
Item, owinge to Edward Clawson	11. 0. 0.
Item, owinge to his sonne William Sober	4.13. 4.
Item, owinge to his sonne, John Sober	1.10. 0.
Item, owinge to Thomas Gregorie, more for rent of Grainge Cloos	1. 7. 0.
Item, more for Beckfeilde rent	1. 0. 0.
Item, spent in sewte for Beckfeilde rent	2. 6. 0.
Item, for reaping & shearinge the corne and leading and ...[word unintelligible]... the same	4. 0. 0.
Item, for funerall expenses &c	2. 0. 0.
Item, for ingrossing the will and inventory and for a proctor's fees to Thomas Kinge	5.10.
Item, for charges of the probacion of the will and ...[illegible]... of the saime etc and for a comicion	6. 8.

[Parchment, 2 mm., formerly sewn. Will and inventory in different hands.]

48 Mary Throckmortonof Darlington, 1620

In the name of God, Amen, the sixtenth daie of September in the eightenth yeare of the reigne of our most gracious soveraigne lord, James, by the grace of God, king of England, France and Ireland, defender of the faith &c., and of Scotland the fower and fiftie, 1620, I, Marie Throckmorton of Darlington in the countie of Durham, widowe, lait wiefe and relict of Robert Throckmorton, clarke, deceassed, sicke in bodie but of good and perfect remembrance, I give God most hartie thanckes, do make this my last will and testament in maner and forme followinge. First, I give and bequeath my soule into the hands of Almighty God and His Sonne, Jhesus Christ, my Creatour and Redeemer ...[torn]... through whose meritts and death I onelie hope to be saved, and my body, when it please Him to take me to His mercy, to be buried in the parish church or churchyard of Darlington or elswhere as it shall please myne executor hereafter named. And, whereas I have no children unprovided saving onely my sonne, John Throckmorton, whome tender love and affection doth most constraine me to remember to distribute such worldlie goodes as God haith bestowed upon me towardes his better preferment and advancement, therefore I do hereby freelie give and bequeath unto my said sonne, John Throckmorton, all and singular my goodes and chattelles, moveable and unmoveable, quicke and dead, of what kinde, nature, qualitie or propertie soever they be, and in whose handes soever they remaine, within the realme of England, and hereby do ordaine, make and constitute him my full and whole executor of this, my said last will and testament, my debtes and funerall expences deducted. In witnes whereof, I, the said Mary Throckmorton, to this my said last will and testament, have set my hand and seall, the daie and yeare first above said, in the presence of these whose names are underwritten,

Mary Throckmorton

Witnesses hereof, Charles Husband, Phillipp Johnson.

[Paper, 1 f., seal. In hand similar to 6, 10, 11, 12, 14 inventory, 23, 27 will, 35, 36 will, 43, 44, 46, 49, 50, 51 and 56.]

An inventorye of all the goodes and
chattels of Mrs Mary Throckmorton,
late of Darlington, wedow, deceased, and
praised by Mr John Lisle, Mr
Timothy Barnes, Mr Simon Gifford
and Mr Thomas Barnes, as followeth,
the 7th December, 1620

Imprimis, her purse and her apparrell	10. 0. 0.

In the kitchinge

Imprimis, 88 pieces of pewder	3. 6. 8.
Ittem, 5 brasse potes	2. 6. 8.
Ittem, 1 brasse candlesticke	1. 6.
Ittem, 4 pans & a kettell	1. 6. 8.
Ittem, a pestell, a morter, & a frijngpan	6. 8.
Ittem, 2 drippen pans, a girdell Iron, a gibcrooke, a shreddinge knife & a choppinge knife	10. 0.
Ittem, 1 pair of racks & 2 spites	13. 4.
Ittem, a napkin presse, a lanthorne, & a pair of playing tables	6. 8.
Ittem, a trunnell bed, with the furniture	1. 0. 0.
Ittem, certaine trenchers with the case	4. 0.
Ittem, a table, a liverie cubbert, with other implementes	13. 4.

£20 15s 6d

In the hall house

Ittem, 1 table, 3 buffet stooles, 1 fourme, 2 chaires and one little stool	1. 0. 0.
Ittem, a carpett, a cubbord cloath, and 8 quishons	1.13. 4.
Ittem, a presse cubbord, a Flanders hist, & a deske	1. 0. 0.
Ittem, a stand bed, a trunnel bed, with furniture	10. 0. 0.
Ittem, 4 maps, 2 window curtaines, an iron rod, with the hangings, & a grate	13. 4.
Ittem, a seinge glasse, a table with the Tenn Comandementes, a brush, a pair of bellowes, 2 littel casketes with other implementes	8. 0.

£14 14s 8d

In the green chamber

Ittem, a green bed with the furniture	6. 0. 0.
Ittem, 16 pair off fff lin sheates	16. 0. 0.
Ittem, 3 pair of lin sheates of 3 bredes	2. 0. 0.
Ittem, 3 fff holland sheates of thre bredes	4. 0. 0.
Ittem, 7 pair of lin pillebeers	2. 0. 0.
Ittem, a suite of diaper	1.10. 0.
Ittem, a diaper cloth more	10. 0.
Ittem, 6 table cloaths	1. 3. 4.
Ittem, 4 dozen of napkings	2. 0. 0.
Ittem, 3 lin cubbert cloaths, laced & fringed, 3 towels and a drinking napking, with a white worke	2. 0. 0.
Ittem, 3 lin sheats for a trunnel bed	10. 0.
Ittem, 7 strakinge sheats	1. 0. 0.
Ittem, 3 course napkins, 3 towels, & a tablecloth	5. 0.
Ittem, 8 nedleworke quishons & one long on	5. 0. 0.
Ittem, a cubbord cloath, with a green silke fringe	2. 6. 8.
Ittem, 1 pair of vallence of nedleworke, unfinished	2. 0. 0.
Ittem, 2 long quishons of nedleworke, unfinished	1.13. 4.
Ittem, 5 square quishons unfinished	2. 0. 0.
Ittem, a border of nedleworke, unfinished, for a cubbord cloath	13. 4.
Ittem, 14 silver spoones	6. 0. 0.
Ittem, a double gilt salt & a white silver bowle	6. 0. 0.
Ittem, 3 casketes & a nutt	6. 8.
Ittem, a counter & a carpett	5. 0.
Ittem, a liverie cubbert, with a fringed carpet	13. 4.
Ittem, a cruell	3. 4.
Ittem, a bason & ewer, 3 juges, one quishon, & three Cheinar dishes	10. 0.
Ittem, glasse bottles, with certaine glasses	5. 0.
Ittem, a clock & a sunne dyall	2. 0. 0.
Ittem, a cubbert & cloath	6. 8.
Ittem, 6 yardes of linnen cloth	10. 0.
Ittem, a Flannders chist, & a trunke	1. 0. 0.
Ittem, a temps & certaine hangings	2. 6.

£70 14s 2d

The chamber over the hall

Ittem, a bedd with the furniture	4.10. 0.
Ittem, a presse, the cloath, with implementes	10. 0.
Ittem, a candlecase	2. 0. 0.

£7 0s 0d

The street chamber

Ittem, a cubboord, with a cloath	10. 0.
Item, 2 stone of line	6.16. 0.
Ittem, a bedd, with the furniture	3. 6. 8.
Ittem, a tabel, a cloath, a chist, a spinning wheel, a leaden weight, with other implements	1. 0. 0.

£5 12s 8d

In the stabel

Ittem, 2 doores, 3 swales, a tubb, with other peces of wood	13. 4.
Ittem, coales	3. 4.

16s 8d

Ittem, bondes bills, & debtes	200. 0. 0.

Summa £380 3s 8d

Debtes owinge by the testator to her sonne, John Throckemorton	160. 0. 0.
Ittem, more to be paid to the said John Throckemorton, by legasie given by his father, to be paid by the said Mrs Mary Throckemorton	50. 0. 0.
Ittem, her funerall expences	9. 0. 0.

£219 0s 0d

Summa dew to the testator £161. 3. 8.

John Lisle Timothy Barnes Simon Gyffard

[*Parchment, 1 m. In different hand*.]

49 John Atkinson of Darlington, 1622

In the name of God, Amen, and the fowertenth daie of December, 1622, I, John Atkinson of Bongait in Darlington in the countie of Durham, gentleman, weake in bodie yeat of good and perfect remembrance (God be praised), and knowing the certaintie of death and the time to be uncertaine, do willinglie and with a free hart render and give againe into the handes of my most mercifull God and Creator my spirit which He, of His fatherly goodnes, gave unto me when He first fashioned me in my mothers wombe, making me a living and a reasonable creature, nothing doubting but that for His infinite mercies sake, set forth in the precious bloud of His deerelie beloved Sonne, Jhesus Christ, my onely Saviour and Redemer, He will receive my soule into His glorie and place it in the company of the heavenly angels and blessed saintes. And, for my bodie, I commend it to the earth frome whence it came, nothing doubting but according to the article of my faith, at the great daie of the generall resurrection, to receive the same againe by the mighty power of God wherewith He is able to subdew all things to Himselfe. And for the dispocion of the temporall goods, wherewith God haith indued me, I dispose of in manner and ...[torn]... following, revoking and annihilating all former willes whatsoever, heretofore by me maid. And making and ordey...[torn]... this my last will and testament in manner and forme as followeth. Item, I give and bequaeth to the poore people of the parish of Darlington, to be disposed amongst them by the discrecion of my trustie good freindes, Ralfe Blackwell and my cosine, Bulmer Priscott, iij^{li}. Item, I give to my ancient servant, Meriol Wilkinson, in regard of her true and faithfull service heretofore to me performed and done as also to be done, tenn poundes of lawfull English monie and my best cupbord, standing now in my low parlor wherein I lye, and my cowe withall my pewther vessell. Item, I give to my servant, Richard Browne, for and in recompence of his good and faithfull service to me, likewise heretofore done and to be done, six poundes of lawfull English monie, with my bay horse and colinge furniture and my newest browne cloake. Item, I give and bequeath unto Mr Robert Hope, now curate at Darlington, one halfe peece or, in liew thereof, xj^s in monie. Item, I give and bequeath unto my cosine, Bulmer Priscott, another halfe peece or, in liew thereof, xj^s in monie. Item, I give and bequeath to my nephew, John Ward, the annuall rent of fourtie shillinges to be issuing and paid forth yearely of my house or tenement with thappurtenances in Skinnergait, lait purchased of John Gaye, to be paid him in manner and forme following, after my deceasse; that is to say, quarterly and everie quarter of a yeare, tenn shillinges for and during the terme of the liefe naturall of the said John Warde. Item, I give and bequeath to the three children of Christofer Ward, my nephew deceassed, being two sonnes and a daughter, to each of them, fourtie shillinges a peece, to helpe to binde them apprentices. Item, I give more unto my said nephewe, John Warde, twentie nobles. The rest of all and singular my goodes and chattelles, landes, tenementes and hereditamentes whatsoever, not already given and bequeathed, my debtes, legacies and funerall expences discharged paid and deducted, I freely give and bequeath unto my nephew, Thomas Atkinson of Glasgow in the realme of Scotland, whome I make my sole heire and executor of this my said last will and testament, with my last request to him, in all love, to performe these my bequestes faithfully and truely, as my trust is, according to the true meaning hereof. In witnes whereof I, the said John Atkinson, to these presentes have subscribed my name with myne owne hand and sette my seall, the day and yeare first abovesaid, in the presence of these witnesses underwritten,

John Atkinson

Witnesses hereof, Thomas Midleton [mark], Gabriell Wilkinson [mark], Richard Browne [mark], Richard Pickeringe.

[*Paper, 1 f.*]

An inventarie of all & singular, the goodes and chattells, moveable and unmoveable, of John Atkinson of Bongaite, in Darlington, deceassed, praised the xijth daie of Februarie, Anno Domini, 1622[1623], by Thomas Emerson, Ralfe Blackwell, Thomas Husband and Lawrence Cathericke, as followeth,

Imprimis, his purse and apparrell	13. 6. 8.
Item, one browne cloake given his man	13. 4.
Item, one gowne, one pettycote, two kirtles and other implementes belonging to a woman	5. 0. 0.
Item, one longe silke cushion and fower lesse	2. 0. 0.
Item, one fetherbedd teeke	14. 0.
Item, twoe oversea coveringes	5. 0. 0.
Item, one oversea table cloth	1. 0. 0.
Item, two coverlettes	1.10. 0.
Item, one paire of blankettes	16. 0.
Item, one paire of fustaine blanckettes	13. 0.
Item, three trunckes	2. 0. 0.
Item, two fetherbeddes, one bolster & 4 coddes	2.10. 0.
Item, one rugge, 3 coverlettes, one paire of blanckettes and one paire of pladd sheetes	2.10. 0.
Item, two canobies, one beddstocke	1. 6. 8.
Item, two paire of sheetes, 3 pillowberes	1. 0. 0.

Item, one table cloth and tenn napkines	1. 0. 0.
Item, three long towelles and 2 harden towelles and one harden table cloth	10. 0.
Item, three chaires	13. 4.
Item, 3 bowes and 2 quivers & arrowes	10. 0.
Item, one cupborde	13. 4.
Item, one table with cloth and a liverey cupbord	1. 0. 0.
Item, three deskes, fower buffet stooles, with some iron geare	1. 0. 0.
Item, one close stoole, one iron chymeney and a reckinge crooke & one paire of tonges	10. 0.
Item, in glasses	10. 0.
Item, one paire of larke leaves	6. 8.
Item, one glasse lanthorne, one towell sticke	3. 0.
Item, his librarie	6. 0. 0.
Item, one citharon and recorder	6. 8.
Item, one horse locke and boxes, with other implementes	10. 0.
Item, one sworde and three daggers & gyrdle	1. 0. 0.
Item, one silver bowle and broken silver	15. 0.
Item, 2 skelfes and one litle coffer	1. 6.

In the hall

Item, xix^{ene} pewther dublers, vj plates, xvj^{ene} sawcers, one bason and ewer, fower candlestickes, fower pewther pottes, two salts, two chamber pottes, one custarde dish	4. 0. 0.
Item, one still and a limbecke	10. 0.
Item, 2 brass morters, 2 pestilles, xiiij^{ene} brasse candlestickes, one chafing dishe, with other implementes	1. 0. 0.
Item, 4er brasse pottes and 2 pannes	1.10. 0.
Item, 3 speetes, one paire of iron rackes, one dripping panne, one frying panne, 2 reckine crookes, one fire shovell, one paire of tonges, with other implementes	16. 0.
Item, one table and frame with two buffit formes and one long setle	13. 4.
Item, one cupborde	13. 4.
Item, a cawell, one grate for bread, one skelfe and two chaires	8. 0.
Item, one hatchet, an ech, one stone hammer with wombles and other implementes of iron	10. 0.
Item, a fowlling peece, with her furniture	1. 0. 0.
Item, one corslett, a halbart, 2 iron forkes, and other stafes	1. 6. 8.
Item, x cushions, one skeele & other implementes	10. 0.
Item, in the buttrie, one kimlinge, 2 barrelles, one flackett, 3 skelfes, with other implementes	10. 0.
Item, one masking tubb, one great kimling, one seycke loome and a gavelocke, with other implementes there	13. 4.
Item, a chist, with an olde ambrie	5. 0.
Item, a litle truckle bedd, a chist & other thinges, with a mattrisse	13. 4.
Item, in the stable, one carte and furniture	2. 0. 0.

Item, in old woode and fleakes	10. 0.
Item, one bay horse and coaling furniture	4. 0. 0.
Item, in the kilne, 3 tubbes, 2 soes, 5 sackes and kylne hayre, with other implementes	13. 4.
Item, in Thomas Willsons house, one table with frame, one forme & one swall	8. 0.
Item, in bigge, malt & oate malt	36. 0. 0.
Item, a bushell, a pecke, a windowcloth, 3 skeppes, 2 shovelles, 3 bordes, with other implementes	11. 6.

Summa bonorum £118 8s 0d

debts owing to the testator

John Colson for one load of malt	10. 0.
Item, Mathew lorriman, x bushelles of Malt	2. 1. 0.
Item, Jennet Adamson, for iiij^{er} quarters	6.16. 0.
Item, Thomas Willson, for one quarter	1.16. 0.
Item, John Short, for malt	1. 4. 0.
Item, Thomas Glover, in lent monie	2. 0.
Item, Richard Thaddie, in lent mony	5. 0.

Somma debitorum £12 14s 0d
Summa totalis £131 2s 0d

desperate debtes

John Hudson	18. 0.
Item, Roger Jewitt	10. 0.
Item, Robert Coundell	1.10. 0.
Item, Anthony Simson	5. 0.

Somma £3 13s 0d

debtes owen by the testator

Item, to John Hodgshon	1. 0. 0.
Item, to Thomas Richardson	6. 0.
Item, to Thomas Gregorie	4. 0.

Some £1 10s 0d

The funerall expences disbursed as followeth

Item, 2 gallons of wyne	6. 8.
Item, halfe a pound of sugar	8.
Item, for cheeses	1. 3. 0.
Item, for breade	16. 0.
Item, to Mr Hope, for his fees	5. 4.
Item, to Richard Pickeringe, for his fees	2. 0.
Item, to Edwarde Coates	2. 0.
Item, for the coffine and the making thereof	2.10.
Item, for candles	1.10.

Item, to the ringers	10. 6.
Item, paid to the poore people of the parish	3. 0. 0.
Item, paid to John Smart for his journey into Scotland to give	
knowledge to thexecutor	13. 4.
Item, for the wynding of the corpes	6.
Item, for two pound of soape	8.

Some £7 1s 8d

The charges of the probate of the testament

[*Paper, 3 ff., sewn. Will and inventory in hand similar to 6, 10, 11, 12, 14 inventory, 23, 27 will, 28, 35, 36 will, 43, 44, 46, 48 will, 50, 51 and 56.*]

50   George Marshall of Darlington, 1622 [1623]

In the name of God, Amen, the eleaventh daie of Januarie, 1622[1623], I, George Marshall of Darlington in the countie of Durham, yeoman, sicke in bodie but of good and perfect remembrance, I give God most hartie thanckes, do make this my last will and testament in maner and forme followinge. First, I commend my soule into the handes of Almightie God and his Sonne, Jhesus Christ, my Creator and onelie Savior and Redeemer, through whose merites, death and passion, I faithfullie hope to be saved, and my bodie, if it please God at this time to take me to his mercie, to be buried in the parish church or churchyard of Darlington aforesaid, at the discrecionn of my freindes. Item, I give to the poore people of the parish of Darlington five markes. Item, I give to my cosine, Jennet Ellstobbe, five shillinges. Item, I give to my sisters, Agnes Bellamie and Elizabeth Bellamies children, being in number eight, to each of them, sixe shillinges, eight pence a peece. Item, I give to Robert Stainton five shillinges. Item, I give and bequeath unto myne eldest sonne, John Marshall, for and towardes his better preferment in mariage in regard all my landes were estaited to certaine feoffees for uses, the some of ffourtie poundes in full consideracion of his whole filiall and childes porcionn, over and besides the possibilitie of my landes. Item, I give to my sonne, Thomas Marshall, one hundreth markes in full satisfaccion of his filiall and childes porcion. Item, I give and bequeath to Jennet Marshall, my daughter, fiftie poundes in full satisfaccion of her filiall and childes porcion. Item, I give to my sisters, Agnes and Elizabeth Bellamie, to either of them, a peece or xxs in monie. The rest

of all my goodes and chattells, moveable and unmoveable, not
given nor bequeathed, my debtes, legacies and funerall
expences deducted and dischardged, I give and bequeath to
Helen, my wiefe, to whome I whollie referre my trust and
confidence for theducacion of my children during their
minoritie, and do hereby make her my whole and sole
executrixe of this my said last will and testament, in testimonie
of the witnesses underwritten,

Lawrence Cayteryck, John Oswolde, Francis Cathericke, Thomas
Cathericke, Richard Pickering.

[*Paper, 1 f.*]

The inventarie of all and singular, the goodes & chattelles,
moveable and unmoveable, of George Marshall
of Darlington, in the countie of Durham, yeoman, deceassed, praised the xxiijth daie of Januarie, Anno Domini,
1622[1623], by Thomas Emerson, Francis Foster, John
Oswold and George Stevenson, as followeth,

First, monie in his purse and his apparell	4. 0. 0.
Item, in the forehouse, one cupbord	1.10. 0.
Item, pewter in the forehouse, with a brasse morter & candlestickes	
and saltes, with a glasse case and other implementes	3. 6. 8.
Item, two tables, 2 formes, 2 buffet stooles, a chaire and three skelfes	1. 6. 8.
Item, three cushions	2. 0.
Item, salt flesh hanging in the forehouse	6. 8.

In the loft above the low parlour

Item, 3 bedsteades with 2 fether beddes, 3 bolsters, five coddes, 4	
coverletts, 2 paire of blanketes and two happines	7.10. 0.
Item, more in the said lofte, 2 chistes	2. 0. 0.
Item, lether in the same lofte	2. 0. 0.
Item, fower pound of yarne in the same lofte, with one paire of	
sadle trees	5. 0.

in the lofte over the entrie

Item, one ryding sadle, with furniture and other implementes	13. 4.

In the low parlour

Item, one cupbord and pewter vessell upon it	2. 0. 0.
Item, one chaire, 3 buffet stooles and one dozen of cushions	1. 0. 0.
Item, one longe table, 2 formes & one table cloth, a truckle bedd,	
one coffer, with other implementes	13. 4.
Item, another coffer there, with all the lynnen in it	5. 0. 0.

In the kitching

Item, one cupbord with brasse, pewter, 2 rackes, two speetes and other implementes there	2.13. 4.

In the stable

Item, one arke and one kimlaie	10. 0.
Item, one mayre and 2 foales	4. 0. 0.
Item, fower kine and hay	8.10. 0.

Some £45 14s 0d

debtes owing to the testator
at the time of his death as followeth

Item, all the debtes in generall, contained in obligacions, amount to the some of	219. 6.10.

Item, debts owing, not contained in any specialty, as followeth

Item, Rowland Oswold	2. 0. 0.
Item, Marmaduke Willson	2. 0. 0.
Item, William Leadham	5. 6.

Somma totalis £269 6s 4d

funerall charges

Inprimis, to Mr Hope, for his buriall and funerall sermon	9. 6.
Item, to the clark, xij^d, & sexton, xij^d	2. 0.
Item, to the ringers	8. 6.
Item, given to the poore people in p.... dole	3. 6. 8.
Item, for bread and cheese	1.15. 0.
Item, for six peckes of malt	6. 9.
Item, for his funerall dinner at Peter Glovers	4.10. 8.
Item, for his coffin	5. 0.
Item, for the mortuarie	10. 0.
Item, for the lare stall	6. 8.
Item, to Richard Pickering, for writing the will and inventaries	3. 4.
Item, to the Church, for rent	6. 8.
Item, to his maid servant, for her wages	4. 0.

[*Paper, 1 f. Will and inventory in hand similar to 6, 10, 11, 12, 14 inventory, 23, 27 will, 28, 35, 36 will, 43, 44, 46, 48 will, 49, 51 and 56.*]

51 William Bower of Oxen-le-field, 1622

In the name of God, Amen, the thirtenth daie of March, in the xix^th yeare of the reigne of our most gracious soveraigne lord, James, by the grace of God, king of England, France and

Ireland, defender of the faith, &c., and of Scotland, the lvth,
1621, I, William Bower, thelder, of Oxenetfeild in the countie
of Durham, gentleman, not sicke but decrepit in the abilitie of
my bodie, and knowing that death is most certaine, and yeat
not knowinge the time when it shall please Almighty God to
call me to his mercie, and purposing to make tranquillitie
amongst those whome I leave to succeed, do make this my
last will and testament, absolutely revoking, frustrating, and
making voyd all former willes and testamentes heretofore maid
what so ever, in manner and forme following. First and
principallie, I comend my soule into the handes of my most
mercifull God and Saviour, Jhesus Christ, by whose onelie
sacrifice I doe verie faithfully assure my selfe of the
resurrection of my body, forgivenes of all my sinnes and liefe
immortall, and my bodie to be buried, when it shall so please
God to call me to His mercy, in the church or churchyarde of
my parish church of Darlington, at the discrecion of mine
executor hereafter nominated. And for my temporal goodes,
with the which it haith pleased God of his bountious goodnes
to indue me, I dispose of in maner and forme following. That
is to say, I give and bequeath to the poore people of the
parish of Darlington aforesaid five poundes. Item, I give and
bequeath to Simon Curwen and John Curwen, to either of
them, fourtie shillinges, & to my servant, Jane Chambers, xxx^s.
Item, I give unto my brother, Richard Bower, tenn poundes of
currant monie, with the one halfe of all myne apparrell,
meaning yeat hereby the meanest and coursest sort thereof.
Item, I further do hereby confirme unto the said Richard, my
brother, my burgage in Darlington, with thappurtennances (for
the terme of his liefe if he happen to survive me), now in the
tenure of Anthonie Adamson, and the revercion and remainder
of inheritance, after the longer liver of me and the said
Richard, to my nephew, William Bower, according to the true
intent of a deed of feoffement thereof already past, for thuses
therein intended. Item, I give and bequeath unto my said
nephew, William Bower, for and towardes his better preferment
and advancement in marriage, three score poundes of lawfull
English monie, withall thother moytie and one halfe of my
said apparrell, meaning the better sort thereof. Item, I doe
further give and bequeath to the said William Bower, my
nephewe, all such implementes of houshold stuffe as are now
standing and being in the house or burgage on the Head

Rawe in Darlington, now in thoccupacion of Robert Newton, which said house or burgage, with thappurtenances, I have likewise already by a former deed in writing, with livery and seizure there upon executed, given to the said William Bower, my nephewe, as thereby doth and may appeare, provided that the said William, in regard of these my legacies to him hereby bequeathed, shall not charge myne executores for the payment of any rent by me arreare for using of the malt loftes there, during my liefe time. Item, I give unto my kinsman and lait servant, William Rotheram, tenn poundes. Item, I give to my cossine, George Rotheram, xxx⁵. Item, I give unto my cosine, Bulmer Priscott, five poundes. Item, I give unto my servant, Thomas Garmise, three poundes. Item, I give and bequeath unto my brother, Richard Bower, the bed and bedstockes with furniture, which he now lyeth in. Item, I give and bequeath unto my nephewe, William Bower, all such implementes of houshold stuffe as are now remayning and being in the house wherein Anthonie Adamson now dwelleth in Darlington. Item, I give and bequeath unto my sonne-in-lawe, John Wilkinson, sixe daughters, three partes in fower partes, to be divided, of all and singular my houshold stuffe and implementes of houshold at Oxenetfeild, and the fourth part thereof I give and bequeath unto my said nephewe, William Bower, reserved out of the said fower partes the said legacie of bedd and bedclothes formerly given to my brother, Richard. Item, I give and bequeath unto my very loving and kind freindes, Mr Simon Giffard and John Atkinson, to either of them, a Jacobus peece of gold or, in liew therof, to either of them, xxii⁵ in monie. The rest of all and singular my goodes and chattelles, moveable and unmoveable, not yeat given nor bequeathed, my debtes and funerall expences deducted and discharged, I give and bequeath unto my grandchildren, vicz., Robert Jackson, sonne of Stephen Jackson by my daughter Margaret, Francis Anderson, Barbary Anderson and Anne Anderson, children of Roger Anderson begotten by my daughter, Jane Anderson, his lait wiefe, as also to the sixe children of my said sonne-in-lawe, John Wilkinson, that is to say, Mary Wilkinson, Elizabeth, Dorithy, Jane, Phillis and Katherine Wilkinson, to be equallie divided amongste them all, that is to say, to every of my said grandchildren, a like proporcion. Ordaining, making and constituting my said sonne-in-lawe, John Wilkinson, my sole executor of this my said last will and testament. In

testimonie whereof, I have hereunto subscribed my name with myne owne hand and sette my seall in the presence of these witnesses, witnesses hereof
William Bower
Ralph Jackson, John Ward, Anthonie Sotheron [*mark*], Richard Pickeringe

[*Paper, 1 f., seal*]

The inventarie of all and singular, the goodes and chattelles, moveable and unmoveable, of William Bower of Oxenetfeild, in the countie of Durham, gentleman, deceassed, praised the fourth daie of June, Anno Domini, 1622, by John Warde, Nicholas Bellsey, George Chipchase and George Bullman, yeomen, as followeth,

First, xx^tie kyne, with a bull & seaventene calves	52.10. 0.
Item, sixe oxen	26. 0. 0.
Item, fower stottes of three yeares old	9. 0. 0.
Item, twelve stottes of twoe yeares old	18. 0. 0.
Item, seaven whyes of two yeares old	12. 0. 0.
Item, eighteene stirkes of one yeares old	14. 8. 0.
Item, vij^xx and sixteene old sheepe	39. 0. 0.
Item, fower scoore and twelve lambes	13. 0. 0.
Item, three peeces of old hay	4. 0. 0.
Item, the cropp of corne, winter and ware, on thearth	30. 0. 0.
Item, in wooll	10. 0. 0.
Item, three longe waines, one paire of bound wheeles and two paire unbound, 2 Cowpes with stinges and waines, yoakes, teames and all other implementes belonging husbandrie	5. 0. 0.
Item, certain peeces of oake and ash wood, unwrought, with staggarth railles and some other peeces of wood	5. 0. 0.
Item, three swine, with other pultrie	2. 0. 0.
Item, v horses and mares	10. 0. 0.
Item, 2 corslettes, a coate of plait, one calliver, 2 litle fowling peeces, with furniture	3. 6. 8.
Item, in malt, about v quarters, with vj pound of hoppes	7. 0. 0.
Item, in coales	1. 0. 0.
Item, one beehive	10. 0.
Item, a Bible, with the booke of Martyres and other litle bookes	1. 0. 0.
Item, monie in his purse	40. 5. 7.

Implementes of houshold in the hall
First, two tables, a leverie cupbord, 3 chaires, tenn buffitt stooles, a cupbord with gallowbalkes, tonges and some other litle implementes   3. 0. 0.

In the litle parlor adioyning upon the hall
Item, one bedstead with fether bedd and furniture, one livery
   cupbord, a square table, fower cushions, with some other
   implementes   3. 0. 0.

In the lofte above the buttrie and foresaid parlor
Item, 2 bedstockes with furniture, one padd & some other small
   implementes   1.10. 0.

In the buttrie
Item, two silver bowlles and sixe silver spones   4. 0. 0.
Item, in pewther and brasse there   2.10. 0.
Item, a cupbord, with skelves, beare barrells and some other trifles   10. 0.

In the lowe parlor
Item, one fetherbedd, with bedstead and furniture thereupon   6.13. 4.
Item, one square table, a cupbord, a long wrought cushion, 3 chaires,
   3 stooles, a litle truncke, 2 other carpett cushions, 2 low stooles,
   with some other litle thinges there   2. 0. 0.
In the chamber over the lowe parlor
Item, one stand bed stockes with a truckle bedd, both furnished,
   with cloathes and fetherbeddes   5.10. 0.
Item, 3 dozen of napkins of lynnen, three lynnen table cloathes,
   contayning about three yardes a peece, one dyaper table cloath
   of lyke contentes, with 5 codwares   2. 6. 0.
Item, viij[th] paire of lynnen sheetes   4. 0. 0.
Item, one truncke, three Flanders chistes, 3 coffers, 2 buffett stooles,
   2 chaires, with a close stoole with some other implementes   1. 6. 8.

In the chamber over the hall
Item, two beddes furnished, a presse, a great chist, a kimline with
   salt flesh in it, 2 wanded baskettes and other implementes and
   tenn paire of harden sheetes   2.10. 0.
Item, more lynnen occupied daily about the house, vicz., a dozen
   of straking napkines & 7 hand towelles, 2 paire of lynnen sheetes,
   2 lynnen table cloathes and one odd lynnen sheet   1.10. 0.

In the kitchinge
Item, 2 great ketles, three lesse, v brasse pottes   3.13. 4.
Item, 3 speetes, 2 dreeping pannes, 2 reckinges, a paire of iron rackes,
   3 paire of potkilpes, a fyre shovell, a paire of tonges, a broyling iron
   with 2 litle pannes and a chafing dish   1. 0. 0.
Item, a kitching cubbord, 2 tables with brewing vesselles and other
   implementes in the kitching   13. 4.

In the milkhouse
Item, 2 chirnes, one butter kitt, 2 dozen of milk bowles, with
   skelves, cesfattes and other implementes there   1.10. 0.

In the chamber over the kitching
Item, 2 chistes, 2 tunnes, 4 sackes, one wyndring cloath, a tempse,
  with divers other implementes there   1.13. 4.

In Widow Adamsons house at Darnton
First, a bedstead, a fetherbedd, one bolster and 2 coddes, with a table
  and some other implementes there   2. 0. 0.

In Robert Newtons house at Darnton
Item, one bedstead, a cupbord, a long table, with a Flanders chist
  with some other thinges as sparres and such like   2. 0. 0.

Item, the deceassed, his apparrell in generall, woollen and
  lynnen and els what soever of that nature   10. 0. 0.

Somma totalis £365 16s 7d

[Paper, 2 ff., sewn. Will and inventory in hand similar to 6, 10, 11, 12, 14 inventory, 23, 27 will, 28, 35, 36 will, 43, 44, 46, 48 will, 49, 50 and 56.]

52 Robert Garnett, of Blackwell, 1622

An inventorie of all the goodes and
houshould stuffe that can be found
of Robert Garnets of Blackewell, late deceased

In primis, one leverra Cubbard	1.13. 4.
One stand bed	1.13. 4.
One chare	4. 0.
One buffet stole	1. 6.
One buffet firme and one bed poulter	5. 0.
One table frame	2. 0.
One broken coffer	4.
One chist	3. 0.
Sixe plough beames	3. 0.
One chese presse	1. 0.
Thre trow stones	2. 0.
One fleake	8.
For ould brush wood	6. 8.
For timber wood	2. 6. 8.
For thre pare of chaufed wheeles & the tiere stolen of them	3. 0.
One old wane soule	2. 0.
One old arke	2. 0.
One old cubbard and a choping bord	1. 6.

One gan of wheele fellies	4. 0.
For eight whele naves	3. 0.
One gan of wheele speakes	2. 0.
One buffet firme	1. 0.
One irand pot & a dreping pan	3. 0.
One chaufing dish, one pare of tongues, with other implements	2. 0.
Two ould counters, one old chist, one old bedstead, one butterie dore	6. 8.

The totall is £8 12s 8d

John Middleton   Petter Bowbancke [mark] Tobye Corker [mark] Charles
Robson [mark]

[Paper, 1 f.]

January 1622

Whereas sequestracion of the goodes and cattells of Robert Garnet,
late of Blackwell in the parish of Darlington, within the countie of
Durham, gentleman, deceased, was leytelye committed to Mistris
Ann Garnet, his wife, and, for soe much as the said Mistris Garnett
hath crediblie enformed us that much old wood and tymber which
was the said deceasedes and by her entred upon, by vertue of her
said sequestracion, doth lye without house or anie shelter and soe
subiect to stealth and in danger to spoile and rott and cannot be
gotten into anie harbor, we doe therefore thinke fitt and soe doe
order that the said implementes, which cannot with safetie be
preserved, shalbe forthwith solde by the said sequestratrix and the
monye by her to be receyved to be safelie preserved & keept for their
use to whome the same shall of right appertayne.

[The following occurs on the back of the sequestration.]

Thomas Pottes of Gateside, deceased
Roger Younger of Gateside, overman
Raphe Thompson of Over Heworth
Richard Wheldon of Cawsey, hard by Bemish
One   Savage of Gap Leases

These wills are unproved
Thomas Banckes
Robert White de Read Heugh in xvij Janu
John Eltringham de Whagg, def
Dorothy Hamble de Whickham, def

[Paper, 1 f. In different hand from inventory.]

53 Thomas Hodgson of Morton near Darlington, 1621/2 [*filed under 1621*]

In the name of God, Amen, I, Thomas Hodshon of Mortonn nigh unto Darlington, being syke in body but in perfitt remembrance, prayssed be God, I do heare make my last will and testament the xx^th vij day of January, in the yeare of our lord God, 1621[1622]. In primis, I give and be queth my soulle unto Allmighty God, which was my Maker and my Redeemer, and my body to be buried in the church or church yeard of Darlington, to the discrestion of my executors, and, for the porcion of worldly goodes which God haith sent me, I give and bequeth them, as ffolloweth. I give and be queth unto Edmond Hodshon, my sonn, and Agnis Hodshon, my daughter, to eyther of them, xx^li, whom I do make my sooll and joynt executors. Also, I give and bequeth unto William Hodshon, my sonn, x^li. I give and bequeth unto Thomas Faussett, sonn to Oswould Fausset of Darlington, x^li. I give and bequeth unto Thomas Gilpin, son to Anthony Gilpin of Cokerton, x^s. My detts and leogosses payd and my funneralls discharged, and all the reste of goodes I give unto my seaven children to be devided by equall portions, that is to say, to the sayd Edmond and Agnis Hodshon and the sayd William Hodshon & Elinor, Elizabeth, Margerie & Jane Hodgshon.

In witness of this, my last will and testament, Richard Ingldew, John Oswould, Anthony Gilpin, Christofer Wilkinson.

[*Paper, 1 f. In hand similar to 25.*]

An inventory of all the goodes and chattels of
Thomas Hodgson, late of Morton, deceased, praised
by Richard Morley, Henry Oswold, Frances Katerick,
Richard Ingledew and Christofer Wilkinson,
the 31 of January, 1621 [1622]

Christofer Wilkinson, Richard Ingledewe, Francis Cathericke, Richard Morley

Att Morton in the haule

Imprimis, his apparrell & purse	6.13. 8.
Item, ij cubbordes	2. 1. 0.
Item, xxj peece of pewder	1. 1. 0.
Item, v brasse candlestickes, j pewder candlestick	5. 0.
Item, j muskett with furniture	1. 0. 0.
Item, ij chaires, j fourme, j great tubb	5. 0.
Item, x boordes	6. 8.

In the buttery

Item, iij skeeles, ij barrels, iij standes, ij kemlinges, ij ...[*unintelligible*]... v cheesefattes, xviij boulles, v kannes	10. 0.
Item, iiij kettles, iij brasse potts, j iron pott, with other litle implementes	1.14. 0.

In the parlour

Item, j table, j tablecloth	5. 0.
Item, iij cheeses	4. 0.
Item, j bedstock, j fetherbed, iij coverlettes, j paire of blankettes	1. 0. 0.
Item, ij coverlettes, ij coodes	4. 0.
Item, iij paire of linnen sheetes	10. 0.
Item, v paire of harden sheetes	10. 0.
Item, vij tablenapkins	2. 0.
Item, v pellibes	5. 0.
Item, j tempes	8.
Item, iij boordes	1. 6.
Item, lynne and yarne	13. 4.

In the chamber above the parlour

Item, j truckle bed, j coverlett, v happins, iij coodes, j fetherbed teeke	15. 0.
Item, j trucklebed ij happins, with other implementes	6. 8.
Item, iij speetes, j paire of rackes, ij paire of tonnges, j broyling iron, ij Recken crookes	8. 0.
Item, ij choppin knifes, ij paire of pottkilpes	2. 0.
Item, ij payre of wollen cards, ij paire of shews	2. 0.

Att Cockerton

Item, j cubbord, j caule, one stand bed, j arke, ij ladders, j table	3. 0. 0.

Att Morton and Cockerton

Item, j iron bound wayne with wheeles, 1 coupe	3. 0. 0.
Item, j wayne, with wollen wheeles	13. 4.
Item, iij skoore yewes	21. 0. 0.
Item, forty weathers	13. 6. 8.
Item, 39 hogges	10. 0. 0.
Item, xj litle stootes	11. 0. 0.
Item, viij great stootes	16. 0. 0.
Item, ij stootes	2.10. 0.
Item, xiij kyne, j bull & ij calves	21. 0. 0.
Item, x oxen	25. 0. 0.
Item, vj horses & maires, ij foles	12.14. 0.
Item, vij calves	3.10. 0.
Item, iiij swyne hogges	1. 6. 0.
Item, hay	4. 0. 0.
Item, 4 plowes, ij paire of Irons	6. 0.
Item, iij teames	6. 0.

Item, j oxe iron harrow, j paire of iron horse harrowes	13. 4.
Item, ij boltes, ij shakels, j spade, ij axes, j mattock	2. 8.
Item, j chespresse	1. 0.
Item, j paire of axell nayles	1. 0.
Item, j coupe and stanges	5. 0.
Item, xvj threaves of ry	2. 0. 0.
Item, viij threaves of wheat	1. 0. 0.
Item, liij threave of good ootes	10. 0. 0.
Item, xiij skoore threaves of ootes	16. 0. 0.
Item, corne upon the earthe	10. 0. 0.
Item, in the fouldgarth att Cockerton	1. 0. 0.
Item, v yokes geand	4. 0.

[Summa £209 4s 6d]

Debtes owinge to the testator

John Garthorne	11. 0. 0.
Cutbert Robinson	11. 0. 0.
John Vasy	22. 0. 0.
Edward Marshall & Thomas Marshall	9. 14. 8.
Lawrence Katerick	22. 0. 0.
Edward Elgy	13. 4. 0.
Franncis Newby	22. 0. 0.
Lawrence stainsby	5. 0. 0.
Francis Ward	10. 0. 0.
Richard Morley	10. 0. 0.
Henry Moore	20. 0. 0.
Rodger Watsonn	18. 0.
William Staynforth	12. 0.
Thomas Simpsonn	3. 0.

[Summa £148 11s 8d]

Debtes owing by the testator

To Mr Roger Fitzhew, for rent	25. 0. 0.
To Dorithy Marshall	2. 2. 3.
To Oswold Fawcet	2.13. 4.
To Isabell Masonn	6. 0. 0.
For servantes wayg	1. 10. 9.
To Anthony Gilpin	2. 11. 8.
To William Blake	8. 0.
To Richard Hellcott	1. 1.
To Thomas Bowbancke	4. 6.
To Richard Cootsworth	3.13. 4.
Item, for funerall expence	4. 4. 0.

[summa £48 8s 11d]
Suma £69 13s [*very faded*]

[*Paper, 1 f. In hand different from will.*]

54 Ralph Thursbey of Archdeacon Newton, 1622

.A true inventory of all the goodes and chattles,
moveable & unmoveable, of Raphe Thursbey of
Archdeacon Newton, within the parishe
of Darlington, yeoman, lait deceased, praysed
the xxiiijth day of September, Anno Domini,
1622, by Richard Heighington, gentleman,
Thomas Richardson, Christofer Richardson
& Thomas Thursbey, as followeth,

Imprimes, viij oxen praysed to	26.13. 4.
Item, xix^{teine} kyne & on bull	40. 0. 0.
Item, fifteine stottes & whyes	24. 0. 0.
Item, thirteine yong beastes & foure calfes	14. 0. 0.
Item, four meares & ij folles	4. 6. 8.
Item, thre stages	6. 0. 0.
Item, ten score shep	37. 0. 0.
Item, corne in the barne & staggarthe	56. 0. 0.
Item, v teames, ij cowters, ij socke yokes, ij axes, on hay spad, pack sadles, on leap, with other implementes	1. 4. 0.
Item, weynes, whelles, plowes, harrowes, assell trees & beames	1.13. 4.
Item, iiij^{or} hay stakes, j rucke	44. 0. 0.
Item, xiiij bushelles of malt	2. 0. 0.
Item, his purse & apparrell	2.10. 0.
Item, the furniter in the hall, on table, j cobbord, with other implementes	1. 0. 0.
Item, in the chamber, on bed & other implements	10. 0.
Item, in an other chamber, tubes & skelles & other implements	3. 0.
Item, chesses praysed to	1.10. 0.
Item, woll praysed to	8. 0. 0.
Item, swine praysed to	1. 6. 8.
Item, gyse & other pullen	10. 0.
Item, bees praysed to	5. 0.

Sume £272 12s 0d

Debtes that the testator did ow at his deathe

Imprimes, to Mr Henry Blaxton	122.10. 0.
Item, to An Gybson	22. 0. 0.
Item, to Elizabeth Thursbey	10. 0. 0.
Item, to Martyn Stelling	9. 0. 0.
Item, to Christofer Richardson	10. 4.
Item, to Mr Richard heighington	1. 0. 0.

Sume £165 0s 4d

Remanet debitis deductis £167 11s 8d

[*Paper, 1 f. In hand similar to 5, 20 will, 26, 37, 38 and 39 inventories, 40 and 57.*]

55 John Lisle of Bedburn Park, 1623

In the name of God, Amen, I, John Lisle of Bedboorne Parke in the parish of Hamsterley, within the countie of Durham, gentleman, sicke in bodie, but whole in mind, and of good and perfect remembrance, thankes be given unto Almightie God, revoacking all former wills and acts, doe make this my last will and testament, in manner and forme following. First, I give and bequieth my soule unto Almightie God, my Maker and Redemer, by Whome my salvation is wrought in His Sonne, Jesus Christ, which shed His pretious blood upon the Crosse for my redemption, by Whome I stedfastly believe to be saved and by none other, and raigne with Him in heaven, and my bodie to the ground, my mother, from whome I was first taken. Item, I give unto my sister, Isabell Lisle, ten pounds. Item, I give unto Talbot Lisle, my brother sonne, my signit of golde, which I use to weare. Item, I give unto Gilforth Lisle, fyve pounds. Item, I doe give unto my sister, Sibbill Lisle, her sonne, ffower pounds. Item, I give unto everie one of my sister Sibills daughters, twentie shillings. Item, I give unto every one of my sister Bell her daughters, twentie shillings. Item, I give unto my sister Bentley sonne, dwelling at Sedgfield, one sute of apparill and a two and twentie shillings peace. Item, I give unto my sonne, Thomas Barnes, one of my silver beare bowles. Item, I doe give unto my servant, Robert Follansbie, my cloake I weare and a peece of newe cloath to make him a cloake, and a sute of apparill, and a litle trunke at Darlington. Item, I doe give and bequieth unto my sister Bentley sonne, which is travilling in Ireland or elsewhere, twentie shillings, when he shall personally demaunde it. The rest of my goods ubequiethed, my debts paid and my funeraall expences discharged, I doe give and bequeath unto Barbaray, my wife, whome I doe make and ordeine the full and sole executrix of this my testament and last will. In witnesse whereof I have here unto subscribed my name and set my seale, the second daye of March in the twenteth yeare of the raigne of our soveraigne lorde James, by the grace of God, kinge of England, Scotland, France and Ireland, defendor of the faith, &c., and of Scotland the fiftie seven, in the yeare of our Lord God, one thousand six hundred twentie two. Postscriptum: item, I doe give fower pounds to remane unto the pooer people of the parish of Hamsterley for a stock for ever. Item, I do likewise give unto the poore people of Darlington fower pounds to remaine for a stock for ever.   John Lisle

These being present and witnesses, John Dunkay, curate, Robert Follansby.

[*Paper, 1 f., seal*]

The true and perfect inventorie of all the
goods and chattells of John Lysle of Bedboorne Parke, within the comitatu of Durham, gentleman,
which he died seazed, upon the eight daye of
March, in the twenteth yeare of the raigne
of our Soveraigne Lord, James, by the Grace
of God, King of England, Scotland, France and
Ireland, defendor of the faith, &c., and, of
Scotland, the fiftie seventh, Annoque
Domini, one thousand six hundred twentie two [1623],
vewed and praysed by these fower indiff-
erent men, Henrye Follansbye, gentleman,
Edward Blackit, Ralfe Walton and
Henry Atkinson, as followeth,

Imprimis, his purse and his apparill	10. 0. 0.
Item, eight oxen with theire furniture	20. 0. 0.
Item, twelve kine, six calves, a bull and the haye unto them provided	26. 0. 0.
Item, fower score and six ewes and two toopes	18. 0. 0.
Item, thre draught horsses	5. 0. 0.
Item, fower yonge beasse	3. 0. 0.
Item, thre quies and thre calves, with haye	6. 0. 0.
Item, sheepe hoggs and other sheepe, in the medowe feilds, five score and three	16. 0. 0.
Item, wether sheepe upon the fells, seven score	31. 0. 0.
Item, oates in the howse eight loads	4.10. 0.
Item, rye upon the ground	2. 0. 0.
Item, one swine	10. 0.
Item, thre quies gelds & a stott six pounds	6. 0. 0.

In the hall

Item, one presse, one cupboard, two tables with a carpit, a firme a great chist, one coarslit, with the furniture	6. 0. 0.
Item, in the parlor, one table, twelve buffit stooles, thre chayres, one liverey cupboard, one langsettle, one carpit, one cubbert cloath, sixteen cusshings, two lowe stooles, one fyer shovell and a paire of tongues	3. 0. 0.
Item, in the inner parlour, one stand bedd, one feild bed with their furniture, a little cupboard, a liverey cupboard, a glasse case with the glasses, a chist, a foote pace, a chandle chist, a seing glasse, woling yearne and lining yearne, with other implements	4. 0. 0.
Item, in the buttery, one presse, one hogseheade, seven barills, seven candlesticks, six table cloathes, five dozen of napkins, six towills, with juggs and glasses	2. 0. 0.

Item, in the kitching and the larder, eight & thirtie peeces of
  puter, nyne sawscers, fower brasse potts, fower kettles, one driping
  pane, spitts, a payre of iron racks with reckon crookes, a brazin
  morter, a pestell, one cawill, with the brewing toobes and other
  implements   4. 0. 0.

Item, in the mylch howse, two dozin booles and two chirnes   10. 0.

Item, in the roome over the hall, two standbedds with theire
  furniture one table, a hanging cubbard, a trundle bed, two chists,
  a chayre, one cushing and still with a table in the iner roome,
  with other implements   3. 0. 0.

Item, in the roome over the parlour, one presse, one livery
  cupbord with a cloath, thre chayres, two cushings, a payre of
  tongues, thre trunkes, eighten payre of sheets, six paire of
  pillowebeers and one table, fyve puter chamber potts   2.10. 0.

Item, the chamber over the inner parlour, one standing bedd
  with the furniture, one litle cupbord with a cloath, one trundle
  bedd & one little greene chayre   3. 0. 0.

Item, in the maydes chamber, two beds, with the furniture   1. 0. 0.

In the menservants chamber, one bedd with the furniture, with
  certaine lowse wood   1. 0. 0.

Item, two gesse, a stege, two ducks, thre hens, a cocke, two capons   6. 8.

Summa totallis £178 6s 8d

Henrye Follansbye, Edward Blackit [mark], Railfe Walton, Henry Atkinson

[Paper, 2 ff., sewn .]

An inventorye of all the goods and chattells of John Lisle, late
of Darlington, gentleman, deceased, which were at Darlington, praysed the
xviij[th] day of March, 1622 [1623], by Simond Geffoord, John
Bygott, George Rickatson, Raiph Jackeson, as followeth,

Imprimis viij oxen, with all the wain and ploughgeare   24. 0. 0.
Item, the corne in the barne   13. 6. 8.
Item, the corne on the ground   24. 0. 0.

In the hall
Item, the tables, chaires, formes, two carpett clothes and quishons
  and one liverey cubboord, with a cloth   2.10. 0.

In the buttery
Item, one old cubboord, with barrells, pewther and some
other implements there   5. 0. 0.

In the parlour
Item, one standing bed with the furniture and other
implements of howshould stuffe there, with some other
implements in the closset   3. 0. 0.

In the kitchin
Item, the bruing vessell, the brasse vessell, spitts, racks and other
implements belonging the kitchin   5. 0. 0.

In the parour next the kitchin
Item, one standing bed, furnished, with one presse, one truncke,
two liverey cubboords and other implements there   6.13. 4.

In the maids parlour
Item, one bedd, furnished, with other things there   1.15. 0.

Item, one the backe syde of the howse, two ladders, the coles and
a furre sparre   8. 0.

In the streete chamber
Item, One standing bed, furnished, a liverey cubboord with
chaires, stooles, quishons, and other things there   8. 0. 0.
Item, one chist theire, two truncks and a litle coffer, with the
linnen therin   10. 0. 0.

In the closset
Item, all the plate there, with glasses and some other
implements   24. 0. 0.

In the great chamber
Item, one table, a liverey cubboord with carpet clothes and
cubboord clothes, stooles, chaires, quishons, and other
implements there   6.13. 4.

In the chamber over the butterye
Item, one standing bedd, furnished, a liverey cubboord with the
cloth, a table, a chaire, with other implements   3. 0. 0.

In the chamber over the litle parlour
Item, one standing bed, furnished, a presse, a table, a liverey
cubboord, with chists and other implements there   5. 0. 0.

In the chamber over the kitchin
Item, one bedd, furnished, two tables and some other things there   1.15. 0.

Item, mault in the garnoure   13. 4.

Summa totalis £250 14s 8d

Simon Giffarde, George Rickatson, John Bygott, Raiph Jackeson

Debts owinge to the testator
In primis, the righte reverende father in God, Richarde, lorde
   bishopp of Durham, for his fee for the bailiwicke of Darlington   20. 0. 0.
Item, by Brabant Rippon   41. 0. 0.
Item, by Thomas Parkin   1. 3. 0.
Item, by Mr Tymothie Barnes   18. 0.
Item, by Anthony White   12. 0.
Item, by Samuell Grinwell   2. 0. 0.
Item, by George Rickatson   16. 0.
Item, by Edwarde Blackett   15. 2.
Item, other small debts by severall persons   1. 2. 0.
Item, by Thomas Gregorye   1. 4. 0.
Item, recyved of Wall and Ablesonn   31.10. 0.

Summa totalis £100 0s 2d

Debts owing by the testator
Imprimis, to Elizabeth Barnes, his daughter in law   60. 0. 0.
Item, to his daughter in lawe, Jaine Barnes   100. 0. 0.
Item, to Mr John Clemett   1. 4. 5.
Item, for the hindes and other servannts Waigs   7. 0. 0.
Item, for the tithe of Bedburne Parke   15. 0.
Item, his funerall expences   10. 0. 0.
Item, given to the poore at the churche   2. 5. 0.
Item, charges aboute the probacion of the will   2. 5. 4.
Summa totalis £183 9s 9d

[Paper, 1 f.]

56 Lawrence Catherick of Darlington, 1623

In the name of God, Amen, the xviij[th] daie of Aprill in the xxj[th] yeare of the reigne of our most gracious soveraigne lord, James, by the grace of God, king of England, France, and Ireland, defender of the faith, &c., and of Scotland, the lvjth 1623. I, Lawrence Cathericke of

Darlington in the countie of Durham, yeoman, sicke in bodie but of
good and perfect remembrance, God be praised, do make & ordaine
this my last will and testament, in manner and forme following. First
and principallie, I commend my soule into the handes of Almyghtie
God and His Sonne, Jhesus Christ, my Saviour and Redeemer, by
whose merites, death and passion, I onely hope to be saved, and my
bodie, if it shall please God to call me to His mercy at this time, I
commend to the earth frome whence it came, to be buried in the
parish church yarde of Darlington, as neare unto my lait deceassed
most loving wiefe, as can conveniently be devised. Item, I give and
bequeath unto the poore people of the parish of Darlington three
poundes, to be distributed at the discrecion of my children and
freindes. Item, I give and bequeath unto my sonne, Lawrence
Cathericke, my best cupbord in the hall house. Item, I give unto my
daughter, Hellen Marshall, the next best cupbord, likewise standing
in the hall house. Item, I give to my daughter, Jane Robinson, one
cupborde now standing in the buttry chamber where I lye. Item, I
give and bequeath to my daughter-in-lawe, Margaret Cathericke, my
sonne Thomas wiefe, one other cupbord, now standing in my
daughter Hellen Marshall stable, with my best bedstockes, which
were lait widowe Glover's, now standing in the lofte over the hall
house. Item, I give and bequeath to my daughter Alice, my sonne
Francis his wife, one other cupbord, now standing in my low parlour.
Item, I give to everie of my grandchildren, in number thirteene, to
each of them, a gymmer lambe, or so much monie as will buy everie
one of them a gymmer lambe. Item, I give another gymmer lambe to
the child now in my daughter, Jane Robinson's bodie, as yeat
unborne. Item, I give and bequeath unto my said sonne, Lawrence,
for and in consideracion of his filiall and childes porcion, three
poundes, to be paid him by my sonne, Francis yearely, with his dyet
and sufficient apparrell, all to be paid him and founde at the charges
of my said sonne, Francis, for and during so long as the said
Lawrence shall live, or like thereof. And, if the said Lawrence shall
mislike of such dyet and of the said annuall rent of three poundes
and apparrell, as I have formerly hereby bequeathed, then my will is
that my sonne, Francis, shall (upon such his refusall and mislike of
such his dyet, apparell and yearly payment of three poundes to him
so formerly bequeathed) in further, full recompence of his said filiall
porcion, secure the said Lawrence, by some sufficient and reasonable
securitie, for thannuall and yearely payment of tenn poundes per
annum, for and during his liefe naturall, and thenceforth to
maintaine himselfe where he shall best like of. Item, I give more unto
my said sonne, Lawrence, my gray colt. Item, I give and bequeath

unto my sonne, Thomas Cathericke, and his heires for ever, my burgage or tenement, with thappurtenances, on the Head Rawe, wherein my sonne Francis now dwelles, provided that my said sonne, Thomas, shall releasse all future clame to be pretended by him, of ingresse, egresse and regresse, to & from the well of the backside of my house, wherein I now dwell, being a covenant contained in certaine articles formerly agreed upon betwene me and Robert Ward, touching a mariage maid and solemmized betwene the said Thomas my sonne and Margaret, now his wiefe, daughter of the said Robert. Item, I give to my said sonne, Thomas, two silver spoones. Item, I give to my sonne, Lawrence, another silver spone. Item, I give to my daughter, Helen Marshall, two silver spoones. Item, I give to my daughter, Jane Robinson, other two silver spoones. Item, I give to my sonne, Francis, sixe silver spoones. Item, I give to my said sonne, Lawrence, my great chist in the buttery chamber. Item, I give to Mary Ellstobb, my servant, an ewe and a lambe and one paire of bedstockes in the bigg loft. Provided alwaies that my will is further that, whereas I have formerly given and bequeathed a legacie of tenn poundes per annum to my sonne, Lawrence, upon his dislike of iij^{li} per annum and meate, drinck and cloathes with my sonne, Francis, that notwithstanding the said former bequest, my mynd, will and true intent is that, if the said Lawrence, my sonne, shall, at anie time after my deceasse, goe about to sell, morgage or convey the said annuall rent of tenn poundes (by me to him so bequeathed) to anie person or persons whatsoever, without the full assent and consent of my other two sonnes, Francis and Thomas Cathericke, that then and thence forth, the said legacie of the said x^{li} per annum utterly to discontinue, ceasse and be voyd, any former act, gift or bequest above said in anie wise notwithstandinge. The rest of all and singular my goodes and chattelles, not given nor bequeathed, my debtes, legacies and funerall expenses deducted and discharged, I give and bequeath unto my sonne, Francis Catherick, whome I make sole and whole executor of this my said last will and testament. In witnes of us,

John Stephenson Anthony Mylner Ralph Blackwell [*mark*] Richard Pickeringe

[*Paper,* 1 *f.*]

The inventarie of all and singular, the goodes and chattelles, moveable and unmoveable, of Lawrence Catherricke of Darlington, in the countie of Durham, yeoman, deceassed, praised the first day of May, Anno Regis Jacobi Anglie, &c., xxj^{mo}, 1623, by Thomas Emerson, John Steele, Ralfe Blackwell and Bulmer Priscott, as followeth,

In the hall house

First, his purse and apparrell	6.13. 4.
Item, two cupbordes, xxˢ a peece	2. 0. 0.
Item, one table, 3 chares, a counter with a liverey cupbord, 2 shelves, a callever, a musket with furniture, and other implementes as 2 reckines, speetes and other small necessaries	2.10. 0.
Item, all brasse and pewter in the hall	3. 0. 0.

In the butterie chamber

Item, one cupbord	1. 0. 0.
Item, 13 silver spoones	4. 6. 8.
Item, iijᵉʳ brasse pottes, with 20 peece of pewter	2.10. 0.
Item, one great chist	10. 0.
Item, 2 bedstockes, with their furniture	3. 0. 0.
Item, a litle chist, with a chaire & other buttery vessell	10. 0.

In the milke house

Item, bowles, skelfes and other woodden vessell there	1. 0. 0.

In the lowe parlour

Item, one cupbord	1. 0. 0.
Item, 4ᵉʳ pewter dublers	5. 0.
Item, 2 bedsteades with furniture, a long table, a forme, a paire of tonges and a buffet stoole	8. 0. 0.
Item, a Flanders chiste, five paire of lynnen sheetes, 3 of harden, sixe codwares, with table cloathes and napkines	4. 0. 0.

In the chamber over the hall

Item, one bedstocke, with a cupbord in Elinor Marshall stable	1. 0. 0.
Item, 2 paire of bedstockes, 3 fether beddes, with coveringes and other furniture and other implementes there	4. 0. 0.

In the chamber over the shopp

Item, xvᵉⁿᵉ bushelles of bigge, with other implements	5. 0. 0.
Item, one paire of bedstockes	6. 8.

In the kitchinge

Item, 2 kaldrons, a cheese presse, 2 litle ketles, a paire of iron rackes, with all other implementes there	2.13. 4.

In the barne on the backside

Item, corne as yeat unthresht	6.13. 4.

In the lofte over the stable

Item, iiijᵉʳ loade sadles, iiijᵉʳ bordes, ix iron forckes, with all other implementes there	1. 0. 0.

In the malt lofte over the kitching and low parlor

Item, xx^{tie} quarters of bigg and oate malt	35. 0. 0.

Item, xx^{tie} quarters of bigg and oate malt — 35. 0. 0.
Item, hay in the stackgarth, on the backside of the house — 10. 0.
Item, v calves — 1.13. 4.
Item, one gray colt — 5. 0. 0.
Item, v horses and mares, with a stagge — 12. 0. 0.
Item, 3 paire of iron bound wheeles, 3 cowpes, a coaling waine, three long waines, with ploughes, yokes, teames and all other implementes of husbandrie — 12. 0. 0.
Item, viijth oxen — 32. 0. 0.
Item, viijth kine, 3 whies, a bull stircke and a why stirk — 23. 0. 0.
Item, iij^{xx} and eight sheepe — 20. 0. 0.
Item, harde corne and ware corne of thearth, in Grainge Feild — 35. 0. 0.
Item, harde corne and ware corne upon the earth, growing of the glebe land — 43. 6. 8.
Item, more corne on the said glebe landes, growing at the garthes end — 5. 0. 0.
Item, dunge on the backside of the house with stackgarth railles — 1. 0. 0.

Summa £286 8s 3d

Debtes owing to the testator at the time of his death

Imprimis, Richard Bishoppricke of Crofte — 3.18. 0.
Item, the said Richard, more — 4. 8.
Item, Thomas Worthie of Crofte — 4.14. 0.
Item, James Hawkinges of Crofte — 3.16. 0.
Item, Widow Bradeley — 1.16. 0.
Item, Cuthbert Hodgson — 5.12. 0.
Item, Widowe Clarke, alias Johnson — 1. 4. 0.
Item, Edwarde Hall — 3.15. 0.
Item, Robert Parkinson — 5. 0.
Item, Richard Patteson — 1.16. 0.
Item, the said Richard, more — 8. 4.
Item, Christofer Robinson — 1.10. 0.
Item, Mathew Lorriman — 10. 0.
Item, John Walker — 3. 0.
Item, Cuthbert Hodgshon, more in lent monie — 2. 0. 0.
Item, the said Cuthbert, more — 1. 0. 0.
Item, Charles Merrington of Long Newton — 1. 9. 0.
Item, Widow Glover of Darnton — 13. 6.
Item, the said Widow Glover, more — 14. 0.
Item, Richard Reerton of Haughton — 15. 0.
Item, Andrew Russell — 7. 6.
Item, Henrie Oswold — 7. 6.
Item, the said Henrie, more — 5. 0.

Item, William Carre of Darnton	18. 0.
Item, Widow Wood of Darnton	8. 4.

Somma £40 10s 10d
Somma totalis £326 18s 2d

Debtes owen by the testator as followeth
Imprimis to Richard Wood, tutor for Lawrence Cathericke, sonne

of John Catherickes, for his use	22. 0. 0.
Item, to Widowe Hodgshon of Cockerton	22. 0. 0.
Item, to Anthonie Rainton	10. 0. 0.
Item, to Mr Robert Crompton	5.10. 0.
Item, to Agnes Fawcett, widow	2. 2. 0.
Item, to Richard Thaddie, for the remainder of his next	
Whitsondaie rent next	18. 0.
Item, to Henry Robinson, for the said Richard Thaddy	19. 0.
Item, to Anthony Tinckler	1.10. 0.
Item, to John Stevenson	2. 5. 0.
Item, to Ralfe Blackwell	3. 3.11.

Somma debitorum debentium per testatorem £70 7s 11d
Summa totalis debitis deductis £256 10s 3d

Item, more debtes contained in the testators debt booke, supposed	
to be desperate, amountinge to the some, in all, about	20. 0. 0.

[*Paper, 2 ff., sewn. Will and inventory in hand similar to 6, 10, 11, 12, 14 inventory, 23, 27 will, 28, 35, 36 will, 43, 44, 46, 48 will, 49, 50 and 51.*]

57 Antony Stainsbey of Cockerton, 1623

In the name of God, Amen, the 19 day June, Anno Domini 1623, I, Antony Stainsbey, of Cockerton within the parish of Darlington, sicke in my body, nevertheless of good & perfite remembrance, laud & prayse be to Allmightie God, make & ordaine this my present testament, conteyninge herin my last will. First, I comend my soulle to Almightie God, my onlye Maker & Redemer, & my bodye to be buried within the church earth of Darlington. First, I geve to Martyn Stainsbey xxˢ by legacie. Item, I geve & bequeath to my daughter, Isable Stainsbey, by legacie ten pound which Bartle Jackson of Byshopton oweth to me, to be payd at Martenmes next. Item, I give & bequeath to my daughter, Isabel Stainesbey, by legacie other ten pound which John Bucke & William Allyn oweth to me. Item, I give to my son, Roberte Stainsbey, all my wayne geare & all my plow geare, yoke & teames, & all other implements that belongeth, either to wayne or ploughe, that be now remaininge about my house, by legacie. Item, I give to my son, Roberte Stainsbey, by legacie iij^{li} v^s 8^d that John Hall oweth to me. Item, I give & bequeath to my son, Roberte Stainsbey, one bay meare by legacie. Item, I give & bequeath to my son, Mathew Stainsbey, ij^o oxen by legacie. Item, I geve to my wife, Katheron Stainsbey, & to my daughter, Isable Stainsbey, by legacie all my howshould stuffe that is now remaininge in the hall, in the chamber & in the mylke howse. All the residue of my goods & chattles, moveable & unmoveable, my debtes, legacies & funerall expences discharged, I give & bequeath to my wife, Katheron Stainsbey & Mathew Stainsbey, my youngeste son, whom I make jointley executors of this my last will & testament. Item, I geve to Margreat Mason, my mayd servant, tow shillings & therefor I have caused these premises to be written. Witnesses herof, William Marshell, Lawrence Stainsbey, Mathew Thompson, Roberte Stainsbey & Thomas Mason.

Anthony Stainsbey [*mark*]

[*Two copies, both 1 f. of paper.*]

A trew inventory of all the goods & chattels of
Antony Stainsbey of Cockerton, in the parishe of [Darlington],
lait deceased, praysed the first day of Julye, 1623,
by William Marshell, Raphe Blackwell,
Lawrence Stainsbey & Mathew Thompson,
as followethe,

First, his purse & apparrell	2. 0. 0.
Item, ij oxen, given to Mathew Stainsbey by legacie	9.10. 0.
Item, iiij^{or} oxen praysed to	19. 0. 0.
Item, hard corne of Newbey More	3. 6. 8.
Item, ware corne of Newbey More is	10. 0. 0.
Item, xxvij lames, in the bottome	3.13. 4.
Item, vij ould shep praysed to	1.10. 0.
Item, one bay meare, geven to Roberte Stainsbey by legacie	3. 6. 8.
Item, one gray meare prsysed to	2. 6. 8.
Item, vj yearinge calfes is	5. 0. 0.
Item, iij whyes & ij stots is	8.10. 0.
Item, winter corne in his owne field, wheat, rye & some ware corne	17. 7. 0.
Item, xx^{tie} ewes praysed to	5. 0. 0.
Item, viij kyne praysed to	20. 0. 0.
Item, vij calfes praysed to	2. 0. 0.
Item, one swine praysed to	4. 0.

Item, one long wayne, j pare of iron bund whells, with plowes,
  yokes, teames & other Implements of husbandry, geven to Roberte
  Stainsbey by legacie   3. 6. 8.
Item, one cubbord, xx^te peece of pewther & v candlestickes   2. 0. 0.
Item, one cawell, iiij^or pots, iij panes, with other
  implements praysed to   2. 0. 0.
Item, one bord, ij formes, ij chayrs, ij bufet stoles, with
  other implements   10. 0.
Item, cheses, the chese bord ...[illegible]...   1. 0. 0.
Item, in the mylke house praysed to   1. 0. 0.
Item, ij pare of bed stockes, j feather bed, with other
  implements, praysed to   3. 6. 8.
Item, iij stone of wooll, praysed to   1. 0. 0.
Item, iij coverleds, ij pare of bleankets, v quishings   3. 0. 0.
Item, iij pare of harden shetes, iiij pane of lynen shetes, xxx^ti yardes
  of harden cloth, vj cood worth, v table napkins, j lynen bord cloth   3. 0. 0.
Item, ij chests & j coffer praysed to   8. 0.
Item, iij saddles, iiij sackes, with other implementes belonging ther to 10. 0.
Item, one winder cloth, j chese prise, with other implementes   10. 0.
Item, vj henes & viij gyse, praysed to   7. 0.

Debts owne to the testator
First, Barth Jackson   11. 0. 0.
Item, John Bucke & William Allen   10.10. 0.
Item, John Hall   3. 5. 8.
Item, John Garthorne   5. 2. 0.
Item, Thomas Simpson   5.10. 0.

Sume £169 10s

Debtes owen by the testatore
Item, for ij oxen to Thomas West   9.10. 0.

[Paper, 2 ff., sewn. Will and inventory in hand similar to 5, 20 will,
26, 37, 38 and 39 inventories, 40 and 54.]

58 Peter Glover of Darlington, 1625

In Dei nomine, Amen, ultimo die Aprilis, Anno Domini 1625, et anno
regni regis Caroli, Dei Gratia &c., primo, I, Peter Glover of
Darlington in the countie of Durrham, yeoman, not sicke in bodie but
partlye infirme, yett perfect in memorie, and knowing the certeintie
of death and the tyme to bee uncertaine, desirous to settle the estate
God hath indued mee withall, in peace both for my owne satisfaccion
& the good of my children, do make this my last will & testament,

revocating and adnullating all former wills by mee either made by word or wryting. First of all, I comend my soule & bodie, whensoever it shall please God to take mee to His mercie, into the Handes of my most mercifull God and his Sonne, Jesus Christ, my onelye Saviour and Redeemer, by and through whose onelie deathe & passion I faithfullie beleeve to bee saved. And for my worldlie estate, I dispose of it as followeth. Item, I give and bequeath unto my daughter Jane, as yet unadvanced in mariage, in full satisfaccion of her filiall and childes porcion, one hundreth poundes, to bee paid her within one yeare and a halfe after the daye and tyme of her mariage. Item, I give and bequeath unto my daughter, Magaritt Glover, likewise yett unadvanced, one hundred poundes, one obligacion of fortie poundes, with condicion for payement of twentie poundes, payable upon the eleaventh daye of November next, to mee and the said Margarett jointlye, made by Mr William Pudsey, to bee allowed her in parte of the said hundred. Item, I give and bequeath unto my daughter Dorothie, in full satisfaccion and payement of her filiall and childes porcion, one hundred poundes, to bee paid her in the daye of her mariage, and that hee, who soever shall marrie her, and shee, shall, upon receipt or securing therof, give a full bequittance or discharge therof to my executor hereafter nominated. Item, I give and bequeath unto my sonne, Tobie Glover, one hundred poundes in full satisfaccion of his filiall and childes porcion, to bee paid him in manner and forme followeing, that is to saye, thirtie poundes within one quarter of a yeare next after the expiracion of the terme of his apprentishipp served, and at the end of one whole yeare then next following, other twentie poundes, and other twentie poundes within one other yeare after, and thirtie poundes, last part of the said hundred poundes, at the end of foure full yeares to bee expired after the terme of the said Tobie his apprentishipp served and compleat. Item, I give and bequeath unto Raphe Millner and John Milner, my grandchildren, to either of them, five poundes a peece, to bee paid them and either of them, at their and either of their accomplishement of full age of one and twentie yeares, if they shall happen to bee then liveing. Item, I give and bequeath to Peter Mottershedd and Dorothie Mottershedd, likewise my grandchildren, to either of them, five poundes a peece, to bee paid them at their full age of one & twentie yeares, if they shall bee then liveing. Provided alwaies that my true intent and meaneing[sic] Item, I give & bequeath to Dorothie Parkin and Jane Parkin, other two of my grandchildren, to either of them, five poundes a peece, to bee paid them likewise at their accomplishment of full age of one and twentie yeares, if they shall hapen to be then liveing. Provided alwaies that my true intent and meaneing is that if anie of the aforesaid sixe children shall dye before their accomplishment of full age of one and twentie yeares, that then the said legacie shall utterlie cease and bee extinguished. Item, I give to the poore people of the parrishe of Darnton, to bee distributed at the churche door, foure poundes. The rest of all and singular my goods and chattles, moveable and unmoveable, of what nature, kind or qualitie soever, my debtes, legacies and funerall expences freed, acquitted, paid & deducted, I give and bequeath, freelie and absolutelie, to John Glover, my sonne, whome I make my whole and sole heire and executor of this my said last will and testament, ordeyning here by my right trustie and deere beloved brothers-in-lawe, John Kettlewell and Jesper Kettlewell, my supervisors, to see the execuion hereof performed, as my trust is, and to bee aydinge and assisting my said executor in all thinges with their best advises. In remembrance whereof I give and bequeath to either of them a Jacobus peece of gold as a token & pledge of love and last farewell, referring everie ambiguitie, if anie shall arise in this my said will, to bee expounded, construed and explayned by my supervisors aforesaid. In witnesse hereof, I have putt to my hand & seale, the daye and yeare first above said, theis witnesses as followeth, John Kettlewell, Jasper Kettlewell, Richard Pickering and John Hodgeson. Vicesimo octavo die Septembris, Anno Domini, 1625.

[*Register copy, Borthwick Institute, York, another copy in County Record Office, Northallerton.*]

GLOSSARY

This glossary contains those words which are likely to need elucidating for the modern reader of 17th-century wills and inventories. Some are unfamiliar words which describe items for which there is no modern equivalent; others are familiar words which have changed their meaning over the years. A number have been included because their strange spelling may make them appear unintelligible. Not every variation of spelling has been listed because words were frequently spelt phonetically and if pronounced out loud become immediately clear. However, some spellings are obscure, perhaps distorted by personal idiosyncrasy or dialect, so these are included and grouped together.

Words have been given in the singular, unless only the plural form is correct. All sources used have been listed in the bibliography.

Angel. Gold coin worth 6s 8d.
Aqua-vit. Any fiery spirit e.g. brandy.
Ark. Chest, box or coffer.
Armery, aumbry, ambry, almery, amb-rie. Cupboard with doors pierced for ventilation used for storing food.
Armytage. The Hermitage, a property in the Bank Top area (see Carswe).
Asselltree. Axletree, the spindle or axle of a wheel.
Axe. 1, axe; 2, axle.
Aye. Hay.
Badderhaie. Possibly 1, badelar, a short broad sword curved like a scimitar; 2, slasher, billhook (from haie meaning hedge?); 3, finery, jewellery, a corruption of bawdry?
Bailiwick. Office or area of a bailiff's jurisdiction.
Balk. Beam of a balance (see Beam).
Barkhouse. Tanning house.
Barktub. Tub for storing bark, used in tanning.
Barrey. Hand-barrow.
Bartries, barretrees. Wooden frame for the warp (weaving term).
Battledor. 1, leaf of paper containing the alphabet (often also the ten digits, some elements of spelling and the Lord's Prayer) protected by a thin plate of transluscent horn and mounted on a tablet of wood with a handle; 2, flat wooden instrument resembling a cricket bat used for smoothing linen after washing.
Beam. 1, transverse bar of a balance from which scales are suspended; 2, the great timber of the plough to which all the other parts of the plough tail are fixed.
Bedstocks. Bed posts.
Bellies. Bellows.
Bend leather. The thickest kind of

leather used for the soles of boots and shoes.

Bey. Bay wood; a quantity of wood; a finished article of wood?

Bigg. Barley.

Binke. Rack, usually for crockery.

Blonglemear Possibly a form of bolymong, a mixture of oats and tares; or a crop of mixed corn and peas?

Bodie. Bodice.

Bole, boole. Bowl.

Bollinge lace. Bobbled lace.

Bolster. Long stuffed pillow.

Bord. Board, table-top; the legs and rails are called the frame.

Bout cloath. Bolt cloth, fine cloth for sifting flour.

Bows. 1, yokes for oxen; **2,** two pieces of wood laid archwise to fit a horse's back.

Brackotilloe. Brocatelle, a fabric similar to brocade, made on a jacquard loom.

Brake. 1, bread brake, q.v.; **2,** wooden frame placed over a tub to support the strainers used in brewing and dairy work; **3,** toothed instrument for breaking flax or hemp.

Brandred, brandrith Gridiron or iron trivet for supporting a pot on the fire.

Braying stones Used like pestles for pounding in a mortar.

Bread brake Wooden slatted crate suspended from the ceiling for bread storage, also bread grate.

Brede Unit or piece of material of the full width.

Brewe grater. Brewing grate or sieve.

Broyl iron, brynling iron, broylyron Broyling iron, gridiron.

Budgett, budget Tin can shaped to fit the back, used for carrying milk.

Buffaine, buffine. Buffin, a coarse cloth used for gowns.

Buffet firme Buffet form, frame for a buffet stool.

Buffet stool. 1, stool for use at a long table; **2,** low or foot stool.

Bullaines 1, coarse linen cloth? **2,** bullion, gold or silver lace or braid.

Bulting ton, boulting tunne. Large cask or barrel used in sifting flour.

Burgage. Land-holding in a borough.

Bushell. 1, vessel used as a bushel measure, of eight gallon dry measure; **2,** circle of iron on the hub of the wheel to prevent it from wearing.

Busk Piece of bone, wood or whalebone used in the front of a woman's stays.

Bustiane. Bustian, a coarse type of fustian (see fustaine).

Butter. 1, small tub in which newly made butter is washed; **2,** bolter, a cloth used for sifting flour.

Buttery. Room for storage of food and drink.

Calderon, Cawtheron. Cauldron.

Calle, caul, cawell, cawill, cowl. Large tub or vessell with two ears.

Callover, calliver, calever. Caliver, a light musket.

Can. Vessel such as a drinking cup.

Candlecase. Case or box in which to put candles.

Canobies Canopies, hangings suspended over a bed.

Card. Implement made of wires, set in leather, used to part and comb out the fibres of wool, hemp, etc.

Carpet Used at this time for covering tables, beds and other furniture, not on the floor.

Carssae, kersey See kersey.

Carswe Causeway going to the Hermitage; the River Skerne at this time spread itself widely over the low lying land in the Clay Row area. The river was crossed by a stone bridge at the bottom of

Tubwell Row, but this was not long enough to span the whole wet and marshy area and a causeway was needed to reach to the Bank Top area where there was a property called The Hermitage.

Casier, kayser. Caser, a coarse sieve.

Cesse. Tax, rate or fee.

Chandle Candle.

Chaufed wheels Worn, scuffed wheels?

Chaufing dish Chafing dish, a warming dish for food.

Cheinar. China.

Chesfatt. Cheese vat.

Childer Children.

Chirnestaffe, kirnestaffe Churn staff, for agitating the milk in the churn.

Chymbneyes. Chimneys.

Cinkar, cinkarthe. See sincker.

Citharon. Cithern, a sort of guitar, strung with wire and played with a plectrum. Nearest modern instrument is a zither.

Close presse Clothes press, a wardrobe.

Close stool. Stool to hold a chamber pot.

Clowt. Leather or hide leather for patching.

Coate of plait. Plate armour.

Cobirons, cobberons Pair of irons which support the spit.

Cod, code, codd. Pillow.

Codware. Pillowcase.

Coole rack. Coal rake, implement like a hoe for raking coals, ashes.

Coop, coup, cowp, cowpe. 1, Cart or wagon with closed sides and ends, thus fitted for carting dung, lime etc; 2. Cup.

Copheaded. Probably polled or hornless; high peaked or tufted head as on polled cattle.

Copweb lawn. Cobweb lawn, a sheer linen fabric.

Copyhold Right to hold land according to the custom of the manor, by copy from the roll of the Lord's court.

Corslet Piece of defensive armour covering the body.

Cortines, courtings Curtains.

Costrell. Costrel, a large bottle or wooden keg with ears, by which it could be suspended from the waist.

Cottell. Small iron wedge for securing a bolt.

Counter Table or desk for counting money.

Coverlet, coverlid Covering placed on top of the bedclothes.

Cowllyer. Cooler, a large cask or tub for cooling malt liquor.

Cowter. Coulter, the iron blade fixed in front of the ploughshare in a plough, to cut the soil vertically.

Crester. Cresset, kitchen utensil for hanging a pot over the fire.

Cruell. Crewel 1, thin worsted yarn used for tapestry and embroidery; 2, embroidery needles.

Cuftes Cuffs.

Cushing canvis. Cushion canvas.

Daker, daycar. Dicker, ten, half a score, being the customary unit of exchange especially in hides and skins.

Diaper Twilled bleached linen.

Draftub. Tub used in brewing and making beer or ale.

Dragge Drag, heavy harrow for breaking up ground.

Dressing bord Table for dressing meat, removing skin and offal.

Droppingpan, dreepingpan Dripping pan, to catch dripping off roasting meat.

Dubler. Doubler, large plate or dish.

Eatish. Eatage, area of grazing.

Ech, eache. 1, eche-hook, a hook attached to the cart or wagon through which the rope passes in binding on a load; **2,** edge, a tool with a non-serrated cutting edge.

Fash tub. Mixing tub.

Fellie. Felloe, the exterior rim, or part of the rim, of a wheel, supported by the spokes.

Feoffee Trustee, one entrusted with an interest in land.

Ferme. Yearly amount payable as rent.

Field bed. Portable bed, equivalent of modern camp bed.

Firdaille. Plank of pine or fir, usually about 6 feet long, 9 inches wide and not more than 3 inches thick.

Firkin. Small cask for liquids, butter, etc., originally holding a quarter of a barrel; also a measure of capacity of 9 gallons or 56lb of butter.

Firme, furme Form, bench.

Flakit, flacket. Flask.

Flanders chest. Chest carved and ornamented in the Flemish manner.

Flecke, fleeke, fleak. Wattle hurdle sometimes used as a temporary gate.

Fleshecrook. Meat hook.

Flicke. Flitch, the side of an animal, usually beef or bacon, cured and hung from the ceiling.

Fogge. Fog, the long grass left standing through the winter.

Foote pace. 1, carpet or mat; **2,** small platform or step (but see **Pace**); **3,** a measure.

Forehouse See Hallhouse.

Fowling peece Fowling piece, a light gun for shooting wild fowl.

Frame. Legs and rails of a table.

Freyse. Frieze, a coarse woollen cloth with a nap on one side only.

Fryons. Type of textile? A placename?

Furre sparre. Spar of fir wood.

Fustaine. Fustian, a fabric of mixed cotton and wool with a silky finish, often used as a substitute for velvet.

Fyershowle Fire shovel.

Gaie. Ornamental? Perhaps dialect, gay, gae, for fairly big.

Gaintreies, gauntries Gantry, a four-footed stand for barrels.

Gallow bawke Gallibaulk, a transverse bar in the chimney or over the fireplace, from which pot hooks are suspended.

Gan. Gang, a set, e.g. of wheel spokes.

Garne. 1, provisions; **2,** yarn, coarse worsted fabric, possibly hemp yarn for sewing leather.

Garth. Enclosed yard, garden etc.

Gate, gait. Right to place an animal on the common pasture, in Darlington the Brankin Moor.

Gavelock Iron crowbar or lever.

Geand. Joined?

Geares. Heddles, the small wires through which the warp is passed on the loom; different gears allowed different types of cloth to be woven on the same loom.

Geastes. Joists.

Gibcrook Hook on which to hang meat.

Gimmer Young ewe sheep.

Girlfatte, guylefatt, guylfatt, gyllfatt. Fermenting tub for malt liquor.

Girth tub. Barrel with a hoop of wood or iron about it.

Goulden Golden.

Gowded. - ?

Grape, gripe. Muck fork.

Grat, grate. 1, gridiron **2,** see **bread brake.**

Groat. Silver four-penny piece.

Grogram Grograin, a coarse fabric of mohair and wool, sometimes mixed with silk; often stiffened with gum.

Grootes. Groats, hulled oats.

Grudhes Grises, horse-girths; leather

bands for securing pack or saddle.

Hack. Pickaxe, mattock or large hoe.

Hacke. See hack or hecke.

Haernes Harness.

Halbart. Halberd, a cross between a spear and a battle-axe, mounted on a handle 5-7 feet long.

Hallhouse, hawlehouse Forehouse, the principal and often only room in a small early modern house.

Hammerstaff Hammerhandle.

Happen, happine, happing Covering, bedclothes.

Harbage. Herbage, natural pasture.

Hard. Hardcorn, a general name for wheat or rye.

Harden, harne. Coarse linen fabric.

Haver. Oats.

Hayre. Colour of a hare

Head Perhaps a container or lid?

Head piece Piece of armour for the head, a helmet.

Hecke Rack for animal fodder.

Hekelte. Heckled, flax in which fibres have been combed out.

Helmes. 1, haulms, stalks of straw, stubble; 2, quantity of rye or oats 3, plural form of helme, a field shelter.

Hempline String made of spun hemp.

Hewer iron. Reaping hook.

Hingers Hinges.

Hogges Young male sheep, not yet shorn.

Hogshead Large cask for liquids; in brewing, 54 gallons.

Holdfast. A locked small chest, a safe.

Holland Fine linen fabric, named after the province of Holland in the Netherlands where high quality flax was grown.

Holmes Fustian made at Ulm in Germany.

Hopper. 1, container for grain; 2, a kind of cheese vat.

Horse lock Hobble or shackle for a horse's foot.

Huswyfe cloth. Grade of linen cloth, between fine and coarse, for family use.

Hydg maryll. Hayseed?

Inkle. Linen tape or braid.

Jacke. 1, contrivance for turning a spit; 2, vessel for liquor.

Jacobus Coin, the (unofficial) name of an English gold coin struck in James I's reign; it passed originally for twenty shillings, later for twenty two or twenty four.

Jarsey. Jersey, worsted wool; wool combed and ready for spinning.

Jeanes Type of fustian, originally from Genoa.

Jeasts. See Geastes.

Joyned Joined, i.e. made by a joiner with morticed and tenoned frames and joints secured with wooden pegs, as distinct from furniture made by a carpenter of planks or trestles.

Judice.- ?

Kaddrene. Cauldron?

Kaul. See calle.

Kayser. See kersey.

Kersey. Coarse cloth, usually ribbed, woven from wool.

Kette, kit. Small tub or bucket with handle.

Kilnehaire, kylne hayre. Horsehair cloth which held malt in the kiln.

Kilpe. Kilp, an iron hook in a chimney for hanging pots on.

Kimlaie, kimlinge, kinnlings, kymlyn Tub used for brewing, kneading or salting meat or other household purpose.

Kine, kyne Cows.

Kirchiffe Kerchief, head-scarf.

Kirne, kirn, kyrne Churn.

Kirtle Woman's gown or outer petticoat.

Knack tubb, knock tub, knopp tub. Tub in which bread was kneaded.

Lark leaves. Possibly planks of larch.

Latten, lattin. Mixed metal of yellow colour, either identical or very similiar to brass.

Latts. Laths, thin narrow strips of wood used to form a groundwork for slates, tiles or plaster.

Laver. Basin.

Layd saddle. Load saddle.

Layrestall. Laystall, a burial place.

Leade, leede. Large lead container e.g. cistern or cauldron.

Leap, leape. Basket.

Lecker panne. Pan used to draw off the fermenting liquid from the mash tub or brewing tub.

Len. Linen.

Lensey woolasey, linsey wallasey. Material made of a mixture of wool and flax.

Limbeck. Alembic, old distilling apparatus.

Line, lyne. Fine long threads of flax or hemp separated by heckling.

Lint. Linen, flax.

Liverie cubbert. Livery cupboard, a cupboard with perforated doors in which food was stored.

Longracea. Bodice laces?

Lowse crook. Implement for unyoking horses.

Lynte. Linen.

Lyvery table. Table upon which a livery cupboard would stand.

Mand, mauns, mawnd. Wicker or woven basket with handles.

Map, mappe. Tablecloth, napkin.

Mark. Never an actual coin in circulation in England, it represented the sum of 13s 4d.

Mashe fat, mask fat, mashing maske fatt, mass fatt. Mashing vat, a brewing vessel, tub.

Maunger. Manger.

Mell. Heavy hammer of metal or wood.

Millaine. Coarse fabric made in Milan.

Moccadoe. Mockado, a popular cloth in the 16th and 17th centuries, originally made of mohair.

Moldrake, moldraik. Mould-rake, a rake in the plough.

Morean. Morion, a kind of helmet without beaver or visor, worn in the 16th and 17th centuries.

Mortuall. Mortuary, fee paid to cleric for funeral services.

Napprie ware. Napery, household linen.

Nave. Central part or hub of a wheel.

Noble. Gold coin worth 6s 8d.

Nonage. Period of infancy, minority.

Nutt. Nut, a small vase.

Oversea. Foreign.

Oxgange. Measure of land, varying locally, but usually between 10 and 20 acres.

Pace. Weight or a container of equivalent capacity (but see **foote pace**).

Padd. Cushion.

Pallion seat. Pillion, a light saddle used by women and placed behind the normal saddle.

Part-cloth. Partlet, a kerchief or neck-covering?

Pearke. Perk, a wooden frame or pole over which leather or cloth was drawn.

Peck. Vessel holding two gallons (a quarter of a bushel).

Peeck. Pick, perhaps pitch fork.

Penny. Small silver coin.

Pensharis. Pinchers.

Pented cloth. Painted cloth, a cheap substitute for tapestry, used mainly for wall or bed hangings.

Percer. 1, piercer; 2, a rapier or short sword.

Perpetuan. Perpetuana, a durable fabric of wool.

Philip and Cheyney. Obsolete English fabric of unknown construction.

Phillisselloe. Filoselle, a silk and

wool worsted cloth.

Pike, pyke. 1, pointed or peaked stack of hay made up temporarily in the hayfield; 2, weapon with a long wooden shaft, with a pointed iron or steel head.

Pillowbere, pyllyver, pilliver, pilobarre, pyllyner. Pillowcase.

Pirled. Purled 1, twisted or ribbed; 2, embroidered with figures of gold or silver thread.

Plough beam. See **Beam 2.**

Ploughshare Large curved blade of a plough.

Poke, pook 1, small sack; 2, contrivance fastened on cattle or pigs to stop them breaking through fences.

Pole, Powle, Pule. 1, stake; 2, long tapering wooden shaft fitted to the forecarriage of a vehicle and attached to the yokes or collars of the draught animals, serving to guide and control the vehicle; 3, long handle of a scythe; 4, clothmaking term - a long pole used for working the wool or cloth in dyeing.

Polke. Cupboard.

Porr. Poker.

Posnet. Small cooking pot with feet and handles.

Possett. Drink of milk curdled with ale, wine or vinegar.

Pottell pot. Half gallon drinking vessel.

Pottindiche. See **pottinger.**

Pottinger. Small basin used for e.g. porridge.

Pouder, puder, puther. Pewter.

Powder-blue Used in the laundry, to whiten linen.

Powle, powll. Pole?

Poynts. Points 1, laces; 2, needles.

Praysed, prised, praised Appraised, valued.

Presse. Large (usually shelved) cupboard especially one placed in wall recess.

Prichell. Pritchel, a sharp pointed tool used to make holes; frequently used by cobblers.

Pullen. Poultry.

Punche. Punch, an instrument or tool for piercing.

Pyck. Pitch.

Quartern. Consisting of or made with a quarter part as of flour in quartern-loaf?

Quell. Twill.

Quishings, quishions, quysshons. Cushions.

Quy. Heifer of up to 3 years, or until she has calved.

Raill. Garment, cloak or neckerchief.

Raills. Fence posts.

Rash. Smooth textile fabric made of silk or worsted.

Ratles. Part of machinery of loom.

Rawed Red? Raw? Rowed?

Rayle. Railed, fitted with a railing.

Razine. See **rossell.**

Reale. Spool of a spinning wheel.

Reckingcrook, reckyncrook, rackancrook Pot hook hanging in the chimney.

Reek. Rack.

Relict. Widow.

Remland, remling Remnant.

Rome Portion of land.

Rosell, rossett. Rosin, cobblers wax.

Rucke, ruck Rook, a small pile or heap.

Ryal. Fine gold coin valued at 10s.

Saae, sae, say. Bucket with two ears through which a pole may be passed for carrying.

Sacer, sawcer. Saucer, ie. a dish for sauce.

Sadd hayre. Dull, sober coloured.

Saddletree. Framework forming the foundations of the saddle.

Saint tillinmas. St Helen's mass.

Samar, samaron, sammering,

samoring. Sammaron, a cloth of textile between linen and hemp.

Say. Sey, a cloth of fine texture resembling serge.

Scammer, skamer. Skimmer 1, of iron to take ash from the hearth; 2, of some other metal for use as a skimmer.

Sciac. Scia 1, opening of the gown into which the sleeves are inserted; 2, sey (see above).

Scoath. Pole , bar or forked stick.

Seafe. 1, sieve; 2, safe, a ventilated chest or cupboard for keeping provisions, e.g. a meat safe.

Seckine 1, coarse cloth of which sacks are made; 2, solid colour flannel for women's robes.

Seinge glass. Looking glass, a silvered glass or mirror.

Seth, sith. Sithe, sieve or milk strainer.

Settle. Long wooden bench with arms and a high back.

Shank panne. Small pan having a long handle.

Sheve Scythe.

Shilling. Silver coin worth 12d.

Shotte. Shoat, a young weaned pig.

Shoule, showle. Shovel.

Sile. See **syle.**

Silmes. Simes, a straw rope or cord for holding down the thatch of stacks.

Sincker, sinker, cinkarthe. Circular board for pressing curds down into a cheese vat.

Sith. Scythe.

Skeal, skeele. Wooden bucket or tub for milk or water.

Skeas. Pair of wooden bars passing through each end of an ox-yoke, to which the neck-straps are fixed.

Skelf (pl. **skelves), skelse.** Shelf or shelves.

Skepp. Skip, 1, large basket; 2, a bowl-shaped vessel with handles

for ladling.

Slomber Possibly a stomber or stumper, i.e. a pestle.

Sned Snead, a handle for a scythe.

Snype. Boggy, poor pasture.

Sock Ploughshare.

Soe. See **saae.**

Spark. Fragment, remnant.

Sparre. Spar, piece of timber.

Spattle staff. Spade-handle.

Speet Spit.

Spence Cupboard.

Spoakes Spokes of a wheel.

Spur-ryal. Gold coin valued at 15s.

Stag, stage. Colt or stallion.

Staggard, staggarth. Stackgarth, a stack yard or rick yard.

Stakes Planks or timber supporting a grain or hay rick.

Stamp. Quantity (of hay).

Stand bed. Bed with posts.

Stang, stinges. Wooden beam or bar, forming, e.g. the side of a cart.

Statine. Stettin? (place-name).

Stee, steighe, stey. Ladder.

Steepeleade. Brewing vessell.

Steer Young ox, generally castrated.

Stelle, still. Stell, a stand or framework to support barrels.

Stiddye, stoddie. Stiddy, anvil.

Stirk Young bullock or heifer.

Stock. Bed.

Stole. Stool.

Stommer. Scammer?

Stopping stick. Wood inserted into the shoe to hold it in shape while the cobbler was working on it.

Stott. Young ox, steer.

Strakine Straikin, a small roll or bundle of flax when dressed.

Strakinge sheets. Coarse linen sheets.

Stralines See **strakine.**

Stress. Roof timber.

Stupe Stoup, bucket or pail.

Swall, swawle, swill. 1, swale, plank; 2, swill, a tub for pig swill.

Swingk. Wooden instrument for

beating and scraping flax or hemp to cleanse it of woody or coarse particles.

Swinglestock. Wooden trough or box in which cloth was placed to be beaten by the swingle.

Swingletree Cross bar in a plough, pivoted at the middle, giving freedom of movement to the shoulders of the draught animals.

Syle Sile, 1, strainer for milk; 2, One of a pair of the main members in a timber-frame house.

Synair table. Writing table? The Sinaic or Sinaitic Table?

Table. Top or board of a table; the legs and rails are called the frame.

Taftay. Taffeta, a light thin stuff with considerable lustre or gloss, very popular in the sixteenth and seventeenth centuries.

Taster, teaster. Tester, a bed-canopy.

Teamce, temps, tempts, tempze. Temse, a sieve, particularly of fine hair for sifting flour.

Teame Part of the gear by which oxen were harnessed to a plough, etc.

Teck. Tick, the case or cover containing feathers or flocks forming a pillow or mattress.

Tewe iyeron. Tew iron, a pipe leading from the bellows to the base of a blacksmith's fire.

Thearth The earth, e.g., **corn of thearth** = still growing.

Thrall Stand for barrels or pans.

Thrave, threeve, threfe, threve. Measure, varying in different localities, three but often two stooks of corn, generally containing 12 sheaves each.

Throwe Thrown, i.e. turned as opposed to joined furniture.

Tiere stolen. Metal rim of a wheel?

Tiffany. Very thin semi-transparent French silk fabric, a lightweight sheer muslin, used in 17th century veils.

Toope. Tup, ram.

Towe. Tow, the shorter fibres of flax or hemp separated by heckling from the fine, longer threads of linen, i.e. prepared for spinning.

Towel sticke. Cudgel.

Trayll steed Type of sledge cart.

Trensher, trencher. Wooden plate.

Tresses, trisses. Trestles.

Triakle. Treacle.

Trindlebed, troklebed, trucklebed, trundlebed Trunnellbed, a low bed on castors (or truckles) and pushed under a high (or standing bed) when not in use.

Trowe. Trough or vessel used in brewing.

Tuft Tufted?

Tuition Guardianship.

Tun. 1, large cask or barrel usually for liquids, especially ale, wine or beer; 2, large vessel in general, e.g, tub or vat.

Turne Spinning wheel.

Tutchbox. Touchbox, a box for touch powder, a kind of gunpowder placed in the pan over the touch-hole in a firearm.

Tutor. Guardian.

Valens Valencia, a lightweight twilled fabric, made of wood sometimes mixed with silk.

Wadnell Wadmal, a coarse woollen material.

Wain, wane, wayne. Large, usually four-wheeled, agricultural waggon or cart with high sides.

Wanded. Made from wand, the young shoot of willow, i.e. wickerwork.

Wane soule. Tapering stick or stake.

Ware. Spring, e.g., **ware-corn** = spring corn.

Water seat. 1, close stool? 2, bucket?

Wayne blaydes Wain blades, shafts

for the wain.

Webb Large sheet or piece of cloth, leather, metal etc.

Webster Weaver.

Wether Castrated ram.

Whelestone whetstone Stone for sharpening edged instruments.

Whye. See quy.

Windle Appliance for winding a skein of yarn into a ball.

Womble Wimble, 1, gimlet or auger; 2, crank with a hook at its tip, for twisting hay ropes.

Wortstone. Utensil used in brewing.

Wyndo leaf, wyndo lease, window-lease. Removeable windows of both glass and frame.

Wyndring cloath. Winding cloth, 1, large cloth on which corn is winnowed; 2, shroud.

Yeardwand. Yardstick.

Yearing Yearling, an animal a year old or in its second year.

Yew. Ewe sheep.

Issac Lowden's books [see pp. 123-4 above]

Gualthe upon Luke. *An hundred, threescore and fifteen homelys or sermons upon the Acts of the Apostles, written by St Luke; made by Radulphe Gauthere Tigurine and translated out of Latine into our tongue for the commodite of the English reader by John Bridges* , London 1572 (Ward)

Rudolph Walther (Rudolphus Gualterus) 1529-1586, early Swiss Reformer

Peter Martir uppon the Rom: *Most learned and fruitful commentaries of D.P. Martir Vermilius upon the Epistle of St. Paul to the Romans,* London 1568 (B.M.C.) - *Comm. in Epistolam ad Romanos,* Basle 1558, 1560 (Ward)

Peter Martire Vermigli 1500-1562, Augustinian prior. Took refuge in Zurich and Basle (1542) before taking up appointment as professor of Theology at Strasbourg. Came to England in 1547, granted government pension of 40 marks. Regius professor of Divinity, Oxford 1548. Reappointed professor of Theology, Strasbourg 1554. Professor of Hebrew, Zurich 1556. Maintained correspondence with Jewel, Cox, Parkhurst and Sandys (O.D.C.C.)

Lambert uppon Luke *In divi Lucae evangelium commentarii,* Nuremberg 1524 (B.M.C.)

Francis Lambert 1486-1530, b. Avignon. Franciscan, left order in 1522 and established relations with Zwingli and other Swiss Reformers. Helped to establish new Protestant 'Church order'. Professor of Exegesis, Marburg University. (O.D.C.C.)

Erasmus Paraphrase uppon Matt: *Paraphrasis in Evangelium Matthaei,* Basle 1522 (Ward)

Erasmus 1467-1536, the most renowned scholar of his age. Professor of Greek and Divinity, Cambridge.

Jacobus de voragne. *Sermones quadragesimales,* Basle 1474 etc.

Jacobus de Voragine, archbishop of Genoa, 1230-1298, best known for *The Golden Legend* which was written between 1255 and 1266. The purpose of its engagingly written narrative, full of anecdotes and curious etymologies was to foster piety. A medieval manual of ecclesiastical lore, it contained lives of the saints, commentaries on church services, and homilies for saints' days. Caxton's English version was compiled from various sources. (Ward, Bennett [1], O.C.E.L.) However, *Sermones quadragesimales* seems more likely here.

Urstitius Arethmeticke *The Elements of Arithmeticke most methodically delivered. Written in Latine; and translated by Thos. Hood, M.D.,* London 1596. (Ward)

Christianus Urstitius, professor of Mathematics, Basle University.

Cesars Comentarie. *Julii Caesaris Commentarii, novis emendationibus illustrati,* London, 1585, 1590, 1601 (S.T.C.)

Hermanus Bodius. *Certein places gathered out of Austen's book, intituled De Essentia Divinitatis by Herman Bodius and now translated into English,* London 1548 (Ward, P & R)

This was Martin Bucer, 1491-1551, the German reformer who sought to reconcile the views of Lutherans and Calvinists and who in exile in England became Regius Professor of Divinity at Cambridge. The writings on original sin and predestination of St Augustine of Hippo exercised a great influence on Calvin and his followers. [O.D.C.C.]

Theodorettus. *The mirror of divine providence containing a collection of Theoret his arguments, declaring the providence of God to appeare notably both in the heavens and in the earth - taken out of his workes De Providentia* [ed J.C.] printed by T.C. for J. Smethick 1602 (B.M.C.)

Theoderet, bishop of Cyrrhus, c.393-c.458 (Ward)

Titlemans physickes *Libri duodecim de consyderatione rerum naturalium,* Antwerp 1530 etc. (B.M.C.)

Franciscus or Frans Titelman, 1502-37, German Capuchin, Old and New Testament scholar.

Erasmus Apothogemes *Apothegmes, that is to saie, prompte saiynges,* translated by N. Udall, 1542, 1564 (Ward)

Used in 16th century grammar schools as an aid to Latin composition (Bennett [1]

A scapula - *Lexicon Graeco-Latinum,* Basle 1579, 1594, 1605, 1627, 1665 etc. London 1619.

A one-volume work, pirated from the four-volume *Thesaurus Linguae Graecae* , published by Henry Stephanus (Paris and Geneva 1572), for whom Joannes Scapula worked as a corrector. The smaller, cheaper book sold well to students and resulted in the bankruptcy of Stephanus. (Ward)

Gualthers homilies. Possibly *The homilies of M.R. Gualther Tigurine upon the prophet Joel, trans. by J. Ludlam* . . . 1582 (B.M.C.); or *Certain godlie homilies upon the prophets Abdias and Jonas . . . made by R. Gualther of Tigure and translated into Englishe etc,* 1573 (B.M.C.)

Hugo Cardinalis upon the whole Bible. Possibly *Opera omnia in Vet. et Nov. Testament* 1498 etc., 7 vols. (Ward)

Hugh de St. Cher. Dominican, cardinal, d. 1263

Homers Illiades. First English translation, 1581.

Brittaynes resurrection. *Great Britaines resurrection: or the Parliaments passing bell...* London 1606.

By William Hubbard, chaplain at the Tower of London.

Direction to Death. *Teaching man to die well that being dead he may live forever: made in the form of a dialogue for the ease and benefit of him that shall read it the speakers therein are Quirinus and Regulu s,* William Perneby 1599 (Ward)

Simon de Cassia - *Gesta Christi, seu Comm. in IV Evangelia XV libris,* Cologne 1533, 1540 (Ward)

The Reformed Catholicke, *or a declaration shewing how neer we may come to the present Church of Rome in sundrie points of religion; and wherein we must for ever depart from them,* William Perkins, Cambridge, 1597, 1598 (Ward)

William Perkins, 1558-1602, Protestant writer, fellow of Christ College, Cambridge 1584-1594. An earnest and effective preacher, outspoken in his resistance to anything which savoured of Roman usage. His reputation during the closing years of his life was unrivalled at Cambridge and few students of theology quitted the university without having sought to profit from his instruction. Respected by his Catholic critics. Thirty years after his death, he was referred to as 'our wonder . . . . living though long dead'. (D.N.B.)

Chemnisius 4or tom: *Examen Concilii Tridenti IV partibus,* France 1596, 1609, English translation by R.V., London 1582 (Ward)

An attack on the Council of Trent by Martinus Chemnitius (Martin Chemnitz 1522-1586), Lutheran theologian

Theophilactus uppon the fower Evangelistes - *Commentaria in Evangelia,* Rome 1542 (Ward)

Theophylactus, archbishop of Achrida, d. c.1100. His commentaries were marked by lucidity of thought and expression and closely follow the scriptural text (O.D.C.C.).

Calvins institution - *The institution of the Christian religion,* Basle 1536 (6 chapters). The final edition contained 80 chapters. Earliest English edition, trans. Thomas Norton 1561.

The text book of Reformed non-Lutheran theology and the most influential single manual produced during the Reformation. (O.D.C.C., Enc.Brit.)

Christes Triumph Possibly *Christ's victory and triumph in heaven and earth over and after death,* Giles Fletcher, Cambridge 1610 (B.M.C.)

A poem by Giles Fletcher, c.1588-1623, rector of Alderton, Suffolk, educated at Trinity College, Cambridge.

Granadoes Meditacions - *Of prayer and meditation, wherein are conteined fowertien devoute meditations for the seven daies of the weeke. bothe for the morninges and eveninges and in them is treyted of the consideration of the principall holie mysteries of our faithe written first in the Spanish tongue, by the famous religious father F. Lewis de Granada, trans, into English by*

Richard Hopkins, Paris 1582, London 1592 (Ward)

Louis de Granada, 1504-1588, Spanish Dominican, mystic, preacher and writer, confessor of Catherine of Portugal. He attributed great importance to the inner life and mental prayer. Saw outward ceremonies as unimportant compared with inner religious life. Adaptations of his works, purged of Catholic doctrine, were produced for the Protestant market. (O.D.C.C., Bennett [2])

Mr. Deeringes lectures. *XXVI lectures or readings upon part of the Epistle written to the Hebrews,* Edward Deering, 1576, 1578, 1584, 1590 (Ward)

Edward Deering, Puritan preacher, d. 1576

Dux Peccatorum. [The Sinners' Guide] by Louis de Granada, Cologne 1587 (Ward)

Sheppardes Callender Possibly *Le compost et Kalendrier des bergiers,* Paris 1483. First English translation 1503.

Popular lore concerning the seasons and the weather, upon which Edmund Spenser based his pastoral allegorical poem, *The Shepheard's Calender.*

Setons log. *Dialectica,* John Seton, 1572.

John Seton, 1498-1567, chaplain to Bishop Gardiner, teacher of philosophy (St. John's, Cambridge). His *Dialectica* was recognised for almost a century as the standard treaty on logic. (D.N.B.)

Mr. Estie workes. *Certaine godly & learned expositions upon divers parts of scripture as they were preached and afterwards briefly penned by* . . . G.E., 2 parts, 1603 (B.M.C.)

George Estie, 1566-1601, educated Caius College, Cambridge, divine and writer.

Bartasias de mundi creatione. *The first day of the world's creation,* Guillaume de Salluste du Bartas, Edinburgh, 1600 (Ward)

William de Salluste de Bartas, 1544-1590, French poet.

Aulus Gellius

Aulus Gellius, celebrated grammarian, born c.130 A.D. His *Noctes Atticae* Rome 1469 etc. (B.M.C.), a miscellany of literature, history, philosophy, philogy and natural science, was important as containing extracts from many lost authors and was commended for its singular style. According to Ward, 'this work is very little known in this country, since here there has been no edition worthy of notice published, or at least known'. (Ward, O.C.E.L.)

Comedia Sacra. - (not traced)

Petrarch de remedijs utriusque fortunae. *De remediis utriusque fortunae,* Petrarch, written 1366. Published Strasbourg 1468, English trans. Thomas

Twyne 1579 (S.T.C.)

Petrarch, 1304-1374, Tuscan poet, father of Italian humanism, the initiator of the revived study of Greek and Latin literature. (O.C.E.L.)

Quintilians Institutions. *De Institutione Oratoria*, Marcus Fabius Quintilianus, Rome 1478 etc. (B.M.C.)

Marcus Fabius Quintilianus, c.42-c.124, rhetorician. During the Renaissance his *De Instituione Oratoria* was revered as the greatest educational treatise ever written. (Enc.Brit., O.C.E.L.)

Brittaynes deliverance *Great Britaines great deliverance, from the great danger of popish powder*, William Leygh, London 1606.(S.T.C.)

William Leigh, 1550-1639, a popular preacher and influential divine, tutor to Henry, prince of Wales, and writer of this title upon the Gunpowder Plot.

Directions to the holy land. Possibly *Informacion for pylgrymes...* London 1500?, or *The way to the Holy Land*, 1515, 1524, or *Instructions for Pylgrymes unto the Holy Land* (Ward)

King uppon Jonas - *Lectures upon Jonas*, John King, London 1597 (S.T.C.)

John King, 1559?-1621, chaplain to James I, dean of Christ Church, Oxford, and vice-chancellor, bishop of London from 1611.

Bilsons Controversies *True difference between Christian subjection and unchristian rebellion, where the princes lawful power to command and bear the sword are defended against the Pope's censure and Jesuits' sophisms in their apology and defence of English Catholics*, Thomas Bilson, Oxford 1585. (D.C.T.)

Thomas Bilson, 1546-1616, bishop of Winchester 1597-1616. A noted preacher, a principal maintainer of the established church.

Calvin upon the Epistles. Impossible to identify precisely.

Calvin wrote several commentaries on the Epistles. As the doctrine of justification by faith is rooted in Paul's thought, it was from the Pauline letters that the Protestant reformers drew their most effective arguments. (B.M.C., D.C.T.)

Gualther upon the small prophetes *Homiliae in prophetas duodecim, quos vocant minories*, Tigur [Rudolph Walther] 1563 (Ward)

The golden Chayne. *A Golden Chayne, or the decription of theologie; containing the order of the causes of salvation and damnation, according to God's word*, William Perkins, 1591, 1597. (Ward)

Hall's Epistles. *Epistles*, 3 vols, Joseph Hall, London 1608-11 (Ward)

Joseph Hall, bishop of Exeter and Norwich, a moderate clergyman who was suspected by Archbishop Laud of showing favour to Calvinists and Puritans.

Imprisoned by Parliamentarians in 1641 and ejected from his palace and diocese in 1647. (D.N.B.)

An exposition of 2 chapters of the proverbes Perhaps *A plain and familiar exposition of the 9th and 10th chapters of the proverbs of Saloman* (with the text by J. Dod and R. Cleaver) London 1608, or *A plain and familiar exposition of the 11th & 12th chapters of the proverbs etc.* London 1608, or *A plain & familiar exposition of the 13th & 14th chapters* . . .London 1609 (B.M.C.)

Hemmeng uppon James. *Commentarius in Epistolam Jacobi Apostoli,* Nicholas Hemmingsen, London 1577 (Ward)

Nicholas Hemmingsen (Hemmingius), Danish divine and theologian, 1513-1600.

A part of Titus Livius.

Titus Livius [Livy], d. 17 A.D., most prolific of Roman historians. Only 35 of his 142 books extant. English edition 1589 (Ward)

Salust.

Caius Crispus Sallustius, b. 86 B.C., Roman historian. Wrote the history of the Cataline Conspiracy and the history of the Roman war against Jugurtha. Many editions printed from 1470 onwards. (Ward, O.C.E.L.)

The pedegree of popish heretiques *The Pedegrewe of Popish Heretiques, wherein is truely and plainley set out the first roote of heretiques began in the churches since the time and passage of the gospell, together with an example of the offspring of the same,* J. Bartlett, minister, London 1566 (Ward)

Bartlett - Calvinist (McA)

Dr Playfayres sermons *Ten sermons by that eloquent divine of famous memory,* Thomas Playfere, Cambridge 1610 (N.C.B.)

Thomas Playfair, D.D., 1561?-1609, Lady Margaret professor of Divinity, Cambridge. (Ward)

The Anotomie of Abuses, *containing a discovery or brief summary of such notable vices and imperfections as now reign in many countries of the world but especially in a famous island called Ailgna* . . . *together with examples of God's judgements,* Philip Stubbs, 1583 (B.M.C.)

Philip Stubbs, a Puritan pamphleteer, became identified with extreme Puritan views, although the preface to the first edition of *The Anatomy of Abuses* sanctioned some plays, dancing and private and moderate gambling. It is a principal source on contemporary social and economic conditions. (O.C.E.L.)

Gritches sermones quadragessimales. Sermons for Lent, Joannes Gritschius, Nuremberg 1475 etc.

Talens Retorique *Rhetorica,* Omer Talon (Audomerus Talaeus), Paris 1543 (N.C.B.)

A greek Testament & a Clenardes grammar. *Meditationes Graecanicae in artem grammaticam,* Nicholas Clenard, Paris 1549

Absolutissimae Institutiones in Graecum linguam. His adjectae sunt meditationes in linguam Graecam, Antwerp 1545 etc. (B.M.C.)

Nicholas Kleinarts, 1495-1542, b. Diest, Brabant, professor of Greek and Hebrew, Louvain and Salamanca, tutor to the brother of the king of Portugal, professor of Latin, Braga. (Brinsley)

One volume of Tullies Orations. *Orationes,* Marcus Tullius Cicero, London 1585 etc.

Marcus Tullius Cicero, d. 43 B.C., one of the greatest orators of antiquity (Ward, O.C.E.L.)

Piscator upon the Epistles - *Analysis logica omnium Epistolarum Pauli . . . una cum scholiis . . . autore,* M.J. Piscatore, Basle 1594 (B.M.C.)

John Piscator, 1546-1626, b. Strasbourg, professor of Divinity, Herborn. Translated Bible into German.

Gibson's meditations. *Meditations upon the 116th psalm with an application to the present times,* Thomas Gibson, minister, 1607. (S.T.C.)

Ramus log. *Dialectica* , 1576. *The logicke of P. Ramus, newly translated by* M.R.Macilmenius, 1574.

Peter Ramus (de la Ramee), celebrated French mathematician and philosopher, murdered in St. Bartholomew's Day Massacre, 1572. The rise of natural sciences called for a new approach to logic which was provided by Peter Ramus. Taught in British universities (notably Cambridge) from the late 16th century. (Ward Bennett [2], N.C.B., Enc. Brit., O.C.E.L.)

Valerius Flaccus Argo. *Argonauticon* (poem on Argonautic expedition), Bologna 1474 etc.

Caius Valerius Setinus Balbus Flaccus, d. c.93 A.D., poet. (Ward)

Catullus, Tibullus & Propertius.

Caius Valerius Catullus, Albius Tibullus, Sextus Aurelius Propertius, Roman poets, many editions of their works, often issued together (Ward)

Five bookes of moses in laten with a commentarie. Possibly *In quinque libros Mosis commentarii,* John Calvin, 1595 (Ward)

A treatise of Christian Equititie. *Epiekeia, or a treatise of christian equitie,* William Perkins, London 1604 (S.T.C.)

For Perkins, see earlier note.

The treasure of Evonimus, *conteyning the wonderful hid secretes of nature touchinge the most apte formes to prepare and destyl medicines for the conservation of helth: as quintessence, aurum potabile, hyppocras, aromatical wynes, balmes, oyles, perfumes, garnyshing waters, and other manifold* *excellent confections whereunto are joyned, the formes of sondry apt fornaces and vessels required in this art; trans. with great diligence and laboure out of the Latin by* P. Morwyne, London 1559 and 1565 (Ward)

Peter Morwing, 1530?-1573?, of Magdalen College, Oxford, clergyman, Marian exile and translator.

Michaell de Hungaria. *Sermones,* Strasbourg 1487 etc.

Litosthones Apothegmes *Apophthegmatum ex optimis utriusque linguae scriptoribus per C.L.,* Lyons 1574, Geneva 1602 (Brinsley)

Conradus Lycosthenes, 1518-1561, b. Ruffach, Alsace. Taught grammar and logic, Basle 1542.

Tullies Tusculan quest *Quaestiones Tusculanae per Erasmum,* London 1577, (Ward) *Those five questions which marke Tullye Cicero disputed in his manor of Tusculanum, Englished by* J. Dolman, London 1561 (B.M.C.)

Salust - (See above)

Brocard upon the Revellations. *Commentary on the Revelations of St. John,* Jacobus Brocardus, Leyden 1580. *A commentary upon the Revelation,* trans. by J. Sandford, London 1584 (Ward)

Clenardes greeke grammer & Clarke de Aulico - see above for Clenard. *De Curiali sive aulico* ... Baldassare Castiglione, translated by Bartholomew Clerke, London 1571.

Baldassare Castiglione, 1478-1529, Italian diplomat, author of *The Courtier,* a work translated into every European tongue. Bartholomew Clerke, 1537?-90, Cambridge scholar, M.P., and ecclesiastical official.

The English secretarie, *wherein is contayned a perfect method for the inditing of all manner of epistles and familiar letters, etc.,* Angel Day, London 1586.

Many editions. The most important book on the art of letter-writing in the late 16th century, planned 'for the unlearned to whom the want thereof breedeth so diverse imperfections' who knew 'how greevous it is to participate their moste secreat causes to an other's credite'. The 1592 edition, printed by Richard Jones, was entitled *The English Secretarie; or plaine and direct method for enditing of all manner of Epistles or Letters, as well familiar as others; the like whereof hath never hitherto beene published. Studiouslie now corrected, refined, and amended, in so far more apt and better sort than before, according to the Author's true meaning, delivered in his former edition. Together (also) with the second part, then left out, and long since promised to be performed. Also a Declaration of all such Tropes, Figures, or Schemes, as either usually, or for ornament sake, are in this method required. Finally, the Partes and Office of a Secretarie, in like manner ample discoursed.* (B.M.C., Bennett [2])

Index of places and personal names

Robert (13), 11, 21, 25, 82-5.
Lowden, Isaac (31), 6, 11, 12, 13, 19,
    30-3, 83, 86, 116, 122-5, 215-22.
Lowton, Gilbert, 118.
Lowyck, Christopher, 51.
Lomle(y), Lumbley, Lumley, John
    (29), 9, 15, 16, 86, 118; Thomas,
    9, 86, 166, 167.
Lyons, Mr John, 85.

Maltyn, Sir John, 90.
Manfeild, John, 161.
Marshall, Marshell, Ann, 96;
    Dorothy, 96, 189; Edward, 62,
    96, 107, 121, 137, 138, 139, 149,
    158, 189; Francis, 96; George
    (50), 8, 11-2, 28, 43, 80, 100,
    178-80; Henry, 96; Helen, 8,
    179, 196, 197; Isabel, 96; James,
    150; Janet, 178; John (20), 10-1,
    39, 62, 96-7; Katherine, 96;
    Margaret, 96; alias Tipladie,
    Percy, 166; Richard, 96; Tho-
    mas, 149, 158, 178, 189; Wil-
    liam, 58, 59, 62, 64, 96, 97, 119,
    120, 122, 137, 140, 150, 161, 201.
Mark(i)nfeild, Martinfield, John,
    110, 146, 147, 150.
Mason, Mayson, Anne, 151; Eliza-
    beth, 140, 141; Gregory, 141,
    142, 149; Henry, 99; Isabel, 189;
    Margaret, 201; Ralph, 151; Tho-
    mas, 5, 11, 19, 58, 63, 96, 107,
    137, 149, 151, 201.
Maugham, Christopher, 64.
Mawer, Richard, 93.
Merrington, Charles, 199.
Messenger, Thomas, 158.
Metcalfe, Brian, 117.
Middleham (North Yorkshire), 125.
Middleton, 90.
Middleton(n), Midletonn, Middl-
    tonn, Myddleton, Cuthbert, 19,
    62; John the elder, 131, 159;
    John, 150, 186; John the youn-
    ger, 159, 161; Thomas, 175,
Middleton Tyas (North Yorkshire),

116.
Middridge (Durham), 17, 161.
Milbanke family, 35.
Mil(l)ner, Mylner, Anthony, 197;
    John, 203; Ralph, 203.
Mitchell, William, 98.
Moore, Andrew 90; Henry, 189.
Morley, Richard, 111, 187, 189.
Morton (Durham), 21, 187.
Morton, Raynold, 98.
Mottershed, Dorothy, 203; Peter,
    203.

Naitbye, Natby, Naytby, Christop-
    her, 90, 99; John, 98.
Nattrisse, Henry, 72; John, 72.
Newby(e), Francis, 189; John, 119,
    158.
Newby Moor, 201.
Newcastle-upon-Tyne, 29, 39, 92,
    97.
Nicholdson, Nichol(e)son, widow
    -, 95; Agnes, 100; Christopher,
    6, 73, 76, 80, 95; John, 99;
    Margaret, 101; Ralph, 62, 90;
    Thomas, 155.
Norman, alias Cowherd, Richard,
    99.
Northallerton (North Yorkshire),
    35, 104.
Northern Rising (1569), 2, 34, 37.
Northumberland, 1; earl of, 2.
Norton, 131.
Nawton, Newton, Norton, John,
    82; Robert, 24, 116, 182, 185;
    Thomas (17), 17, 73, 92-4, 115,
    154; Mr Thomas, 85.

Oates, Coroner -, 72.
Or...., THomas, 64.
Orray, Thomas, 170.
Oswald, Oswold(e), Oswould, H.,
    119; Henry, 31, 36, 103, 122,
    125, 143, 187, 199; John, 111,
    179, 187; Roland, 180; Toby, 36,
    70.
Oxen-le-field, 21, 34-5, 36, 180.